LANDLORD AND TENANT

LANDLORD AND TENANT

by

J. R. LEWIS, LL.B.
of the Inner Temple,
Barrister-at-Law

and

J. ANTHONY HOLLAND, LL.B.
Solicitor of the Supreme Court

Fourth Edition

by

S. J. LEWIS, LL.B.
Solicitor of the Supreme Court

Casdec Ltd.

Published by Casdec Ltd.
Broadwood View
Ropery Lane
Chester-le-Street
Durham DH3 3NJ
© Casdec Ltd. 1988
First Published 1968
2nd Edition 1978
Reprinted 1980
3rd Edition 1981
4th Edition 1988

ISBN Nos. 0 907595 44 8 P/B
0 907595 46 4 H/B

Printed by City Printing Works (Chester-le-Street) Limited
Broadwood View, Ropery Lane, Chester-le-Street, Co. Durham

CONTENTS

PART ONE
CREATION OF THE RELATIONSHIP

PART TWO
RIGHTS AND OBLIGATIONS OF THE PARTIES

PART THREE
PARTICULAR STATUTORY PROVISIONS

TABLE OF CASES

TABLE OF STATUTES

PART ONE

CREATION OF THE RELATIONSHIP

The relationship of landlord and tenant is one which is based upon agreement — though in some cases Parliament has stepped in to create the relationship, or to continue it, even where one party to the relationship desires that it should subsist no longer. The terms of the relationship will differ of course with the type of tenancy, and in this section of the book we shall examine the various kinds of tenancies that may come into existence. It is also relevant to discuss the *means* by which the tenancy arises, and the matter of the lease and of the agreement for a lease may here be examined.

CHAPTER ONE

THE LANDLORD—TENANT RELATIONSHIP

It is a common misconception that a person who owns a freehold estate in land also owns the land in every sense of the word: a misconception because the freehold estate, like the leasehold interest is founded, as is all land law, upon the basic proposition that all land in England is owned by the Crown. It is true that the Crown does not *occupy* all the land, but ownership is nevertheless vested in the Crown. The occupiers are merely *tenants,* who hold the land either directly, or indirectly, from the Crown.

We owe this state of affairs to the Norman Conquest: it was the method William I used to strengthen his grip on the land he had conquered and to reward those hardy followers who had supported his claims by force of arms. The Crown owned the land and certain parts were granted away, not as out and out transfers, but upon conditions. Moreover, these lands were not necessarily granted in perpetuity: they were sometimes granted for limited periods of time.

These two situations—the conditions on which the land was held by the tenant; and the length of time for which the land was held—were fundamental to land law. They were known as the doctrines of tenure, and of estates.

TENURE

The doctrine of tenure simply stated that all land is held of the Crown, either directly or indirectly, subject to certain conditions of tenure (or landholding). The main tenures which existed were *free tenures* and *unfree tenures.*

Free tenures

The free tenures consisted of *tenures in chivalry* (or military tenures) by which in return for the land the tenant would provide some service for the king, such as carrying his banner in war or providing him with a fixed number of horsemen for forty days each year; *tenures in socage* by which the tenant held the land in return for some services of a non-personal nature which commonly amounted to an agricultural service such as so many days ploughing each year; or *spiritual tenures* where the service provided in return for the land was the giving of prayers for the repose of the grantor's soul or similar spiritual services.

Unfree tenures

Free tenure was in the main the system of landholding used by the Crown in its relationship with the Tenants-in-Chief (the barons) and by the landed proprietors and independent farmers.

Below these in the social scale, however, the system of unfree tenures was used. The great unfree tenure in wide use was known as villeinage.

It is beyond the scope of this book to go into detail concerning this tenure and its incidents, as it is to describe in detail the incidents of free tenure. Suffice it to note here that the villein merely *occupied* the land and had no status in connection with the land, his services were more onerous and were unfixed as to quality, and most of the villeins were not *personally* free men.

Villeinage later came to be termed "copyhold" and there was also a variety of this tenure known as customary freehold.

Between 1646 and 1926 most types of tenure had disappeared, with the exceptions of socage tenure and copyhold. This dual system of tenure had great disadvantages for conveyancers: accordingly, in 1926 all land held by copyhold became held by socage (of "freehold") tenure. Even so, the basic principle of land holding remains as it has been for centuries—"the Sovereign remains the lord paramount of all the land within the realm": T. Cyprian Williams (1931) 75 S.J. 848.

The result is that, although for practical purposes the owner of a freehold is the *owner* of the land, legally he is still referred to as the "tenant in fee simple".

ESTATES

The word *estate* is derived from the word *status:* the land that a man held tended to fix his status in the community. We have seen that the system of landholding was such that different *tenures* to the same piece of land were possible. The doctrine of *estates* was concerned not so much with the conditions upon which the land might be held but upon the length of time, the *duration* for which it might be held. While the tenure determined the method and conditions of landholding, estate denoted the period for which it might be held. Nowadays, of course, although, legally, the individual still holds as a tenant, in practical terms and in the lay mind he holds a freehold as though he were really owner of the land. Indeed, the word *estate* has tended to lose the specialised legal flavour that it formerly possessed and is sometimes used to describe the property a person owns generally (for instance, the "executor of the deceased's estate") and "building estates" these days denote areas where a number of houses have been erected in a close proximity.

Even so, it is important to remember that the word "estate" does have a pure legal meaning and when we use the word here it is the legal meaning which is intended.

There were in fact several kinds of estate, several possible interests that could be held in land which were classified according to the length of time that they might be held by the tenant. There were, first of all the freehold estates.

Freehold estates

Until 1926 there were three estates of freehold (see p.7, *post*, for the post-1925 position). The largest of these was the *fee simple*. This was virtually a grant of land which continued for ever, unless the tenant died leaving no heir. The fee simple is the estate which we know today in common parlance as the freehold estate.

Then there was the *fee tail*. This was an estate that continued just as long as the original tenant or any of his "lineal descendants" survived. How did it differ from the fee simple? Quite simply, the word "heir" referred to in the fee simple above would cover persons other than "lineal descendants"—the tenant who died leaving a brother, for instance, would leave an heir but would not be leaving a lineal descendant capable of taking the fee tail.

Thirdly, there was the *life estate*. This was a grant made to a tenant either for his own lifetime or for the lifetime of some other person.

While talking of estates we have so far concerned ourselves with the freehold estates, but there existed another classification of estates. These were the leasehold estates—and it is these with which we are going to be principally concerned in the course of this book.

Leasehold estates

In the early years of the development of English land law the only estates recognised by the law were the three freehold estates noted above. This was not to say that *possession* of land gave rise to no rights. The law recognised the fact that a person could be allowed by the owner of the land to remain in possession of it, but since legally the "tenant" could be ejected at any time he did not have an *estate* in land.

The rigid medieval mind was completely unable to grasp the problem which arose when the commercial possibilities of landholding became apparent. The owner of a freehold estate soon came to realise that it would be sensible and profitable for him to allow another, who held no land, to have the use of his estate. The freeholder could allow the "tenant" the use of the land, for a period specified in the agreement they drew up between themselves, and in return he would receive a specified payment. In this way it became a common transaction for a landowner holding the freehold estate to create what was known and still is known as a "term of years". The tenant would thereby have the right to retain possession for a period of years, and in return would pay the freeholder a rent.

But this is where problems arose. The freeholder was legally entitled to the use of the land, exclusively, and he could enforce this right by what were known as the *real* actions. Real actions gave the right to the return of the thing (*res:* from which comes *re-al*) itself: he could demand the return of the land itself at any time.

But if he did so, where would this leave the tenant? He had a contract with the freeholder which gave him, the tenant, the right to possession of the property for a number of years. The difficulty was that this was contractural right, which gave rise to a *personal* action (*persona*—against the individual who broke the contract) but which gave rise to no right to the return of the thing, the *res,* itself. Quite obviously, the tenant who found himself ejected from the property would be able to bring a *personal* action against the freeholders but this would not give him the right to continued possession and use of the land which generally would be of far more value to him.

It was not until the fifteenth century that the tenant, or leaseholder as he may be described, was fully protected in this way against the freeholder and indeed against other persons who would obviously not be bound by any contract and who could argue that the leaseholder had no estate whereby he could deny *them* entry. But once the leaseholder obtained the remedy of ejectment he became fully protected and he obtained in a roundabout way an estate in the land.

Real property and personal property

But how could this "estate" be classified? The law had already laid down rigid lines. Interests which gave rise to *real* actions (and this in effect meant those interests classified as freehold estates) were classified as real property. Land, broadly speaking, was then definable as real property.

Chattels, personal goods, on the other hand, did not give rise to real actions but to personal actions and so were not classified as real property—they were called *personal* property.

Where could the leasehold fit in? In the fifteenth century it finally attained the dignity of an estate but it was then too late to be classified as real property. Nor could it be classified as personal property, for, although it had formerly given rise to personal actions only it was nevertheless nothing to do with chattel, concerned as it was with an interest in *land.*

The way out of the impasse was discovered by the use of new terminology; somewhat of a compromise, it nevertheless served to distinguish between the lease, which had little connection with chattels, and personal property as such. In future, interests in land which were in the nature of freehold interests could be called *real property*; interests in chattels could be called personal property; the leaseholder, on the other hand, fell somewhere between these two classifications: his interest was designated as a *chattel real.*

Leasehold tenure and estates

The leasehold had emerged, then, from being a merely contractural right to occupy the land and had been elevated to the status of other proprietary interests. Leaseholds had been added to the list of recognised legal estates.

This did not mean that they had been accepted completely within the feudal system of landholding: indeed, they always remained outside this system. Nevertheless, their recognition as legal estates made it very necessary that the fact of tenure should be recognised also, for every tenant must hold by some kind of tenure if he was to be regarded as holding a legal estate at all.

Since the fifteenth century, therefore, the leasehold has been regarded as possessing a type of tenure: the landlord and tenant relationship of necessity gave rise to a tenure in itself. Indeed, it is interesting to note that the decline of "tenure" in the modern law has led to the anomalous position that nowadays it is only the relationship of landlord and tenant that gives rise to any important form of tenure at all.

However, much of the learning relating to tenures and estates, though basic to a true understanding of modern land law, has lost its importance for the student who is required to know the law as it stands today. We may turn, therefore, to a discussion of the modern situation which was ushered in by the property legislation of 1925.

LAW OF PROPERTY ACT 1925

The background to the changes brought in by the Law of Property Act 1925 need not be discussed in detail here; enough has already been said to illustrate that land law was a complex subject in need of considerable reform both as to the substantive law and the mechanics of dealing with the interests that existed. Reforms were carried out by the 1925 legislation which were of basic importance to the land law: here, from the point of view of the landlord and tenant relationship, we need draw attention only to the first section of the Act which in effect laid down the new distinction to be drawn and applied in land law generally.

The effect of section 1 (1) of the Law of Property Act 1925 was to ensure that the number of estates that were to be regarded as capable even of *existence* at law should be reduced. It stated, in effect, that only *two* estates were in future to be capable of subsisting, or of being conveyed, or of being created at law. These two estates were to be:

(1) the fee simple absolute in possession;
(2) the term of years absolute.

It will be noted at once that the old distinction between freehold and leasehold interests in land was retained in the modern law. But gone were the other "estates"—now it was to be two only, and it is with the second of these that we are to be concerned.

But what precisely is meant by a "term of years absolute"? The matter can be dealt with in precise terms when the relationship of landlord and tenant is discussed but it is perhaps relevant to mention here that section 205 (1) (xxvi) of the Act (the definition section) has something to add on the matter.

This section states that the words "term of years absolute" must be taken to mean a term of years that takes effect in possession, or in reversion, and must be either certain or liable to determine by notice, re-entry, operation of law or (as in the case of a term created for effecting a mortgage) by a proviso for cesser on redemption. These particular terms will not be described and explained at this point: they will be dealt with more expansively later but for the sake of completeness this section is noted here. It also goes on to say that it does not include any term of years that is determinable with life or lives or with the ending of a determinable life interest.

The expression "term of years" also includes a term for less than a year, or from year to year: so it includes quarterly and monthly and even weekly tenancies.

We may now look at the relationship of landlord and tenant, its nature, and when it does and does not arise.

RELATIONSHIP OF LANDLORD AND TENANT

At common law the relationship of landlord and tenant arose (a) where one person granted to another an estate in land which was less than freehold and was also less than the estate held by the grantor, and (b) where one person holding land allowed the other to obtain a tenancy at will or a tenancy on sufferance.

These two latter situations we will examine in more detail later. It should be noted that the relationships stated above arose at common law; we have already seen that the matter is affected also by section 1 (1) of the Law of Property Act 1925 and the relationship may arise by statute also—*e.g.*, by the operation of sections 85 and 86 of the 1925 Act where property is mortgaged. But it is necessary to look first at the nature of the relationship that arises between landlord and tenant before we look at the circumstances in which it arises, and an investigation should also be made of the conditions that most necessarily exist before the relationship appears.

Nature of the relationship

The relationship, as we have already seen, is essentially one of tenure between the freeholder (the landlord) and the tenant. Of course, a simple lease of this nature is self-explanatory, but it must be remembered that the relationship will arise also between the assignees of these two parties. If the landlord assigns his interest to A, and the tenant assigns his interest to B and so on, new relationships continually arise which are in fact based upon the same premise.

For this reason, and for the sake of simplicity, it would be as well to explain the particular terminology used in describing the relationships, for they will be used hereafter in this text. If A makes a grant of a lease to B, A may be described either as a "lessor" or as a "landlord", and B may be described either as a "tenant" or a "lessee".

It will be noted from this that there must in effect be at least two persons concerned: a lease by an owner or owners to himself or themselves respectively cannot give rise to the landlord and tenant relationship—it is incompatible with the nature of a tenancy. An interest in the land will remain with the landlord, of course—this interest is called the "reversion" (which is an estate in possession and usually gives the right of receiving rent) and he may thereafter be described as the "reversioner" also.

What then are the general conditions that must be present before the relationship of landlord and tenant can arise?

Conditions for creation of the relationship

(1) *The subject-matter must be land*

Except in those circumstances where the relationship is created by statute there must be a demise of the property concerned and so it follows from this that the subject-matter of the lease must be land.

But what is meant by the word "land"? The term has a wide meaning, extending not only to "coporeal hereditaments" (tangible interests in land) such as mines, houses, flats and even a room which is separately let, but also to "incorporeal hereditaments" (intangible, interests in land) such as easements and *profits à prendre* (the precise nature of which will be discussed later; see p. 118), for example, a right of fishing.

It will not include livestock and chattels. It is true that these may be the subject-matter of a "lease": "It was a surprise to me", said Lord Justice Harman in 1966, "that livestock were also the subject of lettings, but it evidently has been so for centuries now". The fact is, however, that these are rather in the nature of hiring agreements, and they do not give rise to the relationship of landlord and tenant.

(2) *The grant must be of a lesser estate*

The landlord must make a grant of an estate or interest to the tenant which is less than his own. This is important, for the interest that he retains (called the *reversion* because the land "reverts" to him at the end of the tenancy) is essential to the landlord/tenant relationship. If he holds no reversion, he cannot be a landlord. If he grants the whole of his estate or interests he retains nothing for himself; therefore nothing can "revert" to him and he cannot be a landlord. It may perhaps be re-emphasised here that though possession "reverts" to the landlord at the end of the lease, the landlord's estate as an estate is in possession all the time.

An example, perhaps will make the situation clear where the landlord himself does not hold the land as a freeholder:

F, the fee simple owner, leases Blackacre to T for a term of twelve years. After five years, T creates an underlease in favour of U for a term of three years.

Here the landlord/tenant relationship exists between F and T, and also between T and U. F has retained a reversion, and T, in creating an underlease to U, has a reversion also, of four years' duration. But what would be the position if T had given U a lease for *seven* years? Then he would have retained no interest: he would have granted away the full term remaining to him, he would have had no reversion, therefore there would have been no landlord/tenant relationship between T and U. The effect of the grant to U would, in other words, have been the creation of a landlord/tenant relationship by assignment between F and U—and this would have been so even if it had been termed an "underlease" (rather than an *assignment* of T's lease, which in effect it was).

(3) *There must be exclusive possession*

In the case of corporeal hereditament the tenant must be given the right to the exclusive possession of the premises. A mere licence or permission to use them or make use of them in a particular manner would not be enough, even if the licence were exclusive.

For instance, in *Wilson v. Tavener (1901)* A agreed to allow B to erect a hoarding for advertising purposes on the forecourt of a cottage and to use the gable end of another cottage for the same purpose. In return, B agreed to pay A a yearly "rent" of £10. The court held that since there was no right to exclusive possession of any land or building this agreement was merely a licence. As such it could be withdrawn at any time by giving of reasonable notice.

A second example is to be seen in *Jackson v. Simons* (1923). The lessee of a shop allowed part of the shop premises to be used between certain hours by the proprietor of a night club for the sale of admission tickets to the club. The part used was separated from the rest of the shop by a screen which was erected each night and fixed in position by a padlock. The lessee retained the key. The question arose as to whether the night-club proprietor had been granted a sub-lease of that part of the premises by the shop lessee. The answer given by the court was negative: the lessee of the shop has merely given the night-club proprietor a licence to use the premises for specified purposes and times.

The precise nature of the licence, as opposed to the lease, will be examined later.

(4) *The term must be certain*

The term for which the lease is to run must be clearly laid down; the beginning and end of the term of years should be certain, or should be capable of being ascertained with certainty. This does not mean, of course, that leases will necessarily end on the prescribed dates. The parties may agree to bring the term to an end earlier or the lease may be forfeited for breach. In addition, some residential tenancies for terms exceeding twenty-one years fall under the provisions of the Landlord and Tenant Act

1954, as do certain business tenancies. Such tenancies do not end automatically but continue until brought to an end by the prescribed form of notice. This will be dealt with later as will the provisions of the Leasehold Reform Act 1967 (see pp. 29 and 210); suffice it to say here that the term of the lease must be indicated with certainty, or be capable of being ascertained, at the commencement of the term.

(5) *Interesse termini*

Prior to 1926 in many cases actual entry of the tenant upon the property was necessary before the lease took effect. Before he entered he has merely an *interesse termini* which enabled him to maintain an action against any person through whom his entry was prevented, though it did not enable him to maintain an action for trespass. However, the doctrine of *interesse termini* was abolished by section 149 of the Law of Property Act 1925. All terms of years absolute, whether created before or after 1926, by that section, capable of taking effect both at law and in equity from the date fixed for the commencement of the term. Actual entry is therefore no longer necessary.

It should be noted, however, that if a term of years is granted at a rent or in consideration of a fine but is limited after 1926 to take effect more than twenty-one years after the date of the lease (as opposed to the contract to create the lease), that term of years will be void. (This would not, of course, prevent a valid agreement to create a lease 30 years from today, the lease to take effect 15 years after the date of its grant, that is 45 years from today). There are exceptions to this principle in respect of certain terms which take effect in equity.

Express grants and contracts for leases

We have already seen that the relationship of landlord and tenant will often be created by a grant—an express grant by way of demise, to use the legal terminology. But this is not the only way in which the relationship may arise: there may be a creation of the relationship by way of estoppel, for instance, an example being the payment and acceptance of rent which in itself is an acknowledgement of tenancy and is conculsive in the absence of any other evidence (see p.22).

Apart from situations such as these, however, there is the question of a contract for a lease to be examined. This matter will be dealt with again, in more detail, but it may be pointed out there that even where there is no actual legal demise, a contract between the parties to make a lease may, under certain circumstances, create the relationship of landlord and tenant—or, more accurately, have the effect of doing so.

The contract is not in itself a demise, but once the "tenant" enters under the agreement the relationship will arise. Moreover, under the rule in *Walsh v. Lonsdale* (1882) (see p. 37), a tenant who holds property under a contract for lease which is capable of being enforced by a decree for specific performance will hold that land under the same terms, in equity, as if a lease had in fact been granted. In this way the relationship of landlord and tenant may be created in equity.

LEASES AND LICENCES

When discussing *Wilson v. Tavener* (1901) and *Jackson v. Simons* (1923) above, it was shown that the distinction to be drawn between the lease and the licence is that the lease grants exclusive possession of the premises to the tenant whereas the licences in those cases did not.

Unfortunately for the student of land law it is not quite as simple as that. It is true that, in the case of coporeal hereditaments, the relationship is given, it does not follow that if exclusive possession is given the relationship of landlord and tenant *necessarily* arises.

Cases where no tenancy arises

A person may gain exclusive possession of the premises but yet will not be regarded by the law as a tenant if the circumstances negative any intention to create a tenancy. The fact of exclusive possession does give rise to a presumption that a tenancy exists but this can be rebutted by showing that there was no intention to create a tenancy. On the other hand, an agreement which expressly denies exclusive possession may be treated as a sham by the court and interpreted as a lease if it is a blatant attempt to deprive the tenant of statutory protection given to tenants. (See Chapter 15).

What circumstances will negative an intention to create a tenancy? Examples are furnished by:

(a) *Bramwell v. Bramwell* (1942), where the relationship of husband and wife between the parties negatived such an intention where he allowed her to live in his house;

(b) *Foster v. Robinson* (1950), where an act of friendship and generosity whereby the "tenant" was to be allowed to live rent free in future was enough to *change* a tenancy into a licence.

The situation may be summarised thus—if no exceptional circumstances arise the fact of exclusive possession is, if not decisive as to there being a lease, a consideration of the very importance: *Addiscombe Garden Estates Ltd. v. Crabbe* (1957).

Use of terminology

What if the grant uses the words "landlord" and "tenant" to describe the parties? Will this mean that the grant must essentially be a lease?

The answer to this is simply that the creation of the landlord and tenant relationship does not depend upon the terminology used by the parties, but upon the fact and substance of the agreement between them. It matters not whether the grant speaks of a licence or of a lease, or describes the parties as tenant and landlord or licensor and licensee; it is the substance of the agreement that will finally decide whether it is in fact a lease of a licence.

Thus, a grant which is described as a licence, but which gives to the grantee the exclusive possession of the premises for a certain period of time may create a tenancy, not a licence.

On the other hand, if the grant describes the grantor as "landlord" and the grantee as "tenant", neither this nor the fact that it uses other language appropriate to a letting will result in the creation of a tenancy unless the grant in fact gives to the grantee exclusive possession of the land concerned. The House of Lords ruled in *Street v. Mountford* (1985) that save in exceptional circumstances an agreement granting exclusive occupation of residential accommodation for a term at a rent without services creates a tenancy despite the word "licence" in the agreement. Even though the parties intended to create a licence to avoid the Rent Acts they *in* fact made an agreement which did not give effect to their intentions. This case was followed in *Bretherton v. Paton* (1985) where a similar attempt to avoid the Rent Acts failed beacuse of the substance of the agreement.

These rulings should not affect that in *Manchester City Corporation v. National Car Parks* (1982) where an agreement was made for the use of land as a car park between 12.01 a.m. to 2 a.m. and 7 a.m. to 12 p.m. This was held to be a licence although the time restriction was not enforced and the car park was used 24 hours a day. The facts of the agreement are what is conclusive. The subsequent actions of the parties raise different questions altogether.

In other words, it depends upon the construction of the grant: if the substance of the agreement is to confer on the grantee the rights and obligations of a tenant, and upon the grantor the rights and obligations of a landlord, the agreement will be treated as a tenancy agreement.

Particular examples

(1) *Lodgings.* A person who lives in a boarding-house or in lodgings is regarded as a licensee, not a tenant, at all events where the landlord retains control over the rooms the lodger occupies. The test is whether the rooms have become a separate part of which the lodger has exclusive possession, or whether there is just the one dwelling-house over which the landlord retains control.

(2) *Sporting rights.* In the case of incorporeal hereditaments an exclusive licence which is coupled with the grant of such an interest as the right to shoot and carry away game can create an interest which may be regareded as analogous to a term of years absolute. Since such interests do not give rise in all respects to the same rights and liabilities as the tenancy of a corporeal hereditament they may be regarded as not giving rise to the relationship of landlord and tenant.

(3) *Agricultural land.* If agricultural land is let on or after July 12th 1984, to a person for use as agricultural land for an interest less than a

tenancy from year to year, then if the circumstances are such that if his interest were really a tenancy from year to year he would be regarded as tenant of an agricultural holding, the agreement *will* take effect as if it were an agreement for the letting of the land for a tenancy from year to year. This will apply unless the letting or grant was approved by the Ministry of Agriculture, Fisheries and Food before the agreement was entered into.

The important point to be noted here, however, is that this provision of the Agricultural Holdings Act 1986 (in Section 2), is made applicable also to a *licence* granted to a person to occupy land for use as agricultural land.

(4) *Master and servant.* The connotations of the words "master and servant" are unwelcome in modern eyes but the words have strict legal meaning and therefore will be used. The situation here is that although a servant can be tenant of his master this will not be so unless it can be shown that his occupation of the land in question is of right, and not merely a necessary part of his contact of service.

For example:

(a) the servant is permitted to occupy a house belonging to his master for the convenience of his work and as part payment for his services: this gives rise to a *service tenancy* for he is in effect paying a rent or consideration for his occupation;

(b) the servant is required to occupy a house belonging to the master in order that he might carry our his duties more efficiently: here he is not a tenant for his is *required* by his terms of service to occupy the house and is in occupation as a servant not as a tenant. Such an arrangement is a service *occupancy*. In *Crane v. Morris* (1965) it was held that an agricultural worker with exclusive possession of a tied cottage who paid no rent was a licensee and not a service tenant.

How does one explain the absence of a tenancy where there is an exclusive possession? We have already seen the explanation: the circumstances negative any intention to create a tenancy. It could also be explained by the argument that the possession of the servant is still attributed to the master.

But so much for the distinctions to be drawn between leases and licences, and the circumstances where the one or the other arises. What is the importance, and what are the effects of the distinction between lease and licence?

Contrast between licence and lease

There are three kinds of licences: the bare license, the licence coupled with an interest and the contractural licence.

The bare licence is a licence which is not coupled with a grant of any interest in property. It is nothing more than a mere personal privilege which "only makes an action lawful which without it had been unlawful".

Thomas v. Sorrell (1673).

The Licence coupled with an interest is one which does include a grant of an interest in property, e.g. a *profit à prendre.* As we shall see shortly, this distinction is of importance.

The contractural licence is one unconnected with any proprietary interest, being supported only by consideration for the licensor's promise. The basis of the difference between the licence and the lease is that the lease creates a legal estate in the land but the licence confers no rights in land.

(1) *Non-assignability*

The benefit of a lease can be assigned by one tenant to another, in the same way as the landlord may assign his interest. This is not the case with the licence. A licence is personal merely an arrangement between licensor and licensee, and so cannot be assigned to a third person. Thus, in *Roffey v. Henderson* (1851) it was held that a licence given by landlord to remove fixtures at the end of the lease was not binding upon a new tenant in possession.

(2) *Effect on third parties*

A lease gives the tenant the right to exclude others, including the landlord, from the premises; a licence on the other hand, generally gives no such right.

This point is illustrated in *Hill v. Tupper* (1863). A canal company leased land adjoining the canal to Hill. It also gave him the "sole and exclusive right" to let out pleasure boats on the canal. Tupper was an innkeeper who, seeing the commercial possibilities, disregarded Hill's privilege and himself let out boats for fishing purposes. Hill brought an action in his own name against Tupper. The court held that the contract that Hill had with the company was mere licence, personal to himself, but one that gave him no right against Tupper.

However, as it now appears that a statutory tenant under the Rent Act (see Chapter 15) could sue for trespass despite his lack of a legal estate in the land, it would seem that a licensee who has exclusive possession should also have that right. In *Hill's* case there was no such exclusive possession of the canal.

(3) *Revocability*

A tenancy can be brought to an end only in specified circumstances or at the end of the period, but a licence is normally revocable at any time making the licensee a trespasser, although the licensor may be liable to damages unless he gives the licensee reasonable notice to withdraw or to put an end to his commitments. In *Earl of Iveagh v. Martin* (1961) it was held that a week's notice was sufficient to vacate a quay where there were no boats under repair, nor any contract to repair boats, and the licensees were in no difficulty.

It should also be noted that if there is an express or implied contract that the licence will not be revoked for a certain period an action for damages will lie for breach of contract, and to this extent the licence may be close to the idea of a lease, though still unlike it in substance. In *Hurst v. Picture Theatres Ltd.* (1915) for instance, Hurst had purchased a ticket for a seat in a cinema but during the performance he was forcibly ejected by the order of the manager, who mistakenly believed that he had not paid for the seat. The court found (*inter alia*) that the licence granted by the sale of the ticket included an implied contract not to revoke the licence arbitrarily during the performance. And in *Winter Garden Theatre (London) Ltd. v. Millennium Productions Ltd.* (1948) the House of Lords said that a licence made irrevocable by contract cannot be revoked, at least if the contract is capable of being specifically enforced.

If the licence is one coupled with an interest in the land it is irrevocable. It is capable of assignement and covenants may be made to run with it. An example of such a licence is the right to enter on land and enjoy a *profit à prendre,* such as the taking of fish or gravel, or other incorporeal hereditaments.

(4) *Matrimonial Homes Act 1967*

This Act provides that where one spouse owns, or is the tenant of, the matrimonial home the other spouse has "rights of occupation". These rights are a charge on the estate or interest of the other spouse and are registerable as a land charge under the Land Charges Act 1972. (For registered land protection is obtained by registering a notice or a caution).

Moreover, if the matrimonial home is held on a tenancy to which the Rent Acts apply (see p. 165, *post*), or if it is held on a statutory tenancy (see p. 167, *post*), the court has the power, on dissolution of the marriage, to transfer the tenancy from one spouse to another.

THE FREEHOLDER'S POWERS OF LEASING

All persons who do not suffer from some legal disability may grant leases for such terms of years as are not inconsistent with the nature, and the quantity, of the estate which they hold.

The simplest instance is, of course, the lease made by the freeholder, the tenant in fee simple. The general rule is that freeholders who are not subject to legal disability may make leases without limit, and without restraint, for any number of years, and they make such leases upon any terms and conditions they think fit.

The question of legal disabilities will be dealt with in greater detail in a subsequent chapter. But there are two points that should here be made concerning the position of the freeholder. While it is true that he may make leases with complete freedom, this applies only where he is the beneficial freeholder: that is to say, he holds the freehold as tenant in fee simple for his own benefit only. But if the freeholder holds the legal estate as trustee his power to grant a lease is limited; by the Settled Land Act 1925 if he is holding as the tenant for life under a settlement, and by the Law of Property Act 1925 if he is a trustee for sale (see Chapter 5).

But it is not only the fee simple owner who may grant a lease: as we have see, the tenant himself may create an underlease; but again detailed discussion of these matters can be left to a later chapter (see p. 40 *post*). It is now convenient to deal in detail with the types of tenancies that may arise. Briefly, a tenancy may be:

(i) for a fixed period;
(ii) for a series of periods, such as—from year to year, month to month, week to week—determinable at the end of any such period by notice to quit;
(iii) at will;
(iv) on sufferance;
(v) a statutory tenancy.

How are tenancies created? they will arise in one of four ways:

(i) by a lease or agreement for a lease;
(ii) by implication of law, such as where a person without any lease or agreement enters upon land and pays rent;
(iii) by estoppel, and in cases such as where a mortgager attorns tenant to his mortgagee;
(iv) by statute.

These various types of tenancies, and the ways in which they are created, are dealt with in the next chapter.

CHAPTER TWO

TENANCIES

TENANCIES FOR A TERM OF YEARS

Since 1925 the only leasehold interest capable of existing as a legal estate is a term of years absolute. A term of years may be for any length of time, other than for perpetuity, and indeed it is often the case that terms of 2,000 years are created for the purpose of providing security for money advanced upon mortgage.

The simplest kind of term is of course the lease for a fixed number of years. It may be made to commence immediately, or at some time in the future (within twenty-one years), or even at some date which is already past when the lease is executed. The term of the lease must be certain, however, in the sense that it must have a beginning and an end known at its commencement.

Creation

A tenancy for a term of years can be created only by a lease, or by an agreement for a lease.

Lease

A lease made by deed grants to the lessee a legal estate in land. It is a conveyance for the purposes of the Law of Property Act 1925 by virtue of Section 205 and it is a contract between the lessor and the lessee.

Agreement for a lease

An agreement for a lease even if made by deed does not convey an estate as the lease does; it is nothing more than a contract between two parties whereby one agrees to grant a lease to the other. At common law it simply operates to bring about a contractural relationship between the parties but *can* have a wider effect. The matter will be discussed in more detail in Chapter Three but it may be noted here that if the agreement for a lease is one of which specific performance might be granted by the court, and if it has been registered under the provisions of the Land Charges Act 1972 it will have, for most practical purposes, the same effect as a lease. As we shall see, this is not the same thing as saying that an agreement for a lease is as good as the lease itself.

Language used by laymen and lawyers does not always conform to strict legal terminology, of course, and sometimes the words "tenancy agreement" will appear. What precisely does this term mean? Is it a lease or an agreement for a lease?

In fact, it is a covenient expression commonly used to describe a *lease*, but one which is in writing as opposed to one which is made by deed. It may also be used, however, to describe a written *agreement for a lease* under which the tenant has taken possession, so its context needs to be closely examined.

Formalities

At common law a lease of an incorporeal hereditament required a deed; a lease of a corporeal hereditament, on the other hand, could be made by parol—*i.e.*, it could be made by writing not under seal, or it could be made verbally.

Sections 52 to 54 of the Law of Property Act 1925 state that only a tenancy at will can be created if a lease is made by a method other than under seal, with one extremely important exception; a lease which takes effect in possession for a term not exceeding three years at the best rent that can be obtained without taking a fine can be made by parol (section 54 (2)).

The words "not exceeding three years" need examination here. In *Kushner v. Law Society* (1952) it was held that a tenancy will fall within the definition of a tenancy exceeding three years if it is for a definite period of more than three years even though one of the parties has the right to determine the tenancy before three years have elapsed.

If the tenancy is one whereby the tenant has an option to renew the term for a period which would give him a total tenancy of more than three years, it can still be made informally. The fact that the two terms added together exceed three years does not mean that the exception does not apply. It is only where the term originally granted exceeds three years that the formality of a lease under seal will be essential.

Agreement for a lease

The mere fact that a document not under seal is described as an "agreement", or that it uses the words "agrees to let" and "agrees to take" and so on, does not mean that it is necessarily an agreement for a lease. It can still in fact amount to a *lease*, if from the document itself it appears that:

(a) it creates a tenancy for a term not exceeding three years; and

(b) it is the intention of the parties that the instrument should operate as a lease without the execution of any further instrument.

If, on the other hand, the document contemplates that something further should be done, or that some further document should be executed *before* the relationship of landlord and tenant may come into existence, then it will *not* be construed as a lease. In other words, the distinction is based upon the primary fact of intention: if the document appears to intend that a lease, rather than an agreement for a lease, should operate, and the term is three years or less, it will be construed as a lease. But if something more is to be done, it will be nothing more than an agreement for a lease, as where the document contains an express statement to the effect that the agreement is subject to the grant of a formal lease.

TERMS DETERMINABLE WITH LIFE

It will be remembered that formerly the estate that was to be held for one's own lifetime or for the life of another could exist as a legal estate. With the cutting down of legal estates to two kinds only, this was no longer possible after 1925.

At common law it was possible to create a lease for life but this was changed by section 149 (6) of the 1925 Act.

The effect of this provision is that any lease or underlease for life or lives, or for any term of years determinable with life or lives, at a rent or in consideration of a fine, or any contract of this nature shall take effect as a lease, underlease or contract therefore for a term of *ninety years.*

The ninety-year term will be determinable after the death of the person whose life defined the term, by giving at least one month's notice in writing to bring the tenancy to an end on one of the quarter days applicable.

The notice can be given by the lessor or those entitled under him to the leaseholder; it can also be given by the representatives of the deceased lessee or by the lessee where the life specified is other than his own.

The effect of this provision is that the lease determinable with life has been converted into a term of years absolute which can exist as a legal estate, provided it is granted at a rent or in consideration of a fine. The wheel thus turns full circle: what was formerly a legal estate now again exists as a legal estate by virtue of this conversion to a ninety-year term.

The same provisions apply to a lease determinable on marriage—it becomes a term of ninety-years: determinable by notice after the relevant marriage.

REVERSIONARY LEASES

We have seen that a lease may be granted so as to take effect either immediately, or at some date in the future. If it is to take effect at some future date it is known as a "reversionary lease".

At common law such a lease passed no estate to the grantee because of the doctrine of *interesse termini* (see p. 10, above) but this was abolished by section 149 of the 1925 Act.

The effect of a grant of a reversionary lease nowadays is therefore to vest in the lessee a legal estate in the land; a legal estate which will take effect from the date fixed for the commencement of the term. But, although it may be limited to take effect either after a fixed interval of time, or upon the occurrence of a certain event such as the death of an individual:

(i) it will be void (other than in certain exceptional circumstances) if it is limited to take effect more than twenty-one years from the date of the instrument creating it;

(ii) it will be void for creating a legal estate if it is not made by deed (for, as we have seen, it is only leases taking effect *in possession* for a three-year term or less which can be made by parol).

A contract to grant a lease which, when granted, would create a term commencing more than twenty-one years after the date of the lease, would similarly be invalid: *Re Strand & Savoy Properties* (1960).

It is convenient to note here that a perpetually renewable lease, *i.e.*, one which gives the tenant the right to renew it for a further period as often as it expires is converted by section 145 of the Law of Property Act 1925 into a term of 2,000 years while sub-leases of this nature are converted into terms of one day less than the superior lease.

CONCURRENT LEASES

A concurrent lease is one which is granted for a term that commences before a previous lease expires or is otherwise determined. It will be a lease of the *same* premises, but to a *different* lessee.

The concurrent lease thus takes effect in reversion upon the earlier term, which may be either shorter, or longer, than the concurrent term.

This means that a concurrent lease operates from its commencement as an assignment of the reversion—during that period of time that the two terms run concurrently. Since the lessee under the concurrent lease is an assignee of the reversion he is entitled to the rent reserved, in the same way as he is entitled to the benefits of the covenants that are contained in the lease made previously.

As far as creation of a concurrent lease is concerned, as the concurrent lease is effectively and assignment, it must be created by deed; however if created by parol it may take effect in equity under the doctrine in *Walsh v. Lonsdale* (see p. 37).

What if a concurrent lease is granted to the *same lessee*? If this happens and he accepts the grant, it will operate as an implied surrender by him of his previous term: the result cannot be otherwise because the same person cannot be both tenant and reversioner of the same premises.

TENANCY FROM YEAR TO YEAR

A tenant from year to year is a tenant who holds under a grant, express or implied, for a term which may be determined at the end of the first or any subsequent year of the tenancy. The determination may be by the landlord, or by the tenant by notice to quit. If no such notice is given the tenancy will continue from year to year, for any number of years, until the lease is surrendered, or the title of the lessor ceases, or it is extinguished by the Statute of Limitation. It will not be determined simply because one or other of the parties dies.

Creation

(1) *Express grant*

A tenancy from year to year may be created by express grant and will be determinable at the end of the first or any subsequent year by notice to quit.

(2) *Entry into possession*

It will sometimes be the case that the lease granted to the grantee is in fact void because it was not made by deed when it should have been. In such cases, if the grantee can show that he has in fact entered into possession of the premises, and has paid a yearly rent he becomes a tenant from year to year. The reason for this is that the law *implies* in such instances the existence of a tenancy from year to year upon such of the terms of the lease or agreement as are applicable to a yearly tenancy.

A tenancy will similarly be implied where there has been an entry into possession and payment of part of a yearly rent *without* any lease or agreement. The mere fact of payment of the rent or receipt of it will, if it remains unexplained, be an admission of the fact that a tenancy exists. In the absence of any evidence to the contrary this will be deemed to be a tenancy from year to year particularly in respect of premises which are ordinarily let from year to year such as farm premises. Either the receiver or the payer may prove the circumstances under which payment was made so as to rebut the presumption which would otherwise arise. In other words, payment of the rent is only *evidence* of the existence of the tenancy: it does not of itself create a tenancy from year to year.

(3) *Holding over*

If a tenant whose term of years has come to an end then remains in possession of the premises and subsequently pays or agrees to pay a rent at the previous yearly rate a new tenancy from year to year may thus be created, which will be held upon the same terms and conditions as were contained in the expired lease, in so far as they apply to and are not inconsistent with a yearly tenancy.

It should be noted here, however, that a tenancy will only be created in this way where:

(a) there has been *no* new agreement;
(b) the former rent is paid or the tenant agrees to pay it;
(c) the landlord's consent to occupation is obtained; and
(d) there is no evidence to the contrary, which might destroy the presumption that a yearly tenancy has been created.

In *Tickner v. Buzzacott* (1965) the tenant's mistress went to live with him and stayed on after the death for nineteen years, paying the rent, but the court held that she was mere squatter; she did not hold under the lease and could not be a tenant from year to year as the landlord did not know that the tenant was dead and that she was now paying.

The fact that the whole matter is a question of evidence is important. The court will ask: what is fairly to be inferred from their conduct to be the intention of the parties? In *Morrison v. Jacobs* (1945) for instance, it was held that the inference that a tenancy from year to year was created could not be upheld from the mere fact that rent had been accepted, where the tenant of a dwelling-house controlled by the Rent Acts had held over under his statutory right after the determination of his term of years. Similarly, where a tenant holds over under section 24 of the Landlord and Tenant Act 1954 (which will be dealt with later) the presumption does not arise. The fact is, that in such cases as these where there is statutory interference in the contract between the parties, the mere payment of rent cannot be regarded as raising the inference of an intention to create a tenancy from year to year. Thus, it was held in *Dealex Properties v. Brooks* (1965) that the proper inference where the landlord accepts rent from a potential successor to a statutory tenant is that he recognises him as a successor, not that he means to create a new contractural tenancy.

Moreover, the inference of a yearly tenancy will be drawn only where the payment of the rent bears reference to a *yearly* rent. Thus, in *Adler v. Blackman* (1952), the tenancy agreement was for one year and the rent was expressed to be so much per week. The tenant held over after determination of his tenancy but paid the same weekly rent. The court held that only a *weekly tenancy* should be presumed from this, rather than a yearly tenancy, if on the other hand the rent under the original tenancy is calculated by reference to a year, but the machinery of payment provides for weekly payments, and the tenant holds over, continuing to pay, the situation is different: here since the *basis* of calculation is a yearly one, it is a yearly tenancy which will be presumed: *Ladies Hosiery and Underwear v. Parker* (1930).

When a tenancy from year to year does arise as a result of the tenant holding over, and paying rent after the original lease has ended, that tenancy will be determinable on the anniversary of the determination of the original term.

TENANCY FOR LESS THAN A YEAR

If premises are let for an indefinite period less than a year it will depend upon the circumstances and the general custom of the area as to whether the letting will be regarded as a quarterly, monthly or weekly tenancy. Quite obviously, the main basis upon which the question can be settled will be the payment of rent: if the letting is at a monthly rent a monthly tenancy will be presumed; if at a weekly rent, a weekly tenancy.

In the main, these tenancies can be treated in the same way as the tenancy from year to year. If a tenant holds over with the consent of the landlord after the end of the tenancy and pays rent with reference to a week or a month, a new weekly or monthly tenancy will be presumed.

Once again, it will be a matter of determining from the circumstances just what the true intention of the parties might be. Unless a contrary intention is shown, however, the holding will be on the same terms as under the old lease, so far as they can apply to the new tenancy.

It is important to recall the distinction to be drawn between tenancies and the mere hiring of rooms. It will be remembered that the relationship of landlord and tenant does not arise where the situation is one of hire only. The distinction is sometimes not clearly grasped where weekly and monthly tenancies arise, but it is there, nevertheless. If it is a hiring—in other words, if the "tenant" is merely a lodger and nothing more—it is not a tenancy; but the mere fact that the period is as short as a week or a month does not mean that it does not give rise to a tenancy. The length of the period is irrelevant.

The landlord of any dwelling for which rent is payable weekly, regardless of how it is calculated, or whether rates are included, must provide a rentbook, except where there is a payment in respect of board and the value of the board forms a "substantial" part of the rent: S4 Landlord and Tenant Act 1985 (see p.184).

The letting of agricultural land for less than a period from year to year is restricted. As we have already seen (p.13) under the Agricultural Holdings Act 1986 s. 2, such agreements take effect as if they were in fact agreements to let the land for a tenancy from year to year.

TENANCY AT WILL

The tenancy at will does not fall within the definition of a "term of years absolute" and so, by section 1 (3) of the Law of Property Act 1925 it can take effect only as an equitable interest. But what *is* a tenancy at will?

It arises where land is let by one person to another whereby the tenant holds "at the will" of the landlord. The tenant is called a tenant at will because he does not hold any certain estate. Either party can determine a tenancy at will at any time, even if it is expressed to be determinable by only one party.

Creation

How is the tenancy at will created? There are two ways in which it may arise.

(1) *Express agreement*

The first and perhaps obvious way in which it may arise is by way of a lease, which expressly states that the tenancy shall be at will. Such an agreement may provide for a rent to be paid.

If, however, the term of a tenancy is fixed, it will not be a tenancy at will merely because it contains a provision that one of the parties may determine it without notice.

(2) *Implication of law*

If there is no agreement as to the length of time for which the tenancy is to last but a person becomes a tenant of the premises the law will imply a tenancy at will. One example arises where there has been entry on the premises under a lease or agreement which is in fact void or an agreement which is not specifically enforceable. If the tenant has not paid any rent, his tenancy will be a tenancy at will: if he has paid part of a yearly rent, of course, his tenancy will be one from year to year.

If a person is allowed to occupy premises rent free this will be regarded as a tenancy at will and the same situation will arise where the tenant has been let into possession of the premises during negotiations for their sale or their letting to him. Moreover it will remain so until some other interest is granted to him, or is inferred from his payment of rent.

In *Young v. Hargreaves* (1963) a married couple were invited to live in part of a house "for as long as you wish, and I hope that it will be for the rest of your lives". After this the married couple paid rent with reference to the year. The court held that:

(a) the conversation between the parties gave rise to a tenancy at will; and

(b) the subsequent payment of rent converted the tenancy at will to a yearly tenancy.

It should be emphasised, however, that there can be no tenancy at will unless the lessor has given his consent, either expressly or by implication, to the tenancy.

Determination

A tenancy at will has been described as "the lowest estate known to the law" and this observation is justified when the methods by which it can be determined are examined. A tenancy at will may be ended by:

(a) a demand for possession; or

(b) implication of law — which may be by the death of either party, acts of ownership exercised by the landlord, his alienation of the reversion, or by the tenant's leasing or assigning the premises over with notice to the landlord, or by his doing any act which is inconsistent with a tenancy at will.

The determination may occur at any time, by act of either party, and the question of previous notice does not arise, as being unnecessary.

The determination may be *express:* an example is seen in the demand of possession by the landlord. A writ for possession would not amount to a demand: it would seem there must be a demand before the writ. Determination may also be *implied* from the conduct of the parties.

The sudden determination by one party or the other will not be allowed to injure the other's interest: an entry may be made thereafter to cut crops, for instance, and the tenant may also re-enter for a reasonable time to remove his goods.

In some cases a tenant at will may acquire his landlord's title to the land concerned. By section 4 of the Limitation act 1939 no person may bring an action for the recovery of land more than twelve years from the date on which the right of action first accrued and by section 9 (1) of the same Act a tenancy at will is deemed to have determined a year after it has been commenced (unless it has previously been determined) and the landlord's right of action accrues at the date of the determination. Thus, a tenant at will who remains in posession for thirteen years (the year during which the tenancy is deemed to exist plus the twelve years after the landlord's right of action accrues) will acquire whatever his landlord's title to the land is whether the freehold or some lesser interest. But the tenant at will, like any squatter, may perform some action which interrupts the twelve-year period. Thus in *Edginton v. Clark* (1963) the squatter—not, in this case, a tenant at will but the principle is the same—offered to buy the land concerned from the freeholders before the limitation period was up. By so doing he was held to have interrupted the limitation period and could not claim that the owner's right of action had been barred.

TENANCY ON SUFFERANCE

A tenancy on sufference exists where a person has at one time been in possession of land under lawful title, and then, subsequently and *wrongfully,* continues in occupation after his title to the land has expired. Thus, where a tenant for years holds over after the end of the term, or where any person continues in possession even though there is no agreement and his particular estate has ended, a tenancy on sufferance will arise. This does not apply, however, where there is a statutory right to remain.

What then is the distinction to be drawn between the tenancy at will and the tenancy on sufferance?

Distinction

There are several points of distinction:

(i) the tenancy at will is held by right: the consent of the landlord is obtained, either expressly or by implication. The tenant on sufferance on the other hand holds over wrongly after the ending of a lawful tenancy;

(ii) no contractual relationship exists between the landlord and the tenant on sufferance, whereas there is such a relationship in the case of the tenancy at will;

(iii) the tenant on sufferance cannot be sued for rent, for the acceptance of rent by the landlord would act as a consent, thus creating a new tenancy—the tenant is liable, however, to an action for use and occupation.

The reversioner who suffers such a tenant is guilty of some negligence or *laches* (delay in asserting his rights). Since the Crown is regarded as not capable of committing *laches,* there can be no tenant on sufferance against the Crown: such a person would be classified as a mere intruder and trespasser.

TENANCY BY ESTOPPEL

Estoppel is a principle of the law of evidence. It is a principle whereby if a person asserts or admits certain facts and agrees to act on the basis of them, he will not be allowed to deny the existence or validity of the facts asserted. He will be in a similar situation where he makes an admission or an assertion which he knows will induce another person to act: he will be "estopped" from denying the truth of those facts.

Thus, if A grants a tenancy of Blackacre to B he will be estopped during its continuance from denying that he had any estate in Blackacre out of which he could grant the tenancy. In the same way, B will not be allowed during or after the tenancy to dispute A's title at the time the tenancy was created, though it will be open to him to show that it has since determined.

Tenancy by attornment

An example of the creation of a tenancy by estoppel is to be found in that situation where the relationship of landlord and tenant is created by attornment. This is an acknowledgement by one person that he holds land as the tenant of another. There is no question here of a lease or an agreement for a lease: it is a mere acknowledgement by one party of the existence of the relationship.

Thus, if before 1926 a tenant for years agreed to the grant of the reversion to another person, the relationship of landlord and tenant then arose, by attornment, between the tenant and the grantee. This was necessary at common law to perfect the grantee's title but is now unnecessary: section 151 of the Law of Property Act 1925. Again, a mortgage may contain a clause by which the mortgagor attorns tenant to the mortgagee at a nominal rent (*i.e.*, acknowledges that he is the tenant of the mortgagee) with a proviso that the mortgagee may re-enter the premises if the mortgagor is in breach of any of the covenants in the mortgage.

The effect of an attornment is that it estops the person making it from denying the title of the one to whom it was made, and in *Mackley v. Nutting* (1949) it was held that the right to enforce the estoppel passes to the assigns of the tenant. Attornment clauses are now regarded as largely superfluous in mortgages.

Rent under an attornment clause

The situation formerly was that an attornment clause was a rent equal to the amount of the mortgage interest, so that the mortgagee was then given the power to distrain for (*i.e.*, seize goods to the value of) the interest. The Bills of Sale Acts 1878 and 1882, however, deem an attornment clause to be a bill of sale of any personal chattels that might be seized under the power of distress. To that extent, the attornment clause is void unless registered under the terms of the Acts.

The result is that the modern practitioner has tended to dispense with the power of distress under the attornment clause: he reserves a nominal rent only, so that the real relationship between the parties will be that of mortgagor and mortgagee. As the landlord and tenant relationship will not arise it then follows that if the attornment clause provides for one week's notice to quit, the mortgagor will *not* be entitled to four week's notice under section 5 of the Protection from Eviction Act 1977 (see p. 181).

STATUTORY TENANCIES

In most of the types of tenancies so far dealt with the relationship of landlord and tenant has been seen to arise by the intention of the parties. In some instances, however, quite apart from the question of the intention of the parties, a tenancy will be created or extended by virtue of some statutory provision.

Rent Act 1977, Rent (Agriculture) Act 1976.

These Rent Acts place certain restrictions upon landlords which prevent them from recovering possession of certain classes of dwelling-houses. The details concerning these matters will be dealt with later (see p. 165) but it may be pointed out here that when a tenant remains in possession of the premises merely by virtue of the Rent Acts he becomes a "statutory" tenant. His relationship with his landlord is then a statutory relationship, instead of the contractural one which previously existed. The terms and conditions of the contractural tenancy will apply to the new relationship, however, at least as far as they are consistent with the provisions of the Act.

Continuation tenancies

Parts I and II of the Landlord and Tenant Act 1954 have the effect of preventing certain tenancies coming to an end on the termination of the contractural tenancy. Instead, a tenancy continues until brought to an end by the proper form of notice. (These matters are dealt with in Chapters Fifteen and Sixteen). The tenant then has the right to make application to the court for a new tenancy to be granted to him. If the court makes an order to this effect the landlord is bound to execute or make in favour of the tenant a lease or agreement for a tenancy on the terms of the order.

These "continuation" tenancies can be distinguished from statutory tenancies in that the tenant under the statutory tenancy has no estate in the land but merely a right of occupation. A continuation tenancy is, however, a *continuation* of the old estate in the land that was created by the contractural tenancy. It can be assigned and is a valuable asset to a tenant.

Agricultural Holdings Act 1986

This Act regulates another type of security of tenure. A tenancy for a year or less of an agricultural holding (if that tenancy was created before the 12th July 1984) is automatically continued at its expiration as a tenancy from year to year and notice to quit served by the landlord may be paralysed (see Chapter Eighteen).

Leasehold Reform Act 1967

Under the Leasehold Reform Act 1967, the tenant of a long leasehold dwelling-house may be able to extend the original contractural lease for a period of fifty years or purchase, compulsorily, the landlord's reversion (see Chapter Twenty).

CHAPTER THREE

THE AGREEMENT FOR A LEASE

It has already been noted that a tenancy will normally be created by a lease, but that it can also arise by statute or by an agreement for a lease. The bulk of this chapter will be devoted to the matter of the lease itself, its preparation and requisites, its contents and interpretation and other ancillary matters. It is convenient, however, to postpone a discussion of the lease until the contract for a lease, looked at cursorily in Chapter One, has been examined here in more thorough fashion.

AGREEMENT FOR A LEASE

It has already been emphasised that although an agreement for a lease might finally give the tenant the estate which he would have obtained under a properly drawn lease it is nevertheless true to say that the agreement for a lease is not as good as a lease. One reason is the simple and basic one that an agreement, or contract, for a lease is simply an arrangement between the two parties (albeit a legally binding one) that they will enter into a lease at some future time. The lease on the other hand is much more effective in nature since it passes a legal estate to the tenant immediately on completion and that estate will bind any purchaser of the lessor's reversion.

A contract for a lease is a contract to convey or create a legal estate. As such it falls within the Land Charges Act 1972 and may be registered as a land charge in Class C of the Land Charges Register—not only *may* be registered, but must be registered to bind a purchaser of the reversion.

Moreover, the agreement for a lease, to be enforceable must conform with the general law relating to contracts. There must be an offer to take a lease, an acceptance by the other party, and counter-proposals will destroy the original offer. But for the student, perhaps the most important thing to remember in connection with the agreement for a lease is that it falls within section 40 of the Law of Property Act 1925.

SECTION 40, LAW OF PROPERTY ACT 1925

This section (which re-enacts in substance section 4 of the Statute of Frauds 1677) is of such importance that it would be as well to reproduce it completely before examining it in detail. The section runs as follows:

"(1) No action may be brought upon any contract for the sale or other disposition of land or any interest in land, unless the agreement upon which such action is brought, or some memorandum or note thereof, is in writing, and signed by the party to be charged or by some other person thereunto by him lawfully authorised".

"(2) This section applies to contracts whether made before or after the commencement of this Act and does not affect the law relating to part performance, or sales by the court".

The second part of this section need not concern us at this point, though its importance will become obvious later; for the time being we may devote our attention to an examination of subsection (1).

Interest in land

The section begins: "No action may be brought upon any contract for the sale or other disposition of land or *any interest in land* ...". What do these italicised words cover?

They are in fact very wide in their scope, covering any interest for any length of time provided the tenant is given exclusive possession. Thus, they will include an agreement to take furnished lodgings, provided exclusive possession of specific rooms is given.

Agreement

The word "agreement" in the section means a binding and complete contract. For instance, if the parties come to an agreement only as to the terms upon which they propose to make a contract, this will not be a binding agreement of the type envisaged in the section.

It frequently happens that in the course of their negotiations the parties will refer to the ultimate execution of a formal document. In such cases "it is well settled by the authorities that if the documents or letters relied upon as constituting a contract contemplate the execution of a further contract between the parties, it is a question of construction whether the execution of the further contract is a condition or term of the bargain or whether it is a mere expression of the desire of the parties as to the manner in which the transaction already agreed to will in fact go through. In the former case there is no enforceable contract either because the condition is unfulfilled or because the law does not recognise a contract to enter into a contract. In the latter case there is a binding contract—the reference to the more formal document may be ignored" (*Von Hatzfield-Wildenburg v. Alexander* (1912).

The result is that where the agreement contains phrases such as "subject to the preparation and approval of a formal contract" or "subject to the terms of a formal agreement to be prepared" or subject to the terms of the draft lease being "reasonable in the estimation" of one of the parties there will be not binding contract within the meaning of the section.

In *Raingold v. Bromley* (1931) the words "subject to the terms of a lease" were used. The court held that this meant that the agreement was subject to the terms to be contained in a lease executed by the lessor. It followed that a lease would have to come into existence and be executed by the lessor before any legal agreement was reached.

This does not mean, of course, that *all* agreements which make reference to the execution of a later lease will automatically be excluded from the operation of section 40. A concluded and complete agreement is not prevented from being binding merely because the parties also agree that it shall be reduced to formal shape by their solicitors. There is still a binding agreement before such formal lease is executed, and the requirements of section 40 will have been satisfied.

Note or memorandum

The section goes on to say that no action can be brought upon an agreement unless it is in writing or is supported by written evidence in the form of a note or memorandum, signed by the party who is to be sued or by his lawfully authorised agent.

From this it is apparent that it is not necessary to show that the agreement *itself* is in writing. Section 40 refuses action to any agreement of this kind which is unsupported by written evidence. So, even if the agreement is not in writing it is still enforceable if written evidence conforming with the section is produced.

No particular form for the note or memorandum is required provided it acknowledges the existence of the contract; *Tiverton Estates, Ltd., v. Wearwell Ltd.,* (1974): it is not necessary that the note was prepared as part of the contract. Any writing, even a letter written to a third person, could be sufficient. Under certain circumstances two or more documents may be used together to constitute the required memorandum. A signed document, for instance, which makes reference to another, unsigned, document may be used together with the second document. They may then together constitute the written memorandum. And in *Pearce v. Gardner* (1897) a letter and the envelope that contained it were admitted together to constitute the necessary written evidence.

But in what circumstances will this situation arise? Why will such joinder become necessary? The answer to be found in the fact that the memorandum, to satisfy the requirements of section 40, must contain certain particulars. It may be that one document contains only some of those particulars — it will not suffice on its own. In *Pearce v. Gardner* the letter did not contain an adequate reference to the other party to whom it was written. This was supplied by the second document — the envelope.

What are the necessary particulars which must be found in the memorandum in order that the section requirements will be fulfilled? They are the cardinal terms—all those terms that are material to the contract.

The cardinal terms

In order to constitute a sufficient memorandum or note under section 40 the writing (or writings):

(1) must:

(a) identify the parties;

(b) identify the property concerned;

(c) contain all other material terms of the contract, including the length and commencement of the term, and the rent payable, together with any special covenants or stipulations that have been agreed upon. If none have been agreed the "usual" covenants will be implied into the contract, and;

(2) must be signed by the party to be charged on by his lawfully authorised agent. It will be enough for the purposes of the statute to show that the name of the party or of his agent has been inserted by him or his agent in the memorandum as the name of the person with whom the agreement is made. In other words it is quite immaterial *where* the name appears in the body of the document; it may appear at the end or at the beginning. Provided it was intended to authenticate the whole document it matters not what position it takes in the memorandum. In *Evans v. Hoare* (1892), for instance, the name and address of a firm at the head of a letter was held to constitute a signature.

The signature of an agent will suffice if the agent is lawfully authorised. The agent need be appointed by deed only where his is to be authorised to execute a lease under seal. In *Wragg v. Lovett* (1948) it was held that authority to a house agent to make a contract would not be inferred from vague and ambiguous language. A house agent has an implied authority to describe the property or state facts affecting its value, but not to let an intending tenant into possession. The activities of house agents are controlled by the Accommodation Agencies Act 1953. Similarly a solicitor does not have implied authority to sign a contract on behalf of his clients. He must have express authority in order to do so.

Reference has already been made to the possibility that more than one document may be introduced to conform with the requirements. But what are the conditions upon which they will be allowed?

There are two situations where the note or memorandum may be contained in more than one document.

(i) The documents form the component parts of a memorandum made at the one time. We have already seen an example of this in *Pearce v. Gardner* (*supra.* p. 32), where the letter merely began "Dear Sir" but could be supported by the envelope which contained the name of the addressee; or

(ii) the signed writing refers to a previous transaction and a particular document can be identified as being that transaction. In *Long v. Millar* (1879) the signed writing referred to a previous "offer" and the two together constituted a complete memorandum under the Act.

Effect of section 40

What then is the effect of section 40?

Quite simply, it is this. If the agreement for the lease does not comply with the provisions of the Act that agreement is unenforceable.

The word *unenforceable* should be noted. It is not the same thing as saying that the agreement is *void*. It means that the court will not enforce that agreement—though the existence of the agreement could be recognised in a court of law to support other rights arising, for example, as a defence to an action, for the return of a deposit paid by the defaulting party. This could not be the case if the agreement was void, as it would be for illegality—for instance, if the tenant intended using the premises for purposes of prostitution.

Breach of the contract

But if it is assumed that the agreement for the lease is a valid and enforceable one, what rights will the parties have if the one or the other breaks the contract?

There are two remedies available: an action for damages for breach of contract may be brought, or an action to compel specific performance of the contract may be instituted. However, this second remedy may be asked for even though section 40 has not been complied with. In other words, even though the formalities demanded by section 40 are not present—which means that at law there is no legally enforceable contract for a lease—specific performance of that contract may yet be obtained.

Why should this be? The answer is found in the fact that specific performance is an equitable remedy, and the role of equity in part is to ensure that the necessity for legal formalities should not override the principles of fairness and justice. Thus, even though the section 40 requirements remain unfulfilled, in some cases equity will grant specific performance of the contract and call upon the parties to execute a properly drawn lease.

What are the circumstances in which specific performance of this legally unenforceable contract will be granted? They are found in the equitable doctrine of part performance.

THE DOCTRINE OF PART PERFORMANCE

It will be remembered that section 40 (2) runs:

"This section ... does not affect the law relating to part performance, or sales by the court".

From this it will be obvious that although the strict legal requirements of section 40 relating to the provision of a note or memorandum are still necessary, there is nevertheless an escape hatch recognised by the section in the doctrine of part performance. The result is that even though no written note or memorandum can be produced, if the equitable doctrine of part performance is satisfied, a lease binding upon the parties will finally be executed.

But what is meant by the doctrine of part performance?

Requirements of the doctrine

Under the doctrine the plaintiff must have done an act in performance of the contract. The Act must therefore have been done after an oral agreement was reached, but such acts will not all be in performance of the agreement (measuring rooms for carpets, for instance) nor will all acts in performance be acts of part performance.

The courts have held that to show part performance of the agreement the plaintiff must be able to point to:

(a) an act in performance which is referable to the existence of a contract of the type alleged (see *Rawlinson v. Ames* (1925) below); and

(b) other parol evidence of the terms of the actual contract consistent with the act done.

The payment of money will not normally be regarded as an act of part performance because it does not indicate any particular type of contract, although the House of Lords has suggested that such payment could be part performance: *Steadman v. Steadman* (1976). The following have been held to be covered by the term:

(a) entry into possession and expenditure of money to carry out improvements under the agreement;

(b) expenditure of money in alterations by a tenant in possession who is under no obligation to do so;

(c) payment of rent by a tenant in possession at an increased rate.

Mere retention of the premises would not in itself be sufficient because there is no overt act. The application of the doctrine is perhaps best illustrated by reference to decided cases. The ones noted here do not all concern leases but they well illustrate the principles themselves.

In *Rawlinson v. Ames* (1925) Mrs. Ames orally agreed to take a lease of Rawlinson's flat. At Ames' request, and under her supervision, Rawlinson carried out certain alterations to the flat. After the work was done Ames refused to take up the lease and pleaded the Statute of Frauds (now s. 40 of the Law of Property Act 1925) as a defence. The court held that specific performance of the agreement should be ordered since it was fraudulent for Ames to take advantage of the lack of writing, and there had been an act of part performance by Mrs. Rawlinson, which was referable to the existence of the contract, for how else could the conduct of the parties be explained when the alterations had been carried out under the supervision and at the request of Mrs. Ames?

In *Maddison v. Alderson* (1883) on the other hand, an old man induced a woman to remain in service as his housekeeper after she had decided to leave by an oral promise that he would leave her a life estate in the land. The House of Lords denied that her continuing in his service could constitute part performance for there was no change of circumstances suggesting the existence between them of a new contract.

In *Wakeham v. Mackenzie* (1968), however, there was held to be an act of part performance where a woman relinquished her own home and became resident housekeeper for a man on his oral promise that she would have the house when he died.

In *Nunn v. Fabian* (1895) the landlord agreed orally to grant to the tenant in possession a lease for twenty-one years at an increased rent with the option of purchasing the lease. The landlord died before the lease was executed. Payment of rent in advance can never be an act of part performance, without possession, but the court held here that since the tenant was in possession and payment of one quarter's rent at the increased rate was made, this was a sufficient part performance of the contract. Such cases are even stronger, of course, if in addition the person let into or remaining in possession has expended money on repairs or improvements.

PART PERFORMANCE AND SPECIFIC PERFORMANCE

The student sometimes finds an initial difficulty in distinguishing between *part performance and specific performance.*

The doctrine of part performance is the equitable doctrine set out above, whereby the court will accept as evidence of a contract for land, something other than the signed writing which section 40 (1) would require.

The part performance substitutes for the section 40 written evidence.

Specific performance, on the other hand, is an order of the court, calling upon the parties to do what they have promised to do in the first place. It will usually be the case that once the court has found there to be a binding contract by an application of the doctrine of part performance it will then give effect to the contract by making an order for *specific performance* of it. The order of specific performance has a wide application quite apart from the use of the doctrine of part performance. It is equity's remedy for breach of contract whereas the common law remedy is merely damages. Because equity can require the parties to perform their contractural obligations, where there is merely an agreement to grant a lease but no lease has been granted equity will treat the parties as being in the same position as they would be if the court had already ordered specific performance and they were complied with.

This is what happened in *Walsh v. Lonsdale* (1882). Lonsdale agreed to grant a seven-year lease of a mill to Walsh at a rent payable quarterly in arrear, but with a year's rent payable in advance if demanded. No lease was granted but Walsh entered into possession and paid rent quarterly in arrear. When Lonsdale later demanded a year's rent in advance Walsh refused to pay it. The court found for Lonsdale: Walsh held on the same terms as though the lease had actually been granted, since the agreement was one of which the court would order specific performance and "equity looks upon that as done which ought to be done".

Again, in *Kingswood Estate Co. v. Anderson* (1962) the landlord of accommodation which was protected by the Rent Acts wanted to get the tenant and her invalid son out of the premises. He told her that if she moved into different accommodation there would be no need for a new tenancy agreement and they could stay there for the rest of their lives. They moved in reliance on his statement and he gave them a new rent book.

He then gave them notice as for a weekly tenancy and claimed possession. The court held, however, that since the oral agreement had been acted upon by the tenant moving into the new flat, section 40 did not prevent specific performance and the tenant and her son could stay on. (On a matter of procedure the county court was bound to give effect to the equitable *defence* raised by the tenant even though that court could not uphold a corresponding equitable *claim* since that would have been outside its jurisdiction).

But when and under what circumstances will the court grant or refuse a decree of specific performance?

Considerations taken into account

There are several considerations which the court will take into account in deciding whether or not to grant specific performance of the agreement.

(1) *The nature of the contract*

The contract must be complete in itself and definite. It must not contain a material term which is unenforceable. However the court has held that where the machinery is laid down in a contract by which agreement may be reached to make a term enforceable, that term is specficially performable. In *Sudbrook Estates v. Eggleton* (1982) a lessee held an option to purchase "at a price not less than £75,000 as agreed by two valuers" one to be appointed by the lessor and one by the lesee. When the lessor failed to appoint a valuer the House of Lords held that the court could intervene to ascertain a fair and reasonable price and order specific performance on those terms. Similarly in *Lear v. Blizzard* (1983) a clause in a lease for its renewal at a rent to be agreed by the parties was ordered to be specifically performed as a fair rent. The court will not grant the order where it feels it cannot enforce the judgement. It will make no decree where damages would prove an adequate remedy (although where land is concerned damages are rarely considered adequate), or where one of the parties had been mistaken as to the legal effect of the document and specific performance would cause unjust hardship to him, nor where the contract was illegal in nature.

(2) *The conduct of the plaintiff*

If the plaintiff induced the defendant to enter into the agreement by misrepresentation, deceit, or concealment of material facts, an action for specific performance will be dismissed. If the plaintiff has not performed his part of the agreement the decree will be refused as it will where there has been an unnecessary delay on the part of the plaintiff. This is particularly the case where time is of the essence of the contract: where the property is of fluctuating value, for instance, or is wanted for commercial purposes. And if the tenant has committed breaches of covenants after entering under an agreement for a lease he cannot ask for specific performance since he has in effect committed acts of forfeiture.

(3) *Defective title*

If the lessor cannot perform his contract because of a defect in his title specific performance will not be decreed against him, but it is no defence that the person seeking to enforce the contract had no title when the contract was entered into, if he in fact has good title when the action is brought, or if he can then compel some other person to make title.

(4) *Hardship*

If the decree would impose serious and unreasonable hardship upon the defendant the court will take this into account and may award the plaintiff damages instead. This principle is limited, however, and generally a hardship which arises after the contract, or independently of it, will not be taken into consideration.

Lease and agreement for a lease

So we may not return to a question that has already been raised, but only briefly answered earlier. If the agreement for a lease is specifically enforceable, is it not every bit as good as having a properly drawn lease in the first place?

As was noted earlier, the answer is in the negative. It is true that an agreement which is specifically enforceable may in fact create the same rights as if a lease had been executed: *Walsh v. Lonsdale* (1882); but there are disadvantages in merely having the agreement and not the lease:

(i) The agreement for a lease has application only between the parties to the agreement. This means that unless the agreement for a lease is registered as an estate contract under the provisions of the Land Charges Act 1972 it will give the tenant no protection against any person who thereafter acquires from the landlord, for money or for money's worth, a legal estate in the land (Land Charges Act 1972 s. 4). In practice, agreements of this nature are rarely registered.

(ii) It will apply only in a court which could decree specific performance of the agreement, so that it would not apply, for instance, in proceedings in the county court if the agreement is outside the financial jurisdiction of the county court (at present £5000), although the court can give effect to an equitable *defence* even though a corresponding *claim* would be outside its financial jurisdiction: (*Kingswood Estate Co. v. Anderson* (1962). Moreover, it should be remembered that specific performance is in any case a *discretionary* remedy and so depends upon the willingness of the court to grant the remedy.

(iii) By section 62 of the Law of Property Act 1925 a number of easements and other rights are implied in a "conveyance" (which includes a lease) unless the contrary is expressed (see p. 43). By section 205 (1) (ii) of the same Act, "conveyance" includes a "lease ... and every other assurance" do not include an agreement for a lease for more than three years. Therefore an agreement for a lease cannot include items deemed by section 62 to be included in a conveyance though it will attract easements under the rule in *Wheeldon v. Burrows* (1879) (see p. 115).

(iv) A lease gives the lessee a legal estate and an assignment of the lease passes to the assignee the lessee's rights and obligations; a contract for a lease creates no legal estate with which the obligations imposed by covenants can "run with the land", so the assignee here would obtain the benefit but may not be subjected to the burden of the contract. If, however, the assignee seeks equity he must do equity and so may, in any case, have to comply. The matter of assignments will be dealt with in more detail later (see p. 120-127, 128-129, *post*).

Advantages

On the other hand, there are certain advantages connected to the contract which are not enjoyed by the lease:

(a) a contract for a lease entitles the landlord to the "usual covenants" (see pp. 46 and 71), but the covenants implied into a lease are fewer.

(b) the contract for a lease is free from the formalities required in the executed lease since the contract need not be, and in most cases will not be, a deed. Stamp duty is however, payable on the agreement for a lease as if it were a lease.

CHAPTER FOUR

THE LEASE

There is no particular form prescribed by law for a lease, as is the case with some instruments. Nevertheless, there are forms in use which have been settled by long practice. Their effect and their interpretation have been to a large extent determined by decisions in the courts of law, and for this reason alone it is obvious that departures from such precedents may be regarded as dangerous.

An example of a precendent for a lease is to be found in the Appendix. The form of a lease will be dealt with shortly, but first it would be wise to attempt to define precicely what a lease is, and then state what are the necessary requisites for a lease.

DEFINITION AND GENERAL REQUISITES

We have already seen that under the Law of Property Act 1925 the word "conveyance" includes "lease" unless the context otherwise requires, but that an agreement for a lease exceeding three years is not covered by the term.

What then is a lease? It is a conveyance, "by way of demise", of an estate in land: it will grant the right to exclusive possession of the property for a certain term which must be less than the term of the party making the conveyance. It will in most cases be made in return for some annual payment, usually rent, but a detailed description as to what is meant by "rent" must await a later chapter.

What are the general requisites of every valid lease? It is well settled that a good lease must comply with the following conditions:

(a) there must be a capable lessor (the question of capacity is dealt with in the next chapter);
(b) there must be a capable lessee;
(c) there must be a "demise" of land (which includes corporeal and incorporeal hereditaments, see p. 9, above);
(d) there must be a deed except for a term in possession of three years or less;
(e) the term of the lease must be sufficiently defined;
(f) the lessor must express an intention to demise to the lessee who accepts.

FORM OF THE LEASE

It has already been observed that no particular form is prescribed for a lease. Nevertheless, it will be obvious from what has been said in earlier chapters that to create a valid lease in some circumstances a deed must be used.

The matter may be summarised as follows:

(1) A lease for three years, or less, at the best rent reasonably obtainable without taking a fine *may be in writing or oral.* It will be remembered that this does not cover the case of a lease which *could* be determined within three years but is actually for a longer period (see *Kushner v. Law Society* (1952), p. 19, above).

(2) A lease for more than three years must be made by deed, otherwise it is void for the purpose of creating a legal estate in land (Law of Property Act 1925, s. 52): but it will be remembered that a tenant entering into possession under a void lease and paying rent may become a tenant from year to year, and an unsealed lease may operate as an agreement for a lease which may be specifically enforceable.

Before proceeding any further, however, it would be pertinent to ask: what is a deed?

Form and requisites of a deed

A deed is a written, formal document, which is signed, sealed and delivered by the parties. It may be delivered as an *escrow,* to take effect upon the performance of some condition, but the common situation is one whereby the lessor executes one deed and the lessee executes a copy. The former is the lease, and it is handed to and kept by the lessee. The copy is called the counterpart and it is handed to, and kept by, the lessor. In many cases, all parties execute each document.

What if the two documents conflict? The ordinary rule is that the statements in the lease prevail; but this rule is not inflexible and if the mistake is obviously in the lease this will be recognised.

A lease by deed must be written or printed but it need not be in any particular language. It must, however, be properly stamped in accordance with the statutory provisions that apply. The stamping of leases will be dealt with later (p. 48).

As will be seen from the precedent in the Appendix the lease will be divided into several parts. These are:

(1) *The premises.* This means the parts which precede the habendum. They should contain:

(a) the date;

(b) the names, addresses and descriptions of the parties;

(c) the consideration;
(d) the operative words;
(e) the parcels.

(2) *The habendum* which is that part which fixes the commencement and duration of the term.

(3) *The reddendum* or reservation of the rent.

(4) *The covenants*.

(5) *Provisos* or conditions qualifying the estate created.

(6) *Costs* of leases.

Some of these may now be examined in more detail; rent and covenants in particular will be dealt with in detail in subsequent chapters.

CONTENTS OF THE LEASE

The premises

The *operative words* are usually "demise" or "lease" but any words showing the intent of the parties that the one shall give and that the other shall take exclusive possession for any certain term are sufficient. In some cases, as we have seen, the words "agree to let" may be sufficient to create a lease.

The *parcels* contain a description of the property demised and any exceptions and reservations therefrom. The extent of the demised property will depend, therefore, upon the description used in the parcels but it should also be noted that it may be also dependent upon certain implications of law.

How will the property be described? It may be by way of the name which the premises bear or by the name of the occupier, or it may be by means of a plan which is indorsed upon, or to which reference is made by, the lease. The words used in the description are of course matters of fact but a little should be said here about the general law of the construction of leases by deed.

First, it should be noted that leases by deed are themselves the best evidence of their contents, the circumstances, and the intention of the makers. If the intention of the parties is clear but a clause may be interpreted in two ways, one consistent with, and one repugnant to, the parties' intention, the court will give effect to the consistent interpretation; in construction, regard must be had to the whole document.

Similarly, if one part of the description is true and the other false the maxim *falsa demonstratio non nocet* applies, and if the part which is true describes the subject with sufficient accuracy the untrue part will simply be rejected—an untrue statement will not destroy the effect of the whole document.

Secondly, if material words have been clearly omitted by mistake, the lease can be contrued as though the words were inserted in order to give other words their proper effect.

Thirdly, a deed is construed against the party who "proffers" it and therefore, in the case of the lease, against the landlord and in favour of the tenant.

Fourthly, general words at the end of a particular description will not pass any property of a different nature from that specifically mentioned. this is the *ejusdem generis* rule, which is excluded if the words "of what kind soever" are added after the general words, as showing an intention that the rule should not operate.

Fifthly, parol evidence is normally inadmissible to vary statements made in the lease unless:

(a) ambiguity arises from extrinsic circumstances;
(b) the language is obscure;
(c) it is necessary to show a different consideration;
(d) the grant appears uncertain;
(e) it is necessary to show a different time of delivery from the date the deed is purported to have been made;
(f) it is sought to prove a customary right consistent with the deed;
(g) fraud or illegality in its formation is relied upon to avoid the deed.

Apart from the question of extrinsic evidence, it should be noted that anything that is of the essence of the thing granted, or is parcel of it, will pass with it; this is so even though it has been accidentally severed at the time of the lease. The use of particular words in the lease such as "appurtenances" also has particular effect. "Appurtenances" will pass any orchard, yard or garden of a house and so on, but not the land itself, unless this is the intention of the parties. A right of way will not normally pass under the word "appurtenances" unless it is legally incident to the enjoyment of the property. The use of a staircase, on the other hand, usually will be appurtenant to the letting of the upper floors of a house.

It was noted above that the description of the property will be dependent upon the words used; and also upon certain implications of law. What are these matters which are implied by law?

Law of Property Act 1925, s. 62

The situation really is that it is impracticable to describe in a lease all the rights that have arisen in the past in respect of the property. Formerly, the extent of the grant could be enlarged beyond the precise description contained in the lease by inserting in the deed a standard formula of what were called the "general words" so as to include in the grant all the easements and other rights and appurtenances attached to the land or enjoyed therewith. The use of the general words has now been rendered unnecessary by section 62, which applies if there is no expression to the contrary in the conveyance.

Section 62, which has re-enacted similar provisions of the Conveyancing Act 1881, runs as follows:

"(1) A conveyance of land shall be deemed to include and shall by virtue of this Act operate to convey, with the land, all buildings, erections, fixtures, commons, hedges, ditches, fences, ways, waters, watercourses, liberties, privileges, easements, rights and advantages whatsoever, appertaining or reputed to appertain to the land, or any part thereof, or, at the time of conveyance, demised, occupied, or enjoyed with, or reputed or known as part or parcel of or appurtenant to the land or any part thereof".

"(2) A conveyance of land having houses or other buildings thereon, shall be deemed to include and shall by virtue of this Act operate to convey, with the land, houses or other buildings, all outhouses, erections, fixtures, cellars, areas, courts, coutyards, cisterns, sewers, gutters, drains, ways, passages, lights, watercourses, liberties, privileges, easements, rights and advantages whatsoever, appertaining or reputed to appertain to the land, houses or other buildings conveyed, or any of them, or any part thereof, or, at the time of conveyance, demised, occupied, or enjoyed with, or reputed or known as part or parcel of or appurtenant to the land, houses, or other buildings conveyed, or any of them or any part thereof".

Application

These provisions apply to all benefits enjoyed with the land demised, even though their enjoyment is with the consent of the lessor. In *Wright v. Macadam* (1949) the tenants of part of a house were allowed by the landlord to use a coal shed in the garden. A new lease was granted to them later, including the use of an additional room, but no mention was made of the use of the shed. The landlord then attempted to prevent the tenant using the shed. The Court of Appeal held that the use of the shed was a right known to the law and it had been enjoyed with the demised premises at the time of the new lease and so it passed under the new grant by reason of section 62.

A right not known to the law cannot pass under the general words of section 62. On the other hand, the fact that the right is a *new* one in the sense that it has not been recognised previously by the courts before does not mean that it will not pass under the section for, as *Ward v. Kirkland* (1966) shows us, the list of rights is not closed and provided the right is *capable* of existence in law, it will pass under the provisions of section 62.

In *Ward's* case, Kirkland occupied a farmhouse and lands as a tenant of a rector in 1942; in 1954 a cottage adjoining the farmyard was conveyed to Ward. In 1958 the rector sold the freehold estate in the farmhouse to Kirkland.

The only means of access to maintain a wall of the cottage was through the farmyard, and between 1942 and 1954 work to the wall was done with Kirkland's permission. Between 1954 and 1958 Ward did not ask for permission when he wished to do such work. Subsequently, a dispute arose as to whether Ward had a *right* of access.

The question therefore was whether or not a right to enter to repair could exist as an easement and if so, whether one had passed to Ward in 1954 by virtue of the operation of section 62 on the conveyance to him.

The court found in favour of Ward on both counts. Ward was held to be entitled to an easement to go on Kirkland's property for the purpose of maintaining the wall because that was a right capable of subsisting as an easement which had been enjoyed *in fact* and so was transformed into an easement by section 62.

It is essential therefore, if section 62 is to apply that the use is such that it could be subject of a grant of a legal right. In *Green v. Ashco Horticulturist Ltd.* (1966), the landlords, who were coal and horticultural merchants, thrice successively leased premises to Green for a greengrocer's shop. At the back of the demised premises ran a passageway, from the courtyard to the High Street. The leases never expressly conferred the right to use this pasageway, but Green made extensive use of it for getting goods into his shop. There were wooden doors across the entrance and these were sometimes closed. The court found that the use of the passageway was by consent of the landlords but that this consent was given subject to the exigencies of their own business and the requirements of other tenants. The court therefore held that this intermittent consensual privilege to use the entrance was not user that could have been the subject of a legal grant; accordingly, when the freehold was sold to Ashco, Green could not claim that the user had been converted into a legal easement by virtue of section 62.

Agreement for a lease. Section 62 has no application in the case of an agreement for lease for a term of more than three years. Such an agreement is not, as we have seen earlier, a "conveyance" within the meaning of the Act. A lease in writing for a legal term not exceeding three years is, however, a conveyance for the purpose of the section.

Exceptions and reservations

The parcels will contain a description of the property demised, but it will also include any exception or reservations therefrom. An *exception* is the exclusion from the grant of some existing part of the thing demised. Thus, if minerals are retained by the grantor they are excepted. But to be a valid exception, it must be of part only of the thing demised and separable from the whole.

A reservation may be distinguished from an exception in that it is a right newly created out of the subject-matter of the demise. In other words a *reservation* is a re-grant by the lessee to the lessor of something not previously existing, such as a rent or an easement. However, on the principle that the lessor must not derogate from his grant, if he wishes to exercise any right over the land granted he must reserve it expressly in the grant. Rarely will easements or other rights be implied in favour of a landlord against his tenant (see Chapter Ten).

The habendum

The habendum fixes the commencement and the duration of the term of the lease. If the commencement of the term is not stated, it begins, in the absence of anything to lead to a contrary conclusion, from the delivery of the deed in the case of a lease by deed and in the case of a lease not under seal, from the date of entry.

The duration of the lease must be certain. The latest date for expiration must be ascertainable at the commencement of the term. A demise for "one year from the date hereof, and so on from year to year" creates a tenancy for *two* years at the least, determinable at the end of the second year, or any later year, by notice expiring at the end of that year. Similarly, a lease granted for two years certain, and thereafter from year to year until either party gives three months' notice will be a lease for at least *three* years, and will be determinable by the requisite notice at the end of the third or any subsequent year. These are terms of years certain just as are periodic terms which automatically repeat themselves—the term is certain though the number of repetitions are not. We have already seen the effect of a term which is perpetually renewable by the tenant and of a term for life or determinable on marriage (see p. 37).

Because many leases were granted for the duration of the Second War and were therefore void for uncertainty the Validation of War Time Leases Act 1944 was passed, converting such a term into a term of ten years, determinable by landlord or tenant, if the War ended before the expiration of that term, by at least one month's notice given after the end of the war. The act has now lapsed.

The reddendum

The reddendum is a clause in the lease by which the lessor reserves the payment of rent to himself. Since the matter of rent will be dealt with in more detail, later, little more will be said here, other than to note that it is usually made by the words "yielding and paying" or similar expressions, but that the usual reddendum of a formal nature is not strictly necessary in a lease.

The covenants

A detailed discussion of the rights and obligations of landlord and tenant under the lease is contained in Chapter Six. These rights and obligations will be found in the covenants contained in the lease either expressly or impliedly, and the covenants clause should contain all the terms agreed between the lessor and lessee with regard to the tenancy and the use and enjoyment of the demised property. There is no particular form required: any words in the lease showing an agreement that something is done or shall be done will amount to a covenant.

Certain *implied covenants* are deemed to arise in every lease, unless already dealt with by an express covenant—the implied covenant is then excluded. One implied covenant that may be used here by way of illustration is the implied covenant on the part of the lessor that he will allow the lessee the quiet enjoyment of the premises demised; another, on the part of the lessee, is the implied covenant that he will use the premises in a tenant-like manner and, at the end of the tenancy, deliver them up so used, unless prevented by Act of God.

There are also those covenants known as the "*usual covenants*". In the absence of an agreement to the contrary, the parties are entitled to have the usual covenants inserted in the lease. The usual covenants are:

(1) On the part of the lessee, covenants
- (a) to pay the rent reserved;
- (b) to pay tenant's rates and taxes;
- (c) to keep and deliver up the premises in repair;
- (d) to allow the landlord to enter and view the state of repair;
- (e) a proviso for re-entry on non-payment of rent.

(2) On the part of the lessor a qualified covenant for quiet enjoyment, limited to the acts of the lessor himself and persons claiming under him.

Though these are designated the "usual" covenants, it should perhaps be pointed out that the list of usual covenants should not be regarded as a closed one. Lord Maugham, for instance, has said that in his opinion, the list should not be regarded as closed, and in view of the modern practice it is a question of fact whether a covenant is usual in the particular district, and for the particuar kind of property.

Apart from the foregoing the covenants that are contained in the lease will vary according to the nature of the property. The lease of a dwelling-house, for instance, is normally in the simplest possible form. Sometimes it is merely in the form of an agreement, and it will contain few, if any, express covenants. The rights and obligations of the parties in such cases will be governed by the general common law rules and statutory provisions.

On the other hand, mining and agricultural leases will be quite different and more complicated. They invariably include a number of special covenants relating to the method of working the site, or cultivating the land demised. Again, where the lease concerns one flat situated in a block of flats there will usually be a large number of covenants contained in the lease. The tenant will find his use of the flat controlled by these covenants, in the interests of the community of tenants. Conversely, there will be a number of special covenants by the lessor which will govern his obligations to the tenant in this matter.

The precise nature and effect of the covenants in leases will be examined in Chapter Six.

The provisos and conditions

In this part of the lease will be found the limitation which operates to qualify, to enlarge or to defeat the estate which has been created by the grant.

A proviso for re-entry on non-payment of rent is regarded as a "usual" clause and is necessary for the protection of the landlord who would otherwise have no right of re-entry until the lease cam to an end. It will never be implied into a lease but must be expressly included in the lease. A proviso for re-entry upon the breach of any other covenant however is not "usual".

The words "proviso" and "condition" are synonymous and, like convenants, they are construed according to the real intentions of the parties. If the conditions must be performed before the estate can commence, it is called a "condition precedent", if the effect of the condition is to enlarge or defeat the estate already created, it is called a "condition subsequent".

Cost

A draft lease is often settled and approved by the lessee's solicitor but both the lease and counterpart are normally prepared by the lessor's solicitor, for both parties. By the Costs of Leases Act 1958 neither party is obliged to pay the other's costs of the lease unless the parties agree otherwise in writing, but written agreements for leases nowadays often include an express provision whereby the lessee will pay the legal costs of the lessor. An agreement to pay the costs of the lease does not include the costs of the counterpart, and surveyor's charges will not be allowed as part of the costs of the lease other than for a plan included in the lease.

A scale of renumeration for solicitors in connection with the preparation, settling and completing of the lease and counterpart is laid down by the Solicitors' Renumeration Orders 1883-1972.

Stamp duty

By section 2 of the Stamp Act 1891, the lease or agreement of a lease must be impressed by a stamp. The amount of this stamp will vary: the stamp duty payable is calculated on an *ad valorem* basis (*i.e.*, according to the value) which rises in accordance with:

(a) the amount of the rent payable; and

(b) the length of the term. There are four different rates payable—up to seven years, seven to thirty-five years, thirty-five to one hundred years, and terms above one hundred years.

The stamp duty payable on the counterpart will be the same as that payable on the lease if that duty does not amount to more than 50p., and 50p. in every other case, (if the counterpart lease is for some reason executed by the lessor it must be stamped either as the lease itself or more usually, with a blue denoting stamp showing that the lease itself was properly stamped). An agreement for a lease for a term not exceeding thirty-five years, or for an indefinite term is charged with the same duty as if it were an actual lease. In the case of a lease which is granted for a fixed term, and thereafter till determined, it will be treated as a lease for the fixed term *together* with the period which will elapse before its earliest possible determination.

Unstamped instruments

But what is the result if the lease or agreement for a lease is not stamped in accordance with the statutory provisions? It is simply this: the document cannot be given in evidence or made available for any purpose in a civil court. In practice, however, it will be allowed in, provided the solicitor gives a personal undertaking to stamp it and produce it duly stamped.

Normally, however, the instrument will be stamped within thirty days of its execution. If this is not done penalties are provided since failure to stamp constitutes an offence, though the penalty may be mitigated or remitted by the Commissioners of Inland Revenue where they think fit.

REGISTRATION OF THE LEASE

There are two kinds of registration that apply.

(a) Registration at the Land Registry under the Land Registration Acts 1925 and 1936—which is registration of the leaseholder's title;

(b) Registration of an underlease with the superior landlord or his solicitor—this will be done where there is a covenant in the headlease to that effect.

Registration of title

In some cases a leaseholder may register his title, and in other cases he *must* do so.

Registration of a leasehold estate must be carried out where:

(a) the property is situated in an area of compulsory registration and the lease is one with forty or more years to run; or

(b) the title of the reversion is already registered.

Exceptions

While it is true to say that once the freehold or leasehold reversionary title has been registered leases granted out of that title must be completed by registration, there are exceptions to this rule. Thus,

(i) a lease or underlease granted for a term not exceeding twenty-one years at a rent without taking a fine cannot be registered;
and

(ii) a mortgage term where there is a subsisting right of redemption cannot be registered.

Moreover, the applicant for registration must hold under a lease of which more than twenty-one years are unexpired and the lease must not contain an absolute prohibition against dealings *inter vivos.*

Types of title

The holder of the lease may be registered with one of several kinds of title depending upon the extent to which the Registrar is satisfied with the validity of the applicant's title.

Absolute title vests the legal estate in the applicant subject only to implied and express covenants and conditions, incumbrances and entries appearing on the register, overriding interests affecting the registered land and, if the first proprietor is not entitled for his own benefit, minor interests of which he has notice.

Good leasehold title is somewhat less effective from the leaseholder's point of view, being subject also to the enforcement of any rights or interests or estates which might have affected or been in derogation of the lessor's title to grant the lease in the first place. This is because the Registry has not investigated the reversioner's *right* to grant the lease.

Possessory title is a less effective title again, in that it imposes a similar restriction, not only in respect of the lessor's title, but generally.

Qualified title is similar to possessory title but the defect in the title is noted on the register.

There are provisions for the "upgrading" of these lower classes of title to absolute or good leasehold title in certain circumstances.

Notices

The lease may not in itself be a registrable interest. It can nevertheless be protected in that an application may be made to the Registrar for entry of a notice of the lease on the freehold reversionary title if registered. The entry will constitute notice thereafter to any proprietor and persons deriving title from him: it will amount to an "incumbrance" upon the registered land. No application for entry of a notice can be made without a court order or the consent of the proprietor of the title affected, who has to deposit his title certificate at the Registry. A caution may also be entered (without the consent of the lessor) and if the tenant is in actual occupation he will have an overriding interest.

Any tenancy, underlease or agreement for a lease can be protected in this way.

MORTGAGE OF A LEASE

As we have seen, the leaseholder obtains a legal estate in the land and, like the freeholder, he may wish to obtain an advance of money by using the interest which he holds as a security against the advance.

In other words, the leaseholder may mortgage his interest. By what methods may he do so? Section 86 of the Law of Property Act 1925 stipulates that he can do so in only two ways:

(1) by sub-demise—that is, by creating a new term of years which is less by at least one day than his own term (in order that he might have a reversion); or

(2) by a charge by way of legal mortgage—which gives the mortgagee the same powers and remedies as if there had been a sub-demise.

any attempt to *assign* a term of years absolute by way of mortgage will now operate as a sub-demise to the mortgagee, the term being ten days less than the term expressed to be assigned.

Equitable mortgage by deposit

The two methods stated above are necessary for the creation of a legal motgage of a lease but it is possible to create an *equitable* mortgage apart from these provisions.

The situation is as follows. It may be that the lessee has not used either of the two methods stipulated by seciton 86. Instead, he has merely handed the lease itself to the mortgagee by way of security for the money advanced. Quite obviously, in such a situation the mortgagee, or more accurately, the depositee, has no legal title to the lease. His interest will, nevertheless, be recognised in *equity* and the effect of the deposit of the lease with him as security for the loan will be that an equitable mortgage will be created, even though the legal formalities have not been complied with to create a legal mortgage.

An equitable mortgage or charge can also be created without deposit of the lease by an agreement to create a legal mortgage or charge. In this case the mortgagee who desires protection must register his equitable charge as a land charge in the register of land charges under Class C.

Power of sale

What will happen if the lessee mortgages his term of years and then finds that he is unable to repay the money lent? The situation is governed by section 101 of the Law of Property Act 1925, which gives mortgagees by deed a power of sale, and by section 89 (1) of the same Act.

Section 89 (1) states that the mortgagee of a leasehold who sells under his statutory or express power of sale will thereby convey to the purchaser not only the mortgage term, but also the leasehold reversion affected by the mortgage. This will, of course, be subject to any other legal mortgage having priority to the one of which the sale is made.

What is the effect of this? It is simply one of merger. The mortgage term, or the charge by way of legal mortgage, will merge in the leasehold reversion and be extinguished. In other words, the exercise of the power of sale will enlarge the mortgage sub-term by merging it with the reversion.

OPTIONS

Options to purchase the reversion and options to renew the lease are clauses sometimes included in a lease. The option to purchase is registerable by the lessee as an estate contract under the Land Charges Act 1972. Failure to register means the lessee cannot exercise the option against the purchaser.

Exercise of the option

The option should be exercised in writing as a contract relating to land is created. If there is an agreed method of exercise, the method must be followed strictly. Similarly, any conditions must be observed in the exercise, although the lessor may waive the breach of conditions, expressly or by implication.

An option to purchase the reversion "at any time" was held in *Longmuir v. Kew* (1960) to be exerciseable after the tenant had become a statutory tenant under the Rent Acts; it might also be bad as offending the Perperuity Rule.

One difficulty that arises in the matter of exercise of the option is that two separate relationships are apparent. When A grants a lease to B containing an option to purchase the reversion, the relationship of A and B is that of landlord and tenant. But when B seeks to exercise that option the relationship between them will change to one of vendor and purchaser. But at what time does the change take place? It may well be important to discover this, since the matter of the payment of rent will depend upon it.

The general rules would seem to be as follows:

(1) When the tenant *contracts* to purchase the reversion the lease is *not* determined; but

(2) *in equity,* the landlord's right to distrain is suspended until completion of the contract;

(3) if the contract is released or abandoned, or if the right to specific performance is lost to the tenant because of his delay, the landlord may distrain.

CHAPTER FIVE

CAPACITY

The general rule with regard to the granting or accepting of leases is simply that anyone who is not subject to a legal disability may grant a lease or accept one. As far as the granting of a lease is concerned, the grant can only be of a term which is not inconsistent with the nature and the quantum of the estate held by the grantor.

The result is, then, that a person who is, for instance, absolutely entitled in possession to an estate in fee simple, may in general create a tenancy for such period and upon such conditions as he may desire. Similarly, the owner of a lesser interest may create a sub-tenancy for any term, provided it is shorter than the term which he himself holds.

Apart from this, however, there is to be considered the situation involving a statutory power to create a tenancy. Such powers will be dealt with later in this chapter.

For the time being, we may begin by examining the personal disabilities that are placed upon certain individuals with respect to the granting or the holding of a tenancy. We have seen what types of tenancies may exist, what is meant by an agreement for a lease, and a lease, so we may now deal with the matter of capacity, that is, the question who may and who may not grant or accept a lease.

PERSONAL DISABILITIES

Owners in fee simple may make leases without limit or restraint for any number of years upon such terms and conditions as they think fit. Every tenant other than a tenant at will or at sufferance has a right, subject to contrary expression in the contract, to grant a sub-tenancy.

But not all persons in law possess the same rights. Some individuals suffer from personal disabilities that make it impossible for them to grant or accept tenancies. The married woman was formerly in this position. A tenancy created by a married woman without the concurrence of her husband was, at common law, absolutely void. A tenancy *to* a married woman was not invalid, but her husband might dissent and thus divest her interest.

The disabilities to which the married woman was subjected were gradually removed by the Married Women's Property Acts. Now, by the Law Reform (Married Women and Tortfeasors) Act 1935 a married woman is capable of acquiring, holding and disposing of any property without qualification.

While married women are no longer subject to disabilities in those respects the same cannot be said of minors, persons of unsound mind, and corporations.

Minors

A minor in law is any person who has not attained the age of eighteen years. The general rule in respect of minors at common law was that any lease or agreement for a lease made by a minor or to a minor was *voidable.* The means that the lease or agreement could be repudiated, or disclaimed, by the minor without liability, before or within a reasonable time after attaining majority. If the minor took possession under a lease he would therefore be liable under that lease if he did not disclaim it on reaching full age. In addition, a minor can be held liable on a contract, for necessaries supplied to him. Such a contract is valid and binding and in *Lowe v. Griffith* (1835) it was held that the term "necessaries" might be taken to include "lodgings suitable to his condition of life". Section 1 (6) of the Law of Property Act 1925 now provides, however, that a minor cannot hold a *legal* estate in land, and under the Settled Land Act 1925, any land to which a minor is beneficially entitled in possession is settled land. A legal lease in that land can therefore be created only by the person who has power to do so under the Act — the tenant for life, or the statutory owner (see p. 57).

An attempt to grant or assign a lease to a minor will operate only as an *agreement for valuable consideration to execute a settlement* in favour of the minor and in the meanwhile the grantor (or assignor, as the case may be) will hold the land in trust for the minor.

The present situation is, then, that at law a minor can either grant nor accept a legal lease. A minor can, however, acquire and hold and, therefore, also assign, an *equitable interest under a trust of a legal lease,* and if he does not repudiate that interest within a reasonable time after attaining his majority he will be bound by it. In other words a grant by or to a minor will be valid in equity under the device of the trust but voidable, nevertheless, until he becomes eighteen.

Mentally disordered persons

The former description "lunatic" was dispensed with in favour of "persons of unsound mind"; the Mental Health Act 1959 has substituted for the latter description the words "mentally disordered persons".

The general position with regard to the granting of a lease by a mentally disordered person, or his acceptance of a lease, is that the lease is binding upon him, provided that the other party did not know of his condition so as to take advantage of it. If the other party was aware of the mental condition, the lease is voidable by the mentally disordered person.

Like a minor, however, a mentally disordered person may be liable for necessaries supplied to him and it would seem that once again "necessaries" minght include suitable lodgings. However, under section 101 of the Mental Health Act 1959, if a person has been found to be incapable, by reason of mental disorder, of managing and adminstering his property and a receiver has been appointed he is absolutely incapable, even during a lucid interval, of dealing with his property. By section 22 of the Law of Property Act 1925 the power of conveying or creating a legal estate in these circumstances is vested in the receiver of the person suffering from mental disorder.

The Enduring Power of Attorney Act 1985 also gives a person the power to grant powers of attorney which will, once registered, endure when that person later becomes mentally incapable. The attorney would then be able to deal with the mentally disordered persons's property if so empowered by the power of attorney.

Corporation

A corporation exists as a legal person in its own right, but it is subject to certain disabilities which vary according to the method by which the corporation was created.

A corporation may be created by Royal Charter, or Act of Parliament, or it may exist at common law or by prescription, or it may be created under the provisions of the Companies Act 1985.

The general rule is that the corporation has the same contractual capacity as a private person, unless its powers have been restricted by statute. It should be noted, however, that:

(1) a corporation created by Act of Parliament will possess only those powers that are expressly conferred upon it by the enabling Act, or derived by necessary implication from its provisions — any purported granting or accepting of a lease outside these provisions would thus be void.

(2) a company which has been incorporated under the Companies Act 1985 must set out the objects for which it is incorporated in its memorandum of association — any transaction, including the granting or accepting of leases, which is foreign to or inconsistent with those objects will be *ultra vires* (beyond the power of) the company and therefore void however, under section 9 of the European Communities Act 1972 in favour of a person dealing in good faith with the company any transaction decided on by the directors is deemed to be within the capacity of the company.

(3) local authorities have statutory powers to grant or accept leases for their statutory purposes in accordance with the Local Government Act 1972 and the relevant statute.

Other personal disabilities

There are certain other persons who suffer disabilities of a temporary nature that might be noted here. If a lease is made under duress, for instance, or under some undue influence that lease will be voidable. Similarly, if a person was so intoxicated as not to appreciate what he was doing when he entered upon a lease he will be able to avoid liability for that lease if he can show that the other party was aware of his condition. If the other *made* him drunk in order to obtain the lease, of course, the lease can be set aside on the ground of fraud.

What if a person becomes bankrupt? Once again, this amounts to a personal disability, in the sense that his property is then vested in his trustee in bankruptcy (unless the trustee in bankruptcy disclaims the property), and the powers of leasing in such cases will devolve upon the trustee. Where property is acquired by the bankrupt after the bankruptcy order is made and before discharge this also vests in the trustee but until the trustee intervenes the bankrupt is entitled to possession of it and can, indeed, create valid interests, including leases, in it in favour of a person dealing with him *bona fide* and for value.

At common law, convicts forfeited their real estate, but since the Forfeiture Act 1870 persons sentenced to imprisonment have been able to deal with their property as freely as any person not under a disability.

But it may be that the lease which is to be created or accepted involves not a person under disability but the personal representatives of the deceased freeholder, or a trustee or a mortgagee. To what extent can such persons create or accept leases? Their positions are in fact regulated by statute.

STATUTORY POWERS OF GRANTING LEASES

Before 1926 a person whose ownership of land was limited had certain powers of leasing by virtue of the estate or interest held in the land, but with the emergence of the 1925 legislation and the modern system of conveyancing the limited ownership of land can exist only under a settlement. Leasing powers are therefore determined by the statutory provisions to be found in the Settled Land Act.

We discuss these powers below, under the head of "settled land", but it would first be wise to define precisely what is meant by the term "settled land".

A settlement arises in every case (*inter alia*) where land is for the time being limited in trust:

(a) for any persons by way of succession; or

(b) for any person in possession for an entailed interest;

for an estate in fee simple or a term of years absolute, subject to an executory limitation, gift or disposition over; or contingently on the happening of any event; or

(c) for a base or determinable fee or any such interest in leasehold land; or

(d) for a minor for an estate in fee simple or for a term of years absolute.

What then are the statutory powers of leasing in such cases and by whom are they exercisable?

Settled land

Where land is classified as "settled land" the power of letting is vested either in the tenant for life, or in the statutory owner.

Tenant for life

The "tenant for life" is the person of full age who is *for the time being* beneficially entitled, under a settlement, to *possession* of the settled land for his life.

If no-one under the settlement satisfies that definition other types of owner such as a tenant for the life of another not holding under a lease at a rent, or a tenant in tail, can have the powers of a tenant for life.

Statutory owner

If there is no tenant for life, or person with the powers of a tenant for life the trustees of the settlement will hold the powers and are designated the "statutory owners". They then have, of course, a dual capacity.

The powers

By Section 41 of the Settled Land Act 1925 the tenant for life of the settled land may lease the land, or any part of it, or any easement, right or privilege over or in relation to it. The lease may be for any term of years subject to the following maximum periods:

(i) in the case of a building lease, 999 years;

(ii) in the case of a mining lease, 100 years, though it should be noted that coal mines are now governed by the Coal Acts 1938 and 1943, and the Coal Industry Nationalisation Act 1946;

(iii) in the case of a forestry lease, 999 years (that is to say, a lease to the Ministry of Agriculture Fisheries & Food for forestry purposes;

(iv) in the case of any other lease, 50 years.

A building lease, under section 44 (1), must be made partly in consideration of erecting, improving, adding ro or repairing buildings or an agreement to do this and the rent may be nominal for the first five years. The advantage for the settlement is, of course, that in return for a reduced rent the new or improved buildings will be left on the property at the termination of the lease.

However, the tenant for life has no power to grant a lease of the settled land together with land of his own which he owns beneficially, though in *Re Rycroft's Settlement* (1961) it was said that this might be possible where there is a provision for apportionment of the rent.

Conditions of the lease. These are not the only restrictions placed by the Act upon the power of leasing, however. By section 42 (1), except as otherwise provided by the Act, the following conditions are laid down:

(i) the lease must be made by deed;

(ii) it must take effect in possession not later than one year after its date, or in reversion after an existing lease with not more than seven years to run;

(iii) it must reserve the best rent reasonably obtainable in the circumstances, having regard to any fine taken (*i.e.*, any premium) and to any money laid out or to be laid out for the benefit of the land: a valuation of the rent is, therefore, obviously required;

(iv) it must contain a covenant by the lessee for payment of rent and a condition of re-entry on rent not being paid within a specified time not more than thirty days (this is usually included in a lease in any event); and

(v) a counterpart of the lease must be executed and delivered to the tenant for life.

Notice to be given. Moreover, before granting any such lease the tenant for life must, by section 101 (1) of the Act, give to each of the trustees of the settlement notice of his intention to make the lease. This may be done by notice of a general intention to lease.

In some instances, however, the requirements as to notice are relaxed, as can be seen by section 42 (5) of the Act. Notice will not be required if the lease is for not more than twenty-one years, at the best rent that can reasonably be obtained, and the lessee is not exempted from liability for waste. What is meant by "waste" will be discussed later (see p. 120).

Moreover, if a lease made under these conditions happens to be for not more than *three* years it may also be made merely in writing — a deed is not necessary — with an agreement rather than a covenant to pay the rent; in which case a condition for re-entry for non-payment of rent may be unnecessary: *Davies v. Hall* (1954). In no case does the Act require a condition of re-entry for breach of other covenants.

The lease for the best rent obtainable without a fine and not exempting the lessee from liability for waste has obvious advantages therefore, but the relaxation of the statutory requirements may also be allowed by the court in the case of building and mining leases, including the maximum terms possible, if these are out of harmony with what is customary in the particular district or if they make it difficult to grant such leases.

What will be the situation where the proper notice is required but is not given? Will this have any effect upon the lessee? The answer is that if the lessee dealt in good faith with the tenant for life or statutory owner the matter of the giving of notice is no concern of his.

Exceeding the powers. By section 106 (1) (a) of the Act, any provision in a settlement or will which attempts to prohibit the exercise of the statutory powers is void and of no effect, though there is nothing to prevent a settlor from creating *wider* powers of leasing. Every power so given, however, is exercisable by the tenant for life even though given to someone other than the tenant for life.

But what if the lease given is one granted in excess of the statutory powers? Section 18 of the Act states that any such lease is void in that it does not comply with the requirements of the Act. The provision can provide very rough justice for the innocent lessee. Because of this the legislature has taken steps to ensure that such individuals are protected.

The provisions to cure defective leases are as follows:

(a) provided that the lease is not on its face outside the statutory powers (for this would in effect destroy the "good faith" of the lessee) a lessee who deals in good faith with the tenant for life or statutory owner is conclusively deemed to have paid the best rent that could reasonably be obtained and to have complied with all the requirements of the Act (Settled Land Act 1925, s. 110 (1));

(b) a lease which is invalid because it does not comply with the terms of the power to grant may yet take effect *in equity* as a contract for the grant, at the request of the lessee, of a valid lease under the power. The lease must have been made in good faith, and the new lease granted will be to the same effect as the void lease, subject to such variations as may be necessary in order to comply with the terms of the power (Law of Property Act 1925, s. 152). This particular saving provision is subject to further limitations, however:

(i) the lessee must have taken possession; and

(ii) it will not apply if the lease is defective in any way other than a failure to comply with the terms of the power (for instance, a necessary consent not obtained) — thus, only minor irregularities are cured;

(iii) there can be no curing of the lease if the result will be to create a substantially different lease from the one actually granted — though such a substantial departure will not occur simply where a condition of re-entry required under the power is inserted as a variation.

As the reverse side of the coin to his powers of granting a lease the tenant for life also has wide powers of accepting surrenders of leases, and of varying, or waiving the terms of any lease of the settled land. These particular powers may be exercised by him without giving notice to the trustees.

Trusts for sale

The person who wishes to guide the destiny of property even after his death may do so by means of the settlement, but a more favoured method nowadays is by means of the trust for sale. By this system land is granted to trustees to hold the land on trust to sell it and pay the proceeds of sale to a named beneficiary or benecificaries as laid down by the original owner. The important point is that the trustees have the power to postpone the sale indefinitely and allow the beneficiary the use of the land in the meanwhile.

Section 28 (1) of the Law of Property Act 1925 gives to the trustees under a trust for sale all the powers of a tenant for life and of the trustees of a settlement under the Settled Land Act 1925, combined.

Quite apart from these powers, trustees for sale of land can lease the land for any number of years consistent with the estate they hold and such a grant will overreach (*i.e.*, will be binding against) any equitable interest or power affecting the land, *provided:*

(i) it is made to a purchaser of a legal estate;

(ii) the trustees are two or more persons appointed or approved by the court, or their successors, or are a trust corporation; and

(iii) the capital money arising is paid to or to the direction of the trustees or into court (so that the purchaser who pays the money to the tenant for life would not take the land free from the equitable beneficial interests and so could not make good title to a subsequent purchaser of his lease).

These provisions do not apply in certain exceptional circumstances, such as restrictive covenants, equitable easements, estate contracts, and interests protected by deposit of documents relating to the legal estate: these interests will not be overreached.

Personal representatives

If a person makes a will be may appoint an executor or executors to pay debts, death duties and funeral expenses, and distribute the estate to those persons entitled under the will. An executor derives his power from the will (though he must obtain confirmation by obtaining a grant of probate from the court), and it follows, therefore, that he can make a lease before probate. This an "administrator" cannot do before obtaining the grant of letters of administration because it is from that grant that he derives his powers. But what is an "administrator"?

If a person dies without appointing an executor, or if his executor is unable or unwilling to act, someone with an interest in the estate will apply to the court for letters of administration: once appointed, the "administrator" will have roughly the same powers and duties as the executor. If there is no will, simple administration is granted; if there is a will, administration *cum testamento annexo* (with the will annexed) is granted.

Executors and administrators are generally entitled "personal representatives".

By section 39 of the Administration of Estates Act 1925 it is provided that the personal representatives dealing with the real and personal estate of a deceased person shall have the powers and discretions of trustees holding land upon trust for sale:

(a) for the purposes of administration; or

(b) during the minority of a beneficiary; or

(c) during the subsistence of any life interest; or
(d) until the period of distribution arises.

It should be noted, however, that since it is the duty of the personal representative to realise the property within a reasonable time they cannot grant sub-leases unless it is necessary for the due administration of the property. The concurrence of all personal representatives is normally necessary in the granting of a lease.

Mortgagors and Mortgagees

Law of Property Act 1925, s. 99

This section gives powers of leasing to:

(a) a mortgagor of land who remains in possession, effective against any incumbrances (such as the mortgagee);

(b) a mortgagee of land who is in possession, effective against the mortgagor and any prior incumbrancers.

It will be apparent from this that the power of leasing is therefore to be based upon the fact of *possession.* But what are the powers of leasing?

The powers are:

(i) to make an agricultural or occupation lease for any term not exceeding fifty years;

(ii) to make a building lease for any term effect in possession, not later than twelve months after its date. It must reserve the best rent that can reasonably be obtained, without any fine being taken and must contain a covenant by the lessee for payment of the rent and a condition of re-entry on the rent not being paid within a specified time not exceeding thirty days.

Contrary intention. Section 99 applies only if a contrary intention is not expressed by the morgagor and the mortgagee in the mortgage deed, or otherwise in writing (it might be added that this usually is the case in institutional lending — or certainly only with the consent of the institutional lender). It will only have effect subject to the terms of the mortgage deed, or of any such writing. However, the power of leasing cannot be excluded in mortgages of agricultural land: Agricultural Holdings Act 1986, Sched. 14, para. 12.

Section 99 also provides that the mortgagor and the mortgagee, by agreement in writing in the deed or not, may reserve to, or confer on, either of the parties further powers of leasing. If any such further powers are conferred they will be exercisable, as far as may be, just as if they had been conferred by the Act itself.

These provisions are to be construed to extend and apply "as far as circumstances admit" to any letting, and to an agreement whether in writing or not for leasing or letting. The words "as far as circumstances admit" may indicate that a condition of re-entry for non-payment of rent is not required in oral tenancies for weekly, monthly, or even quarterly periods.

It should be noted also that the provisions of section 152 of the Law of Property Act 1925 relating to the curing of leases granted in excess of the statutory or additional powers (see p.68) also apply here.

Leases before the mortgage

What will be the situation where the tenancy was created by the mortgagor *before* the mortgage was made? In such cases the tenancy will be binding upon the mortgagee, and will thus affect the value of the security. Difficulties arise, however, where the mortgagor leases the property before he acquires a legal estate in it and the vesting of the legal estate and the execution of the mortgage deed take place on the same day, *i.e.*, the day the mortgagor acquires the property and mortgages it. The completion of the purchase and the mortgage are simulaneous so that they appear as one transaction. Even so, it must be presumed that the conveyance is completed before the land is charged with the mortgage and therefore on completion of the purchase the tenancy, which until then can only be equitable, is converted into a legal tenancy, the mortgagor having now acquired the legal estate, and that legal tenancy binds the mortgagee. In the case of registered land the tenant's interest is an overriding interest taking priority over the mortgage under s. 70 (1) (*g*) of the Land Registration Act 1925.

Joint owners

Where a legal estate in land is beneficially limited to or held in trust for any person as joint tenants, section 36 of the Law of Property Act 1925 states that the legal estate in the land is to be held on a statutory trust for sale, as if the persons beneficially entitled were tenants in common but not so as to sever their joint tenancy in equity.

The statutory trustees have the leasing powers enjoyed by trustees for sale (discussed above, p. 59); these leasing powers must be exercised jointly; it is only the undivided shares in the proceeds of sale (or the rents and profits until sale) that can be dealt with individually by the respective equitable owners. It was shown in *Sanders v. McDonald and Pringle* (1981) for example that one of two joint tenants is not capable of granting a licence. However as it was held in Greenwich *London Borough Council v. McGrady* (1982) a perodic tenancy is determined when only one of two joint tenants serves a notice to quit, or as in the case of *Parsons v. Parsons* (127SJ 823) when a notice to quit is served by two of four joint tenants. A purchaser must pay to at least two trustees or a trust corporation or pay money into court otherwise the grant to him will not overreach the interests of the equitable owners unless he has no notice of the trust.

But what if there are two joint tenants and one dies? Can the survivor make a valid grant of a lease? The Law of Property (Joint Tenants) Act 1964 states that such a survivor shall be regarded, in favour of the purchaser of the legal estate, as solely and beneficially entitled. If he conveys as beneficial owner. These provisions are subject to two exceptions:

(1) where before the conveyance by the survivor a memorandum of severance has been annexed to or endorsed on the conveyance which vested the legal estate in the joint tenants;

(2) where a receiving order in bankruptcy made against any of the joint tenants, or a petition for such an order, has been registered under the Land Charges Act 1972.

In both these situations, the provisions noted above will not apply.

The Act applies, with the appropriate modifications, to a conveyance by the personal representatives of the survivor of joint tenants, but registered land is excluded from the provisions of the Act.

In *Rye v. Rye* (1962) it was held that a person cannot make a grant to himself and persons cannot grant to themselves a tenancy of property of which they are the joint owners.

Receivers

Where a receiver is appointed by the High Court he can create a valid lease only where this is sanctioned by the court: generally the judge in chambers will give directions as to the management of the estate.

Where leases are granted they will be made in the name of the estate owner, and the reciever must obtain the best terms.

By section 101 (1) (iii) of the Law of Property Act 1925 a mortgagee may, where the mortgage money has become due, appoint a receiver by deed to take the income of the mortgaged property or any part of it, unless the mortgagor loses his power to distrain for rent and the statutory powers of leasing are then vested in the mortgageee. No appointment can be made until the mortgagee has become entitled to exercise the power of sale conferred by the Act.

It should be noted that the reciever, when appointed, has no authority to lease the property unless the mortgagee delegates his power of leasing to the receiver, in writing.

Finally, in dealing with the question of who may grant and accept leases we can deal with the position of the agent, and of the Crown.

THE POSITION OF THE AGENT

If the estate owner wishes an agreement for a lease to be entered into on his behalf by an agent, he can appoint such an agent without formality. If the agent is to make a lease or an agreement under seal, however, the appointment also must be by deed — the agent must, in other words, be given power of attorney.

The execution of a lease or agreement for a lease by a properly authorised agent will bind both his principal and the other party; if the agent exceeds his authority, however, the principal will not be bound and the agent becomes personally liable on the contract he has made.

Estate agents who are instructed to find a lessee, without more, have no authority to make a contract for a lease or to let persons into possession or to take deposits. If an agent acts without the necessary authority, however, his acts may become binding if his principal later ratifies the act — and since ratification relates back to the time when the agreement was first made, the fact that the tenant has since repudiated the agreements is immaterial.

Misrepresentation

In *Armstrong v. Strain* (1952) a house owner instructed an agent to sell the property but did not tell him that the house had been underpinned on several occasions. The agent told the purchasers that the house was in sound condition but after the sale subsidence occurred. An action for deceit failed against the agent because he had not been fraudulent, and against the owner because he had not deliberately kept the agent in ignorance or misled the purchaser. But if either the owner of the agent had acted fraudulently an action would have lain against the fraudulent person. However, in *Gosling v. Anderson,* the owner of a house was held liable for his estate agent's negligent misrepresentation under section 2 (1) of the Misrepresentation Act 1967. An owner may also be liable for his own mis-statements under *Hedley Byrne & Co. Ltd. v. Heller & Ptners. Ltd.* (1964) if he makes the statement as an expert. Fraudulent statements of the agent may be imputed to the pincipal even if he has not authorised the agent to make them. In *Navarro v. Moregrand* (1951) the agent without knowledge or authority of the landlords, extracted an illegal premium from the tenant, and the Court of Appeal held the landlords liable since their agent had been acting within the scope of his *apparent* authority.

But what if the lessee is fraudulent? In *Feret v. Hill* (1854) the lessee obtained the lease by falsely stating that he intented to carry on a lawful trade there; in fact he used the premises for illegal purposes, but it was held that when forcibly evicted by the landlord he could sue to -re-enter, the fraud not having avoided the lease. The landlord could, of course, sue for rescission.

House agents

The house agent who lets property for his employer has certain duties:

(a) he should make reasonable enquiries as to the solvency of the tenant (unless the terms of his employment absolve him from such duties);

(b) he should obtain the best price reasonably obtainable;

(c) until the principal finally accepts an offer he must disclose to his principal any other offers made to him.

The remuneration of house agents and estate agents is normally based upon a scale of commission; the commission payment will depend upon the terms of the agreement between the parties but since the basic principle is that commission is payable out of the purchase price, the agent can claim commission only when he has introduced to the principal a person who enters into an enforceable letting agreement with the principal unless the agency agreement specifies otherwise. If the agent makes the contract of letting, of course, he is entitled to remuneration.

The position may therefore be summarised thus:

(a) the agent is entitled to commission if he effects a sale;

(b) he can obtain commission for *introducing* a purchaser only where the contract so stipulates;

(c) commission on *offers* is payable only where the contract clearly and unequivocally states this;

(d) commission can be claimed if the *principal* repudiates a binding contract of purchase;

(e) no commission is payable if the third party defaults on a binding contract (unless the principal obtains specific performance of the contract).

As for the accepting of deposits it was held in *Sorrel v. Finch* (1976) that if the agent absconds with the money the vendor will not be liable to the purchaser even though he, the vendor, knew of receipt of the deposit, unless the vendor gave the agent authority to receive deposits.

THE CROWN

The Sovereign is a corporation sole. At common law the Crown could grant leases to any extent and thereby bind the successors.

By the Crown Estate Act 1961, s. 3, the Crown Estate Commissioners may lease any part of the Crown Estate for the best consideration which in their opinion can be obtained but no lease can be granted for a term of more than 100 years from the date of the lease. This restriction will not apply where the lease is granted by way of extension of a long tenancy at a low rent and it appears to the Commissioners that, if the tenancy were not a tenancy from the Crown, there would be a right to an extended lease: see the Leasehold Reform Act 1967, s. 33 (3). See further Chapter Nineteen.

The lease must take effect in possessin not later than twelve months after its date, or in reversion after a lease which has not more than twenty-one years to run.

If the property is to be used for public or charitable purposes the Crown Commissioners may make a lease for any term, either gratuitously or for such consideration as they think, for the development, improvement or general benefit of the Crown Estate.

Government departments are also authorised to acquire land for public purposes in some cases: where this happens, their powers of leasing the property are subject to strict compliance with the enabling Act. If the body is to be regarded as the servant or agent of the Crown, it will obviously enjoy the privileges of the Crown, but otherwise no such privileges accrue. Thus, in *Tamlin v. Hannaford* (1949) it was held that the property belonging to the British Transport Commission was subject to the provisions of the Rent Acts not being Crown property.

PART TWO

RIGHTS AND OBLIGATIONS OF THE PARTIES

The creation of the relationship of landlord and tenant must give rise to certain rights and obligations on both sides. These may now be looked at in detail. Obviously, it would be appropriate first to deal with the rights which subsist during the existence of the tenancy. Later in the section, however, the rights and obligations of the parties on termination of the tenancy will be discussed as will the situation where the terms of the tenancy have been broken by one of the parties.

CHAPTER SIX

COVENANTS

A covenant is a contractural obligation imposed or created by *deed.* A lease can impose covenants in two ways, either expressly or by implication. In the former the covenants are set out in the lease between the parties, but in the latter case covenants are implied by law under the normal rules of contracts. In addition, there are to be considered in this chapter what covenants are included by the expression "the usual covenants"; the construction of express covenants, the results that arise from their inclusion in the lease and their relationship with implied covenants. Finally, covenants which run with the land demised both at law and in equity will be dealt with.

IMPLIED COVENANTS

Certain covenants are implied by law into a lease to give full effect to the parties' intentions as the law understands them. They are implied by virtue of the use of certain technical expressions used in the document and, by the nature of the dealing entered into by the parties. It is as well to point out that these implied covenants do not arise where the parties make express provision on the particular point in question. In other words, implied covenants arise in the absence of an express provision on the point and subject to express provision to the contrary.

Landlord's obligations

On the landlord's part there are implied covenants as follows:—

(1) *For quiet enjoyment.* This covenant is implied wherever the relationship of landlord and tenant exists since it is basic to the whole nature of such a relationship; it permits occupation by the tenant free from unlawful interference. This implied covenant for quiet (meaning freedom from interruption, not noise) enjoyment is qualified only, that is it does not extend to eviction by title paramount to the landlord. Similarily a landlord cannot be held liable for the breach of this covenant by his predecessor in title as it was shown in *Celsteel v. Alton house Holdings No. 2* (1985).

(2) *Not to derogate from his grant.* The landlord must not be anything to make the property sustantially unfit for the purposes for which he let

it in the first place. Some examples will be given to illustrate this obligation which may will assist a tenant in some cases:

(a) In *Harmer v. Jumbil (Nigeria) Tin Areas* (1921) the tenant stored explosives by licence which laid down that there should be no adjoining buildings within a certain distance. His landlord, who owned the land adjoining the property demised, constructed some buildings there. The result was that the tenant no longer complied with the terms of his licence. The court held that the landlord was derogating from his grant — in other words, by his own action he was preventing the tenant from using the demised property in an authorised fashion.

(b) In *Aldin v. Latimer Clark, Muirhead & Co.* (1894) the landlord demised part of his land to the tenant for the purpose of drying timber. The landlord erected on his adjoining part a building interfering with the flow of air to the tenant's part, thereby preventing the timber from drying. The court held that the landlord again had derogated from his grant by his own actions.

(c) In *Malzy v. Eichholz* (1916) the landlord owned two adjoining properties, letting one to a restauranteur and the other to a shopkeeper; the latter held mock auctions which resulted in a crowd gathering on the front of his shop and overflowing on to the pavement blocking the entrance to the restaurant. the court held that the landlord had not derogated from his grant since he did not participate in the auctions and had not let the shop specifically for this purpose. Nor indeed did the acceptance of the rent from the shopkeeper-tenant make him liable; neither was he liable to take steps to stop the nuisance.

Under this heading it is noteworthy that a landlord is not liable for interference with the privacy of a tenant by an adjoining tenant nor is he liable for the payment by the tenant of higher insurance permiums caused by his use of adjoining land to that demised. Finally, non-derrogation is the basis of the *Rule in Wheeldon v. Burrows* (see p. 115) under which quasi-easements will pass to the tenant.

(3) *To repair.* The basic rule is that there is no implied covenant or obligation on the part of the landlord to repair. this, however, as will be seen in Chapter Nine, has been somewhat eroded by statutory intervention so that in certain situations an obligation to repair devloves on the landlord: section 11 of the Landlord and Tenant Act 1985 and section 8 of the Landlord and Tenant Act 1985 have this effect. The reader is referred to Chapter Nine for details but save for these statutory obligations the basic rule remains as before.

Tenant's obligations

On the tenant's part there are implied covenants as follows:

(1) *To pay rent.* Where the words "yeilding and paying" are expressed in a lease there is imported an obligation in the form of a covenant by the tenant to pay the rent. This obligation is, however, imported even if

the words are omitted where the tenants hold at a fixed rent. Where the obligation to pay rent is so implied the landlord must in theory come to the demised premises to collect the rent, otherwise where there is an express obligation the landlord must be sought out by the tenant. Under the Landlord and Tenant Act 1985 a landlord must provide a rent book giving prescribed information form for premises let at a weekly rent (see p. 183).

(2) *To pay the rates and taxes except*

(a) income tax charged on the landlord; and

(b) subject to contrary agreement Tithe Redemption annuity and rates when they are assessed on the landlord.

(3) *To repair.* The position here is a variable one dependent on the length of the tenancy. Basically, of course, a tenant is always liable for voluntary waste. In addition:

(a) A weekly or monthly tenant although under *no* duty to repair must use the premises in a "tenant-like" manner. For example he must cause the chimneys to be swept and mend electric fuses.

(b) A yearly tenant must use the property in a "tenant-like" manner and when the property is agricultural it must be cultivated by the tenant according to custom in a husband-like manner.

(c) A tenant for a fixed term is liable for repairs, however, the parties to a long lease will invariably make express provision for repairs.

(4) *Not to repudiate the landlord's title.* The effect of this obligation is that, if the tenant *intentionally* sets up an adverse title to the landlord or prejudices the landlord's title, a forfeiture arises by operation of law but the landlord must elect to act upon it by re-entering or suing for possession.

Finally it must be noted that there is *no* implied covenant on the part of the tenant to allow a landlord to enter and view demised premises unless there is an express covenant by the landlord to repair them or he is under a statutory obligation to do so. These matters will be touched upon again, later.

USUAL COVENANTS

At this juncture it is as well to mention what are called the "usual covenants and conditions"; since the parties, instead of setting out in full the obligations they are to undertake, may merely refer to "the usual covenants and conditions". Although what this includes is a question of fact for the determinaiton of the court and may vary according to locality and custom, the following are deemed in any event to be included by such a phrase (it might be added that the covenants below can be insisted upon also under an open contract for a lease).

By the landlord

(i) A *qualified* covenant for quiet enjoyment.

By the tenant

(i) To pay the rent;
(ii) to pay the tenant's rates and taxes;
(iii) to keep and deliver up the premises in repair;
(iv) to permit the landlord to enter and view the state of repair;
(v) a *provisio* for re-entry for non-payment of rent.

It may be noted that the following are *not* usual; a covenant by the tenant *not* to assign without the landlord's consent; a covenant by the tenant *not* to carry on a certain trade or business; and a proviso for forfeiture or re-entry on the tenant's bankruptcy.

EXPRESS COVENANTS

Clearly, the nature of the covenants will vary according to the type of property demised, but the most common will be discussed here and their construction explained. The ordinary rule of construciton is that all covenants are construed according to the intention of the parties as ascertained from the natural ordinary meaning of the words that are used: this rule is displaced only where the words that are used appear to be used in a different sense either because of the context in which they occur or where a mánifest inconsistency or absurdity would result from applying the rule.

It might be added that a covenant is construed by looking at the lease as a whole, and if its meaning is clear, it is not permissible to look beyond the document containing it. If there is doubt as to its exact practical application however, regard can be given of the property and purpose for which it is suitable, but not, for example, to the conduct of the parties, not past history nor any drafts of the covenants which appear in papers held by the parties.

The most common of the express covenants will now be considered; some, such as the covenants to pay rent, and rates and taxes, are considered elsewhere under separate chapter headings where they merit individual appraisal. Others, such as the covenants to repair which are the considered in specific chapters later must also, for the sake of continuity and understanding, be dealt with here.

(1) Covenant for quiet enjoyment

As has been explained earlier (p. 69), if this covenant is implied it is qualified only: see *Jones v. Lavington* (1903). If the covenant were expressed to be absolute, it would extend to acts of those through whom the landlord claims.

In its usual form however, an express covenant extends only to acts or omissions (from the date of the term of the lease) of the landlord or persons rightfully claiming by, through or under him. In each case naturally the exact wording is taken into account in construing the liability of the landlord under the covenant. It may be as well to set out in full the general form of such a covenant:

"The landlord hereby covenants with the Tenant that the Tenant paying the rent hereby reserved and observing and performing the covenants and conditions herein contained and on his part to be observed and performed shall and may peaceably and quietly possess and enjoy the premises hereby demised during the term without any interruption from or by the Landlord or any person rightfully claiming from or under him".

(i) Disturbance of the tenant by title paramount is not a breach of the covenant. An example of this situation is *Kelly v. Rogers* (1892) where a head-landlord evicted a sub-tenant whose landlord — the tenant had committed a breach of covenant. The sub-tenant had no remedy against the tenant since the head-landlord in pursuing his remedy of eviction is not claiming "by, through or under the tenant". The tenant would be only liable for the acts himself or someone claiming through him, which the head-landlord was not.

A further example of a title paramount is an order made by a local planning authority under the Town and Country Planning Acts.

(ii) The unauthorised acts of other tenants of a landlord are not a breach. This is aptly illustrated by the already discussed case of *Malzy v. Eichholz* (1916) where the restauranteur whose restaurant entrance was blocked by the actions of a neighbouring tenant had no action against the landlord.

(iii) The act or omission must occur *after* the date of the lease. This is illustrated by *Anderson v. Oppenheimer* (1880) where a water pump, that had been placed in the demised property before the commencement of the term, burst causing damage. There was not liability since the pipe had been reasonably placed in the premises for the benefit thereof *before* the lease began to run.

(iv) Interference with privacy is not sufficient; there must be *physical interference* with the premises but there need not be actual entry thereon. For a landlord to cut off electricity for example would be a breach of such a covenant; another example is provided in *Lavender v. Betts* (1942) where the landlord removed the doors and windows in an attempt to encourage the tenant to leave. (This is not the criminal offence of "harassment" under the Protection from Eviction Act 1977 (see p. 181).

A landlord who is in breach of this covenant is liable in damages to the tenant who, however, remains liable under the terms of the lease, save for the rent where he has been evicted.

The covenant, express or implied, extends only to *lawful interference* by third parties — not, for example, to interference by a trespasser.

(2) The covenant to repair

(a) *By the landlord*

Although a landlord's express covenant to repair in a lease will vary in extent, dependent on the type of property and the length of the lease, there are certain basic principle which must be considered. First, such a covenant entails the principles that the landlord has the right to enter on the property to carry out the repairs and if the tenant prevents the exercise of this right the landlord is not in breach of the covenant. Secondly, the landlord is not in breach of the covenant unless:

(a) he is clearly aware of the defect or ought to be: or

(b) he is in occupation, possession or control of the part of the property that is out of repair; or

(c) he has failed to repair after reasonable notice has been given by the tenant.

In case of breach the remedy of the tenant is to sue the landlord for damages; Specific performance: *Jeune v. Queens Cross Properties, Ltd.* (1974) and section 17 of the Landlord and Tenant Act 1985 which provides that a residential tenant can enforce a repairing covenant relating to any part of a building in which his dwelling is comprised; or to resort to self-help, i.e. do the repairs and recoup the cost from future rent: *Lee-Parker v. Izzett* (1971).

The tenant, however, cannot decline to pay the rent to force the landlord to repair.

(b) *By the tenant*

The general covenant to repair will receive further treatment in Chapter Eight but it is as well to comment on it here. Like the landlord's covenant to repair its extent depends on the type of property and the length of the lease but in addition it further depends on the condition of the property demised at the date thereof.

In general a tenant must keep the property substantially in the same condition in which it was demised to him, at the same time allowing for the natural effects of time and weather. Certain salient points should be made on this:

(i) A tenant need not improve the property — by making good and inherent defect in the property, for example. Thus he need not make damp-proof, walls that are inherently damp.

(ii) A tenant's liability however is not reduced by a deterioriation in the neighbourhood surrounding the property thus lessening the demands of prospective tenants of the property.

(iii) A tenant must rebuild a *subsidiary* part of the property if it is past ordinary repair. In *Lurcott v. Wakeley* (1911), for example, the court held that a tenant was obliged to rebuild a wall fronting the property that was past normal repair.

Thus the covenant generally is one that obliges a tenant not to renew the property nor even to surrender it in the identical condition as it was then demised, but merely to keep it carefully in repair allowing for the effects of the passage of time and considering the type and condition of the property at the date of the demise.

Tenants ought to be aware how onerous an express unqualified covenant to repair may be. In *Smedley v. Chumley and Hawke* (1982) on the particular facts of this case it was held liability of the tenant did in the circumstances extend to repairing defects in the design of the building and extended to work on the foundations. The general construction of such a covenant may be altered if the tenant covenants to "put" or "keep" the premises in good repair; he may then have to deliver them up in good repair even if they were not in good repair when the tenancy began. In leases of old properties a clause is often inserted, a proviso that nothing in the lease should oblige the tenant to give up the premises in any better state than it was — as evidenced by a schedule of conditions.

Fair wear and tear. Where a covenant by the tenant is qualified by the words "fair (or reasonable) wear and tear excepted" the tenant is not liable for damage due to the ordinary operation of natural causes. But he must take steps to prevent further damage flowing from the original damage caused by fair wear and tear. The onus is on the tenant to prove that any damage is the result of fair wear and tear.

It should be added that the fact that a tenant is prevented from complying with his repairing covenant by statutory regulations (such as obtaining a building licence) does not absolve him from liability.

A tenant must rebuild the property if it is destroyed by fire (subject to any express exceptions in the lease). Further the covenant may include in its wording both existing premises at the date of the lease and those (if any) erected afterwards.

The remedy of the landlord for breach of covenant is prima facie damages, though most leases will provide for re-entry and forfeiture.

Measure of damages. By section 18 of the Landlord and Tenant Act 1972 the measure of damages for the breach of the tenant's covenant to repair is the injury to the landlord's reversion, being the diminution in its value caused by the breach, and *no* damages are recoverable if the premises are to be demolished either at or soon after the end of the tenancy. A few points must be added to this statement:

(i) The section does *not* apply where the landlord has a right to a fixed sum in lieu of repairs. Thus in *Moss Empires v. Olympia (Liverpool) Ltd.* (1939) a tenant had covenanted to spend £500 per annum on repairs or alternatively to pay to the landlord the excess up to £500 after deducting the amount actually spent on repair; it was held that this was a debt of the tenant and not damages for a breach of covenant.

(ii) The fact that the landlord can or even has re-let the property at an identical rent without spending the amount by which the value of the reversion has been reduced, or has even negotiated terms by which the new tenant carries out the repairs, does *not* reduce the amount of damages payable.

(iii) If the landlord has an intention to demolish the property at the termination of the lease this is sufficient to exclude damages being payable, even if the landlord later changes his mind. However where a local authority required demolition of premises as being unfit for human habitation, due to its own disrepair as tenant of the property it could not rely on section 18 to escape damages for the disrepair: *Hibernian Property Co. Ltd. v. Liverpool Corporation* (1973).

There are certain requirements before an action is commenced; as to the requirement of service of a notice under section 146 of the Law of Property Act 1925, see p. 106. In certain circumstances it is a condition precedent to an action for forfeiture or for damages for want of repair, that the provisions of the Leasehold Property (Repairs) Act 1938 have been complied with (see Chapter Nine, *post*).

(3) The covenant not to assign or underlet

This covenant is more fully dealt with in the chapter concerning assignments generally (see p. 124). However, certain basic points need mentioning. The covenant is not broken where the assignment occurs by operation of law, for example on the death or brankruptcy of the tenant although there is a breach of the covenant if the resultant personal representative or trustee of the bankruptcy assigns without the consent of the landlord. Likewise a legal charge does not constitute a breach of the covenant but a mortgage by sub-demise does.

Again, as will be illustrated later, if the covenant is not to assign or underlet without the consent of the landlord, such consent is not to be withheld unreasonably. A covenant imposing the bare obligation not to assign is not broken by the tenant granting an underlease, and vice-versa, though there is a breach if the covenant is "not ... to part with the premises for the whole or any part of the term".

Section 19 of the Landlord and Tenant Act 1927 makes various provisions on the matter of the landlord's consent (see p. 124) which will require careful study but it also provides that where the covenant is not to make improvements without consent the requisite consent cannot be unreasonably withheld, and further that where the covenant is not to alter the use of the premises without consent, no fine or increase in rent can be demanded as a condition of the consent of the landlord.

A lease may provide that before applying for consent to assignment the tenant shall offer to surrender the lease to the landlord. This is intended to operate as a condition precedent to the coming into effect of the covenant not to assign without consent so that the tenant must offer to surrender the lease before requiring the landlord's consent to any assignment thus avoiding the pitfalls of section 19. However such an attempt to evade section 19 has been considered recently by the Court of Appeal to not have the effect desired, it being void to the extent that it would defeat section 19. In any event, the right to take a surrender is an estate contract and must be registered under the Land Charges Act 1972 to affect a purchaser of the lease from the tenant: *Greene v. Church Cmrs* (1974).

(4) The covenant to insure

Little need be said concerning this covenant. It is usual to provide that the moneys resultant on a claim should be laid out on reinstatement to avoid the undesirable situation of the other party being unable to insist on this.

THE RUNNING OF COVENANTS

A covenant results in both a burden and a benefit: a burden to the party who undertakes to perform it and a benefit devolving on the party for whose benefit it is performed. Thus a landlord benefits from the tenant's covenants when they are performed; in their performance they are a burden on the tenant. The question arises as to how far these burdens and benefits of both the tenant's and the landlord's covenants can pass on to third parties. Before proceeding to deal with it, two fundamental definitions must be given.

Privity of contract

Where two or more persons make a contract, there is said to exist between them *privity of contract;* that is to say, only the parties to that contract incur obligations and benefit from it generally. This is subject to the limited effect of section 56 of the Law of Property Act 1925 under which a person who is ascertained at the time a covenant is made, may take the benefit of it though not named as a party. Thus between a landlord and a tenant who are parties to a lease there is (*inter alia*) *privity of contract* since they are in a contractual relationship.

Privity of estate

It will be apparent however that not all landlord-tenant relationships will entail *privity of contract.* Thus if the tenant assigns his interest to another tenant (with the landlord's consent, where applicable), between the new tenant and the old landlord there will be no privity of contract but there will be *privity of estate*, that is to say the parties in the relationship of landlord and tenant *pro tem.* are in *privity of estate.* Thus when a reversion is assigned, *privity of estate* is created between the assignee and the tenant, and similarly where a lease is assigned *privity of estate* is created between the assignee and the landlord. On assignment of the reversion on a dwelling, the assignee must give notice to the tenant: section 3 of the Landlord and Tenant Act 1985.

Covenants touching and concerning the land

The next problem therefore is this: which covenants, with their burdens and benefits, that exist between the original landlord and the original tenant, can be passed on to their successors in title? The answer, simply put, is that all covenants which run with the land can be enforced by and are binding upon the respective assignees. Briefly, covenants run with the land in the case of assignment of the lease by the tenant when the "touch and concern" the land demised and in the case of an assignment of the reversion by the landlord when they have "reference" to the subject-matter of the lease". The test in each case appears to be whether the covenant affects the landlord *qua* landlord or the tenant *qua* tenant : if the answer is the affirmative the covenant necessarily runs with the land.

Thus a covenant by a landlord to do something on land other than the land demised or a covenant giving a tenant an option to purchase the land demised is a personal covenant collateral to the relationship of landlord and tenant. In such cases the burden does *not* run with the land or the reversion. It should be noted that the benefit of such an option can of course be expressly assigned and the option is an estate contract.

Examples

The following have been held to be covenants that touch and concern the land:

(a) to pay rent;
(b) to repair the property;
(c) to insure against fire;
(d) to use a private dwelling-house only;
(e) not to assign the lease without consent;
(f) to buy beer only from the lessor.

A glance at these covenants will show that no general definition can be used to cover them; it may therefore be stated that *any* covenant can be classified as one touching and concerning the land if it affects the landlord in his capacity as a landlord, and the tenant as a tenant.

Examples of covenants which have been held not to touch and concern the land are:

(a) to pay for chattels at the end of the lease;
(b) to open no other public house within half a mile;
(c) to pay rates in respect of other land;
(d) to keep other houses in the district in repair.

Conditions

Before the covenant will be binding upon other parties (that is, before it runs with the land) certain conditions must be fulfilled.

1. Where the *lessee assigns* his lease the benefit and burden of the covenant will run with the land, provided:

(a) the lease is made in due form — in *Boyer v. Warbey* (1953) the Court of Appeal held that the covenant will be effective if contained in a lease for three years or less made in writing not under seal;

(b) the whole term was legally assigned — so that the benefit and burden will not run where there has been a sub-lease, nor will the burden pass under the equitable assignement (but the benefit will). A squatter will take neither benefit not burden.

2. Where the *lessor assigns* his reversion, the benefit of a tenant's covenant and the burden of a landlord's covenant will run with the reversion, provided the lease is in due form — but an extension of the *Walsh v. Lonsdale* (1882) doctrine enforceable the same status as a lease for these purposes.

3. If only part of the land is assigned, by either the landlord or the tenant, the covenants are apportioned and run with any relevant severed part of the land.

LANDLORD AND SUB-LEASE

What of the situation where there is no contractual relationship between the parties and no direct relationship of landlord and tenant between them i.e. neither privity of contract nor of estate?

In these circumstances, the covenants are not enforceable except that:

(a) if the covenant touched and concerned the land, at law its benefit could be expressly assigned. Equity has extended this privilege to all covenants, whether they fall into this category or not.

(b) Equity allows the burden to run if the covenant is a *restrictive covenant* — though the purchaser of a legal estate without notice takes the land free from the burden.

With these matters disposed of briefly, we may now proceed to examine the restrictive covenant as outlined in (b) above in more detail.

RESTRICTIVE COVENANTS IN LEASES

A tenant has the right to use the demised premises for whatever purposes he likes — provided they are not illegal or a nuisance or a breach of covenant.

The tenant's use will be subject to the Town and Country Planning Act 1971 which places general restrictions on the use of property, but apart from this the lease itself will often contain a covenant on the part of the lessee whereby he promises *not* to put the premises to particular use. Thus, in the case of a dwelling-house the covenant will often state that no business or trade will be carried on there. There may be a covenant that no building except a dwelling-house is to be put on the land demised. A lease of business premises may contain a covenant that they are *not* to be used other than for specified business purposes. All of these are negative, or restrictive, stipulations, and a such will be enforceable by injunction, while a breach may result in payment of damages or forfeiture (if there is a right of re-entry). Covenants such as these can bind anyone who takes the land, including a squatter, if that person has notice of the restriction when he acquires the land. A sub-lease may therefore be bound. Notice however depends upon inspection of the lease containing the covenant. Restrictive covenants in leases are not land charges.

Continuing nature of the breach

Where the restrictive covenant is to prevent specified uses a breach may be of a continuing nature. The covenant will be broken then anew each day as the prohibited use is continued. The effect of this was shown in *Cooper v. Henderson* (1982). The waiver of the breach by the landlord for one year did not prevent him taking successful forfeiture proceedings later. In the absence of a representation by the landlord the doctrine of *estoppel* could not be invoked.

Letting scheme

It may be that the landlord will covenant not to let neighbouring premises for particular purposes: the landlord who does so covenant can be retrained by injunctions if he acts in breach of the covenant.

In addition, where a landlord grants leases on an estate or of flats in a block in such a way that a building scheme or letting scheme is established i.e. each lessee enters into the same restrictive covenants with the intention that each shall have the benefit of the others' covenants under the scheme, the landlord can be restrained from letting any part of the estate or block for purposes inconsistent with the scheme and any tenant can sue any other tenant for a breach of the covenant despite the lack of privity of contract and privity of estate between the tenants. The covenants, in effect, amount to a local law for the breach of which any tenant or his successors in title can sue, or be sued by, any other tenant or his successors in title provided:

(a) the covenant is negative and touches and concerns the land;
(b) all the tenants derive title from a common landlord.

DISCHARGE OF RESTRICTIVE COVENANTS

Where a lease subject to restrictive covenants merges with the reversion the covenants are extinguished. In *Golden Lion Hotel (Hunstanton) v. Carter* (1965) a covenant not to build on land opposite to that demised was enforceable against a freehold reversion by the lessees of two plots of land. Both leases were subsequently extinguished by merger with the freehold reversion. The court held that the right to enforce the covenant was lost on completion of the merger.

However if one tenant in a letting scheme acquires the reversion on his lease the letting scheme will still be enforceable against him by other tenants in the scheme: *Texaco Antillers, Ltd. v. Kenochan* (1973). However, it is possible that a restrictive covenant in a lease may be still enforceable but it is not in the public interest that it should remain so. The Lands Tribunal has power to modify or discharge restrictive covenants with or without the payment of compensation. Its jurisdiction, which is exercised at its discretion, applies to restrictions on freehold land, and to restrictions on leasehold land where the lease was made for more than forty years and at least twenty-five years have expired, but the powers do not extend to mining leases. In *Ridley v. Taylor* (1965) it was held that though twenty-five years should have expired the court should be slow to exercise its discretion in the case of a restriction re-affirmed within a period of twenty-five years.

The Tribunal will modify or discharge the covenant only where the applicant shows:

(a) that because of changes in the character of the property or the neighbourhood, or other material circumstances the restriction is obsolete, or that the continued existence of the restriction would impede the reasonable use of the land without giving practical benefits to anyone; or

(b) that it impedes some reasonable use of the land for public or private purposes and either it gives no practical benefit of substantial value or is contrary to the public interest and (in either case) money would be adequate compensation; or

(c) that the persons of full age and capacity entitled to the benefit of the restrictions have agreed, either expressly or by implication by their acts or omissions, to the discharge or modification requested; or

(d) that the discharge or modifications would not imjure the persons entitled to the benefit of the covenant.

(The fact that the landlord is prevented from obtaining an increased rent is proof of injury to the landlord: *Ridley v. Taylor* (1965)).

These provisions are to be found in section 84 of the Law of Property Act 1925. If an action is brought to enforce a restrictive covenant the defendant may apply, under this section, for a stay of proceedings so that he can make application to the Lands Tribunal for discharge or modification of the covenant. It was held in *Iveagh v. Harris* (1929), however, that there is no similar power to stay proceedings for forfeiture of a lease where there has been a breach of a restrictive covenant in that lease.

CHAPTER SEVEN

RENT

Rent may be described as the periodical payment due from the tenant to the landlord in return for the landlord's allowing the tenant the enjoyment of the land or other corporeal hereditament which is the subject of the tenancy.

Rent is therefore a profit issuing out of the land: it must always be a profit although there is not need for it to be a sum of money. It usually is money, but it may consist of goods or manual services. As a profit it must also be certain in nature or at least capable of being reduced to certainty by either party. The amount is sufficiently certain if it may be made so by an arithmetical process — the maxim "*ad certum est quod certum reddi potest*" applies. However in *Beer v. Bowden* (1981) it was held where a rent review clause fails to provide machinery for fixing rent, in the absence of agreement, the court may imply a term providing machinery to give business efficacy to the lease. The new rent would be a fair market rent excluding the tenant's improvements.

Rent is also incident to the reversion in the land; this means that on the death of the landlord, the right to recover the rent will pass to the person next entitled to the reversion after the deceased landlord.

Rates paid by the tenant to the local authority are not rent any more than are payments made by him as a result of the landlord's statutory right to repayment in respect of rates which the landlord has been directed to pay. Moreover, it makes no difference what the parties call the payment — for instance, a payment described as a premium has been held really to constitute a rent, while in *Westminster v. Store Properties* (1944) the money paid under an agreement whereby the landlord consented to a breach of covenant was held not to be rent, even though the parties called it by this name.

KINDS OF RENT

The student may well be confused by the various terms used in respect of rent so it would be as well to define them as early as possible. At common law there are three kinds of rent but only one rent-service arises from the relationship of landlord and tenant.

(1) Rent-service

The rent that is due from the tenant of a corporeal hereditament is called a rent-service; it is so called because it takes the place of the services which in feudal times were rendered by the tenant to his lord as incident to, and in recognition of, his tenure.

For the enforcement of these services the lord had the right of distress (which is deal with later, see. p. 130) — which at common law is the essential characteristic of a rent. Accordingly, since distraint can not be made upon an *incorporeal hereditament*, any periodical payment reserved upon grant of one is not, in the strict sense of the term, a rent.

This does not mean that the relationship of landlord and tenant cannot be created by a grant of an incorporeal hereditament for a term of years. In *Lord Hastings v. Northe Eastern Ry.* (1898) on a grant of a wayleave for a term of years there was a reservation of annual payments to the grantor and his heirs and assigns. These payments were described as "rents". The court held that the relationship of landlord and tenant existed between the grantor and grantee and that on the death of the grantor the right to recover the payments to the person next entitled to the reversion.

Where however a single rent is reserved upon a letting of corporeal and incorporeal hereditaments or of corporeal hereditaments and chattels, the whole rent is regarded as issuing out of the corporeal hereditament. So, in *Newman v. Anderton* (1806), it was held that on the letting of a house with furniture, the whole of the rent could be distrained for.

(2) Rencharge

The second kind of rent, called rentcharge, comes into existence when land is charged (in most cases, perpertually) with the payment of an annual sum of money, for which distress can be levied. The distress arises in such cases out of an express clause in the deed and by virtue of section 121 of the Law of Property Act 1925 — but it must be remembered that in the case of the rentcharge the relationship of landlord and tenant does not arise. The owner of the rent has no reversion in the land.

The creation of rentcharges is now (with exceptions) prohibited.

(3) Rent-seck

Rent-seck is really nothing more than a rent reserved by deed or by will, but which at common law could not be enforced by distress. A rent-seck cannot issue out of a term of years and is now obsolete.

RESERVATION OF RENT

It is not essential that there should be a formal *reddendum* in a lease because any expressions which show that the parties intend that a rent shall be payable is a sufficient reservation. In practice, however, the formal lease will usually contain a *reddendum* which will reserve a rent by the words "paying therefore yearly [or as the case may be] during the term the rent of £—". There will usually also be an express covenant by the lessee to pay the rent reserved, and a provision giving the landlord a right of re-entry on non-payment.

The rent is, as we have seen, incident to the reversion so it follows that it can be reserved only to the lessor himself, and after his death to the subsequent owner of the reversion. Accordingly, at common law it was considered the safest plan to reserve the rent generally "during the term" without specifying to whom, in which case it went to the person next entitled to the reversion. The situation was then settled by section 141 of the Law of Property Act 1925.

The section states:

(1) Rent reserved by a lease, and the benefit of every covenant or provision therein contained, having reference to the subject-matter thereof, and on the lessee's part to be observed and performed, and every condition of re-entry and other condition therein contained, shall be annexed and incident to and shall go with the reversionary estate in the land, or in any part thereof, immediately expectant on the term granted by the lease, notwithstanding severance of that reversionary estate, and without prejudice to any liability affecting the covenantor or his estate.

(2) Any such rent, covenant or provision shall be capable of being recovered, received, enforced, and taken advantage of, by the person from time to time entitled, subject to the term, to the income of the whole or any part, as the case may require, of the land leased.

PENAL RENTS

In some cases the landlord will demand that the payment of rent be secured by a bond; the right to such bond will then pass with the reversion. In any action the lessor can sue for the bond or for rent. If he elects to sue for rent, he cannot proceed thereafter on the bond.

The amount of damages for breach of covenants other than payment of rent may also be settled by agreement in advance; this may then take the form of an additional or "penal" rent. The difficulty here is that while the courts are prepared to order payment of liquidated damages (damages agreed to be payable in the event of breach) they have set their faces against bonds or penalties which attempt to coerce tenants into keeping the agreement by stipulating that a totally unrealistic sum be paid in the event of default by the tenant. If the "penal rent" amounts to liquidated damages it can therefore be enforced, but if it is really a penalty then although the lessor can get judgement he will not obtain the sum stated in the agreement — he will be awarded the damages that he has *actually* sustained by the failure to pay.

How are penalties and liquidated damages to be distinguished? Basically, the difference is that liquidated damages amount to a genuine attempt to pre-estimate loss: it is a sum agreed to be paid and intended to be actually paid. A penalty, on the other hand, is not an attempt to pre-estimate loss: it is a payment stipulated *in terrorem,* to coerce the other party. In all cases, however, it is a matter of construction whether the clause will amount to a penalty or not. Some examples might be useful to illustrate the position.

In *Wilson v. Love* (1896) the agreement stated that an additional rent of £3 per ton should be paid by way of penalty for all hay and straw off the premises in the last year of the tenancy. The value of the hay was less than that of straw, and only hay had been sold. The court held that the term was a penalty and unenforceable: only damages (which amounted to 75p to £1 per ton) could be obtained, for the sum of £3 per ton bore no relation to the loss *likely* to be suffered, and so the additional rent was a payment *in terrorem*.

In*Hinton v. Sparkes* (1868) it was held that where a deposit was made to secure the proper performance of the contract, and it is to be forfeited in the event of a breach, this was *not* a penalty.

In *Charrington & Co. v. Wooder* (1914) it was held that a provision inserted in the publican's lease of a "tied house" that the publican/lessee must take all his beer from the lessor, or else pay rent in advance, was valid, provided the lessor supplied good beer at fair prices.

Special provisions relate to agricultural holdings in these matters. By section 24 of the Agricultural Holdings Act 1986 a landlord cannot recover by distress or otherwise any higher rent or liquidated damages in excess of actual damage if such sum is payable under the agreement for breach, or non-fulfilment, of a term or condition.

WHEN RENT IS DUE

The periods for which and the dates at which the rent is payable should be specified in the *reddendum*. If the rent is reserved generally, however, with no mention being made of the periods for which it is payable, it will be due annually. If the periods are mentioned but not dates are specified the dates of payment must be calculated from the *habendum*.

A distinction must be drawn between the times when rent is *due* and when it is *in arrear*. Rent is due in the morning of the day named for payment. It is not in arrear, however, until after midnight of that day.

The time for demand, in order to take advantage of a condition for re-entry at common law, is just before and at sunset, and there are various corollary rules to this which have been laid down by the courts. In practice, however, these rules are avoided by an express provision in the lease itself exempting the need for a formal demand.

Rent is payable to the lessor or to his authorised agent; on an assignment of the reversion the rent will become payable to the assignee after notice of the assignment has been given to the tenant. Section 3 of the Landlord and Tenant Act 1985 requires such notice within two months of the assignment. If the tenant pays the rent to someone other than the reversioner without the necessary consent or authority, the reversioner can still claim the rent from the tenant. On the reverse side of the coin, payment of the rent by a stranger to the tenancy will not discharge the tenant from his liability to pay unless the stranger acts as the tenant's agent or with his authority or subsequent ratification.

Rent expressed in terms of money must be paid in lawful currency, and the ordinary words in the *reddendum* "yielding and paying" imply that payment should be in cash. Unless agreement is reached on the method, payment should not be made by post, but where the landlord directs the tenant to pay by post the landlord will bear the loss if the money is lost in the post.

APPORTIONMENT

If land which is the subject of a lease at a certain rent becomes divided among several individuals, such as where the landlord disposes of part of his reversion by deed or will to other persons, an apportionment of the rent will become necessary.

Where the lessee assigns part of the demised property, the landlord has a choice — he may continue to demand the full rent from the lessee, or he may demand a proportionate part of the rent from the assignee. But even though he has recieved rent from the assignee, the landlord can still rely upon the personal contract between himself and the tenant, so that the tenant can yet be made liable for the whole of the arrears to the landlord.

If the tenant is evicted from part of the leased property by someone who has better title, he must pay a rateable proportion for what he still holds; if he is evicted by the landlord, or the landlord's assignee, however, no apportionment is made. Instead, a supervision of his liability to pay rent takes place.

Apart from the foregoing, however, there is also the question of apportionment as to time, and this matter is dealt with by the Apportionment Act 1870, which states:

"All rents, annuities, dividends, and other periodical payments in the nature of income (whether reserved or made payable under an instrument in writing or otherwise), shall, like interest on money lent, be considered as accruing from day to day, and shall be apportionable in respect of time accordingly".

The terms of this section (s. 2) are comprehensive and apply generally, except in those cases where it is expressly stipulated that no apportionment shall take place. Rent payable in advance and already accrued due is not apportionable, of course: in *Ellis v. Rowbotham* (1900) the rent was payable in advance and the landlord took permission on default being made with an instalment — he was held to be entitled to payment of the whole of the rent.

DURATION OF LIABILITY

It has been decided in a number of cases that the liability of the tenant to pay the rent will continue throughout the term of the lease, even though the premises have been destroyed by fire or by flood, or even where they are occupied by an alien enemy. The reason for this is that the tenant has agreed to pay the rent at particular fixed periods: he has created a duty by his own contract and he is bound to fulfil that duty in spite of any accident that might occur to render his occupation valueless or impossible. If he wishes to escape in such situations, he must ensure that stipulations to this effect appear in the lease when he enters into it.

The tenant who holds under a yearly or other periodic tenancy can, of course, get rid of his liability by giving proper notice to quit, but until the period of his lease is up he will still remain liable in spite of the accidents detailed above.

Attempts have been made to apply the doctrine of frustration to a lease in such cases, but in *Cricklewood Property, etc. v. Leighton's Investment Trust* (1945) the interruption for a time by war of the building contemplated under a ninety-year building lease was held by the House of Lords not to have frustrated the lease and liability for payment of the rent continued. There was some doubt as to whether the doctrine of frustration could *ever* apply to a lease and, until the case of *National Carriers v. Panalpina* (1981) was decided in the House of Lords, it was generally accepted that it can not. In *National Carriers v. Panalpina* (1981) it was held the doctrine of frustration is in principle applicable to leases, although the occasions on which it may be applied are rare. In this case the lease of a warehouse was held not to be frustrated on the facts when the only entry to the warehouse was closed after five years for 20 months. A lease will only be frustrated in exceptional circumstances.

But when will the tenant's liability for payment of the rent be terminated during the period of the lease, if not by fire, flood or other destruction?

Termination of liability

There are several situations where his liability to pay the rent will end, or indeed, never begin.

(1) *Illegality*

If the contract under which the lessee holds the premises is an illegal contract, he will not be liable to pay the rent. This would be the case, for instance, where the premises were to be used for prostitution, or immorality, or blasphemous lectures. If the contract is merely tainted with illegality, this will be enough unless the illegal term is severable as in *Ailion v. Spiekermannn* (1976) where an agreement for a lease required the tenant to pay an illegal premium and the tenant was allowed to enforce the agreement without the illegal term.

(2) *Eviction*

If the tenant is evicted by a person who has a better title to the property than either the tenant or the landlord, the tenant can use such eviction as a good defence to any action for rent payable thereafter by the landlord. But it should be noted that an eviction by the *landlord* or anyone claiming through him will not terminate liability to pay rent; it will merely *suspend* it during the continuance of the eviction. However requisitioning of premises by the government under Defence Regulations does not amount to eviction: *Matthey v. Curling* (1922).

(3) *Lapse of time*

By the Limitation Act 1939 (s. 15) no action can be brought to recover any arrears of rent after the expiration of six years from the date they become due.

Continuance of liability

It follows then that the tenant will remain liable to pay the rent during the continuance of the period of the lease even after:

(a) he has assigned the premises to another; or
(b) he has quitted possession; or
(c) the premises have been destroyed; or
(d) they have been requisitioned under Defence Regulations.

So far as assignment of the premises is concerned, it was held in *Centrovincial Estates v. Bulk Storage* (1983) that an original tenant is bound by a rent revision made by his assignee without his assent, and on the assignee's default was liable to the landlord for the revised rent.

So far as damage by fire is concerned, however, it has long been common to insert in a lease a stipulation that the rent shall be extinguished or suspended in case of damage by fire. Moreover, under the Landlord and Tenant (Requisitioned Land) Act 1942 there are certain provisions for the dsiclaimer of leases of requisitioned land; an example would be the case of the lease of premises for business purposes.

But what will be the situation where a landlord agrees to accept a reduced rate? Is the tenant still bound to pay rent at the original rate? Much will depend upon the question as to whether or not the second agreement amounts to a new tenancy. If it does, obviously the old tenancy agreement is at an end. But what if it is not a new tenancy, but simply a promise which, though acted upon, is not supported by consideration? The question was answered by Lord Denning in *Central London Property Trust v. High Trees House* (1947).

The High Trees case

By a lease under seal in 1937 A granted to B the tenancy of a block of flats for ninety-years at £2,500 a year. B intended to sub-let the flats but under the war conditions in 1940 B realised that the rent reserved could not be paid out of the profits of the flats. After discussions, A agreed in writing that the rent should be reduced to £1,250 a year. this reduced rent was paid from 1941 until 1945. A then claimed that the rent was due at the full rate and arrears of £7,916 should be paid.

The court held that the arrears between 1941 and 1945 were not payable since the parties had acted upon the second agreement, and A was estopped from denying the validity of that agreement — the lack of consideration was therefore immaterial. The original rent payable was due from 1945 onwards, however, since the peculiar conditions giving rise to the second agreement has then ceased.

The *High Trees* case, supplemented by later decisions concerned with the same principle, may therefore be regarded as laying down the following with respect to the payment of rent under a lease: if

(i) the landlord promises the tenant by words or conduct that he will accept a lower rent, and

(ii) this promise is intended to affect their legal relations,

(iii) the tenant acts in reliance on the promise,

the landlord will be estopped from going back on the promise if it would be inequitable for him to do so.

Recent decisions on this principle of "equitable estoppel" have emphasised, however, that the tenant must have acted to his detriment in relying and acting upon the promise, and the promise merely *suspends* the right to demand the higher rent, in the sense that the original payment rate can be demanded again upon the landlord giving reasonable notice to the tenant of his intention to revert to the original agreement if the circumstances have reverted to their original state.

Moreover, it must be noted that the principle gives no *right of action* to the tenant. He cannot *sue* on the second promise; he merely has a good defence if he is sued for the larger amount — it is a "shield, not a sword".

THE CONTROL OF RENTS

Many statutory provisions have been concerned with the control or limitation of rents of dwellings. These have been consolidated in the Rent Act 1977 repealing and replacing earlier legislation (see Chapter 15).

The Agricultural Holdings Act 1986 also makes provisions of this nature. By section 8 of the Act, in certain specified conditions, upon reference to arbitration by the landlord or the tenant the rent may be increased or reduced in accordance with the decision of the arbitrator as to what he thinks should be the rent properly payable in respect to that holding. By section 13 of the same Act the landlord may, subject to the terms of the section, increase the rent without reference to arbitration, where he has carried out certain improvements. The permitted increase is an amount equal to the increase in the rental value of the holding attributable to the carrying out of the improvement.

RECOVERY OF RENT BY ACTION

First of all, what are the remedies available to the landlord who wishes to recover the rent payable under a lease? They are:

(1) the right of action;
(2) the right of distress;
(3) the right of re-entry (if there is a provision to this effect in the lease).

The right of distress is dealt with in Chapter Twelve. The right of re-entry can be dealt with more conveniently under the head of determination of tenancy so discussion of this remedy is postponed to Chapter Thirteen. Here we may restrict ourselves to the recovery of rent by action.

Kinds of action

In order to recover rent the landlord may bring one of two kinds of action. he may bring either an action for rent, or an action for use and occupation. Both these actions are in contract but distinctions are to be drawn between them.

Action for rent lies whenever there is a contract to pay a definite sum as rent. This contract may arise from an express covenant or agreement, or from the fact that the letting is expressed or agreed to be at a certain rent — as, for instance, by the word "yielding and paying" in the habendum of a lease.

The action does not depend upon occupation of the premises by the tenant and so it may be maintained even though the tenant has never been in occupation. This will not be the case where there is some express agreement to the contrary. In *Fox v. Slaughter* (1919) for instance, the agreement to take the premises for three years contained a clause whereby the landlord was to put the premises in repair and the rent was not to be payable until the repairs were completed. Completion of the repairs was therefore a condition precedent to the payment of the rent and no action could be brought until the condition was fulfilled.

Action for use and occupation

An action for use and occupation lay at common law unless there was an actual lease but section 14 of the Distress for Rent Act 1737 provides that where the agreement is not by deed the landlord can recover "reasonable satisfaction" for lands occupied by the defendant, for the use and occupation of those lands, any demise or agreement (not being by deed) being evidence of the amount of damages to be recovered.

The action differs from the action for rent in two respects: it is not maintainable where the rent is due under a deed, and it cannot be maintained unless there has been an actual entry of the premises by the defendant and occupation by him, if he desires.

In *Smallwood v. Sheppards* (1895) the contract stated that the defendant was to have exclusive possession of the land on several occasions, for one fixed sum. He did not occupy the land on each occasion. The court held that the action lay for the recovery of the whole sum even though he did not use the land on each occasion, provided he could have used it had he wanted to do so.

In bringing the action, proof that the land was owned by the landlord and occupied by the defendant will prima facie amount to sufficient evidence to support the action. It may, however, be rebutted by the introduction of evidence showing that the defendant's occupation was adverse to the plaintiff.

If there is an express contract for payment of rent the amount that can be recovered will of course be the amount that is fixed by the contract. In other cases the plaintiff will be able to recover "reasonable satisfaction" — a sum which will depend upon the value of the land during the defendant's occupation.

Defences

There are several defences open to the tenant in an action for the recovery of rent. He may:

(a) show that his landlord's title has ceased since the demise;

(b) plead entry by the landlord and eviction, where rent is claimed under a covenant;

(c) show that the landlord has distrained and from the distress has satisfied his claim, or still holds the distress without having sold;

(d) plead that the landlord has agreed to accept a reduced rent, even if there has been no consideration for the promise (see the *High Trees* case, above, p. 88);

(e) set up a counterclaim, or set off as in ordinary actions;

(f) set up payment or tender on the day when it was due;

(g) plead that the contract was illegal;

(h) show that the deed was void;

(i) plead that the Limitation Act 1939 applies whereby arrears of rent cannot be claimed after the expiration of six years from the time when it was due. It should be noted at this point that as long as the relationship of landlord and tenant continues as a legal relationship the landlord's right to receive rent is not *barred* by non-payment, no matter how long since rent was las paid. Similarly, as it was shown in *Amherst v. James Walker Goldsmith & Silversmith* (1983) delay, however lengthy, will not prevent a landlord from exercising a rent review clause even if it will cause hardship to the tenant. This is so unless the landlord's conduct amounts to estoppel as in the High Trees case. The Limitation Act only applies to bar the *amount* of arrears recoverable. Moreover, an acknowledgement in writing of the liability may extend that amount in the sense that the right to rent is then deemed to accrue *from the date of the acknowledgement in writing.* Thus, even though the right to demand arrears is barred by the 1939 Act, a subsequent written acknowledgement of the debt, signed by the tenant or his agent, will "revive" liability on that rent and start a new six-year period running.

CHAPTER EIGHT

RATES AND TAXES

The general rule is that, in the absence of any contrary agreement, the liability to pay rates and taxes falls upon the tenant. In practice, the usual agreement expressly stipulates that the tenant shall pay all rates, taxes and assessments but if the agreement does stipulate that the liability is to be shared between landlord and tenant there is generally no interference by statutory provisions. An exception is the *tithe rentcharge redemption annuity* which is payable by the estate owner of the land. The term "estate owner" includes a lessee for a term of more than fourteen years at a rent less than a rack rent.

Formerly, there were other exceptions in Landlord's property tax and land tax, both now abolished.

It may be noted that the Finance Act 1965 amended by the Capital Gains Taxes Act 1979, introduced a capital gains tax on assets disposed of after April 6th, 1965. No tax is payable on disposal of a house which was the owner's only or main residence, and where only part of the house has been the residence the gain is apportioned.

In the case of leasehold property of which the lease has more than fifty years to run the ordinary provisions apply; otherwise the lease is a wasting asset and subject to special provisions.

In computing the gain certain expenditure is allowed as a deduction (see Sched. 6, para. 4). Special provisions apply in respect of premiums paid on leases if the lease has less than fifty years to run any premium is treated as rent and is taxed as income.

EXPRESS COVENANTS

The agreement between the parties may be such that the tenant makes himself liable to pay rates and taxes together with all assessments, charges and other outgoings. This would make him liable to pay such outgoings as drainage and sewer rates although as a general rule these will fall upon the landlord. But what if the lessee creates a sub-lease by which the sub-lessee agrees to pay all rates, etc.? It was held in *Read & Co. v. Walter* (1931) that such a covenant could be enforced against the sub-lessee even though the terms of the *head* lease were to the effect that the *lessor* should pay all rates and outgoings.

Moreover, the fact that the tenant is under notice to quit will not absolve him from liability if he has expressly agreed to pay the rates and other outgoings. It could be argued that he will be deriving no benefit from them but he must still pay them, nevertheless, for he has bound himself by contract to do so. It should also be noted that he will be liable for the full amount, notwithstanding any subsequent increase that is occasioned by additions and new buildings, as long as he has the benefit of these during the term of his lease.

Construction

What is the extent of the words "outgoings" or "impositions" and similar terms in the lease? "Rates, taxes and assessments" have been held not to include statutory improvement expenses, but "outgoings" and similar expressions have been held to cover single instances of charges for improvements of a permanent nature, such as the drainage of land, and the paving of footways.

Whether the covenant extends to cover expenses incurred in complying with public health legislation will always be a question of construction of the words used in the agreement and their use in context will obviously be very important.

It is possible, of course, that the meanings of the words used may be qualified by other covenants in the lease so the covenant to pay outgoings must be read with other covenants in the lease to arrive at the meaning. In *Howe v. Botwood* (1913), for instance, the tenant covenanted to pay and discharge all rates, taxes, assessments, charges and outgoings; the landlord to put it in good order. Could the landlord recover the cost from the tenant? The court held he could not, since he could not perform his covenant to keep the premises in repair without doing this work so the cost fell on the landlord in spite of the word "outgoings" used in the lease.

If the words used in the covenant are clear, they are not to be modified by any considerations as to the length of the term, or the condition of the property and so on — these matters are irrelevant to the tenant's liability under the contract.

Apportionment

Some statutes contain provisions for the apportionment of the cost of works to be carried out under the legislation in question. Examples are to be seen in section 170 of the Factories Act 1961 and section 73 of the Offices, Shops and Railway Premises Act 1963. In such cases the county court is given powers to make such apportionment as it considers just and equitable in the circumstances of the case, with due regard being paid to the terms of any contract between the parties concerned.

Remedies

If the tenant fails to pay any rates, taxes, assessments or outgoings when he has promised to do so under a covenant in his lease the landlord may either:

(a) sue him for the breach of the covenant; or

(b) sue for possession *provided* the lease contains a proviso for re-entry for breach of the covenant in question.

Where it is the landlord who is liable to pay any rate or tax, and it is the tenant who has in fact paid, the tenant can deduct the amount from his next rent, unless there is some stipulation or express covenant which prevents him from doing this. He can make the deduction only *after* he has paid the rate or tax, and he cannot claim to do so after the current year or period of the tenancy.

Alternatively, the tenant can bring an action against the landlord for recovery of the amount paid.

RATES PAID BY THE LANDLORD

It has already been noted that statute may provide that it is the landlord who is to pay the rate rather than the tenant. This reversal of the ordinary rule arises usually where the holding of the tenant is of small value, so the rates are collected from the landlord instead. See, for example, Section 55 of the General Rate Act 1967.

TENANT'S LIABILITY

Water rates are always payable by the tenant in the absence of an agreement to the contrary but if the rated *owner* fails to pay the rate the undertaking may not cut off the water supply if the owner is not also the occupier. A covenant by a lessor to pay rates and impositions does not normally include water rates, since the water rate is a liability primarily incurred by the occupier, who will be the tenant. The question will always depend, of course, upon the particular circumstances of every case.

Gas and electricity charges will normally be payable by the tenant. If the landlord supplies the commodity through a private meter and charges the tenant, the tenant is only liable for a maximum charge fixed by the Gas Corporation or the Electricity Board.

CHAPTER NINE

REPAIRS AND DILAPIDATIONS

If there is no express agreement or statutory provision to cover the particular circumstances, there is no implied warranty on the part of the landlord, either on the tenancy of land or an unfurnished house or flat, that it is fit for occupation, or that it is fit for the purpose for which it is to be used. Similarly, there is no covenant implied that he will do repairs, nor is he liable to the tenant, or to the family, customers or guests of the tenant at common law for any loss or injury resulting from want of repair. On the other hand, the tenant, in the absence of any express agreement to the contrary, will remain liable for rent even though the premises have been detroyed by fire or other inevitable accident, as we have seen.

While this is the general position, however, there are certain other matters that must be taken into consideration. there is, first of all, the matter of the usual express provisions to be found in a lease. there is the doctrine of waste to be taken into account; the Occupier's Liability Act 1957 and the Defective Premises Act 1972.

COVENANT TO REPAIR

The lease of a building will usually contain a covenant by the tenant to repair and keep the premises in repair during the period of the lease. There may also be a covenant to repair defects within a particular time after notice. By section 11 of the Landlord and Tenant Act 1985 however, a covenant is implied by the landlord to keep residential premises covered by the Act in repair. The details will be noted shortly, but it is relevant to point out here that if the lease contains a covenant by the *tenant* to repair, and section 11 of the 1985 Act applies, that repairing covenant of the tenant will be of no effect to the extent that it relates to obligations imposed by the Act upon the *landlord.* In other words, the landlord cannot escape this statutory obligation — at least, not unless a county court judge has authorised the inclusion of the clauses in the lease to repair and the covenant to repair defects after written notice, are in fact separate covenants. This does not mean that they cannot be joined in one, but if they are separate the landlord can take proceedings on either or both, if appropriate.

The lease may also contain a covenant on the part of the tenant to allow the landlord to enter upon the premises to carry out those repairs which the tenant has failed to execute after the due written notice has been given and to charge the tenant with the expense of carrying out the repairs. It should be noted that if the landlord does enter and repair under this covenant, he will then automatically lose his rights under a forfeiture clause to forfeit the lease for the disrepair by the tenant.

Distinct from a covenant to repair is a covenant to *leave* in repair at the end of the term, or at the time when the lease may otherwise determine. In *Phillimore v. Lane* (1925) the tenant was held liable even for damage done by burglars without any negligence on his part under such a clause. Similarly, the fact that premises are requisitioned is not a defence for a tenant who is sued under this covenant.

Particularly in the case of a lease of flats or parts of a building, the tenant's express covenant for repair will normally extend only to the inside of the premises, with the landlord, covenanting for the repair of the exterior; if the lease is silent on these points the rights of the parties will depend upon the obligations implied by the law.

Conditions of the premises

A covenant to keep in repair and leave in repair at the end of the term means that the tenant must put the premises into repair if they are not in repair at the beginning of the term. But such a general covenant to repair means only that the premises must be kept in *substantial* repair, and reference will be had to the condition of the premises at the time when the lease began in determining the construction of the tenant's liability under this head. Much will therefore depend upon the terms of the covenant: strictly drawn covenants will impose strict liability. A covenant to keep and deliver up the premises in "as good repair and condition as the same were at the commencement of the tenancy" was held to be broken in *Jones v. Joseph* (1918) where the tenant allowed the property to become infested with bugs.

On the other hand, repair does not mean "improvement", and there is not obligation to repair to the extent that the landlord receives back virtually new property at the end of the tenancy. It is a matter of degree. There is an obligation to deliver up something substantially the same but older, and no more. Similarly, repair is to be distinguished from renewal, although repair will include renewal of *subordinate parts*. An illustration is afforded by *Lurcott v. Wakeley* (1911). The tenant agreed to repair, keep, and deliver up, in repair the 200-year old house leased to him. Shortly before the term ended, the London County Council served a dangerous structure notice upon him and upon the landlord, called upon them to take down the front wall. The tenant refused to do this; after the lease ended the landlord took down the wall, then rebuilt it in accordance with modern requirements. The condition of the wall was caused by decay and the wall could not have been repaired without rebuilding, but the Court of Appeal held that the tenant under the lease was liable for the costs of the works. "The test", said Buckley L.J., "is whether the act to be done is one which in substance is the renewal or replacement of defective parts, or the renewal or replacement of substantially the whole". In this case, it was the rebuilding of a subsidiary part, so the tenant was liable. In *Smedley v. Chumley & Hawke* (1982) a landlord's unqualified covenant to repair was held to extend to liability to work on the foundations of a building which needed repair because of a design defect. The court had to decide what "repair" meant by looking at the precise terms of the lease.

But what if legislation forbids the tenant to rebuild in the way the wall was formerly built? Here, there is no obligation placed upon him to rebuild something different — his obligation is to replace it with something *substantially* the same.

A covenant to repair will also extend to include any buildings erected during the period of the lease, although this may, of course be negatived by the terms of the covenant itself: where it speaks of "the buildings demised", for instance.

Where a covenant by a tenant to keep premises in repair is qualified by the words "reasonable (or fair) wear and tear excepted" the tenant is not liable for damage due to the ordinary operation of natural causes, such as wind and weather or brought about as a normal incident of a tenant's occupation in the course of the reasonable or fair use of the premises, for any of the purposes for which they are let. The tenant is, however, bound to do such repairs as may be required to prevent the consequences flowing originally from wear and tear from producing other which wear and tear would not directly produce, if dealt with at the time. It excepts the tenant only from what directly flows from fair wear and tear, reasonable conduct on the part of the tenant being assumed.

Liability of the landlord

The landlord may, of course, expressly agree that he will be responsible for all or part of the repairs during the term of the lease.

Where the landlord does covenant to carry out the repairs, the tenant must normally give the landlord notice of the want of repair before the obligation will arise. This applies to the express repairing covenant, and to the covenants implied under the Landlord and Tenant Act 1985.

The general principles of the landlord's liability under such covenants are in the main similar to those already discussed above, so if the landlord covenants to keep premises in repair he must first put them in repair and so on.

It should be noted that where the landlord does covenant to repair there will be implied a licence for him to enter the premises to carry out the necessary repairs. The licence is one to enter and remain for a reasonable period for the work to be done. He must give notice of his intention to enter and do the work, though not a detailed specification of what he is about to do. The tenant cannot deny entry at a reasonable time.

If the landlord does not carry out his repairing obligations the tenant may carry out the necessary repairs and deduct the resulting expense from future rent.

IMPLIED OBLIGATIONS TO REPAIR

At common law there is no implied obligation on the part of the landlord of an unfurnished house or flat, or of other land, that the premises will be reasonably fit for occupation, habitation or cultivation nor that the landlord will carry out any repairs.

Landlord and Tenant Act 1985 Section 11

Section 11 of the Act creates an implied obligation in a lease of a dwelling-house granted after October 24, 1961, for a term of less than seven years. A term is treated as one of less than seven years if the landlord has an option to determine the lease in less than seven years and part of any term before the grant of the lease is not taken into account in reckoning the period of seven years.

The section does not apply:

(a) where the tenant has an option to renew for a period which, when taken together with the original term, would exceed the seven years;

(b) where the lease is a tenancy of an agricultural holding within the 1986 Act;

(c) where immediately before the lease, the lessee had another lease of the dwelling-house, or has a lease and an interval in which he was in possession of the house or the rents and the profits and the new lease is subject to the provisions of Part II of the Landlord and Tenant Act 1954, and the old lease was so subject (or would have been but for the provision of section 28 of the Act);

(d) where there are successive leases as in (c) and the earlier one is not one to which section 11 would have applied.

Under section 11, a covenant is implied that the landlord will:

(i) keep in repair the structure and exterior of the dwelling-house, including the drains, gutters and external pipes, which according to *Douglas Scott v. Scorgie* (1984) can include the roof as part of the exterior and structure;

(ii) keep in repair and proper working order all installations in the dwelling-house for supplying water, gas and electricity and for sanitation and for heating space and water.

This implied covenant does not oblige the landlord to carry out works for which the tenant is liable, by virtue of his duty to use the premises in a tenant-like manner, not does it amount to a covenant to rebuild, or reinstate the premises where there has been destruction or damage by fire, tempest, flood or inevitable accident. There is no implied obligation to repair any tenant's fixtures under this section.

Section 11 (6) puts upon statutory footing the implied licence that we have already seen, whereby the landlord is entitled to enter to carry out the repairs. By this section there is implied a covenant on the part of the tenant that he will at all reasonable times permit the landlord (who must give twenty-four hours' notice to the occupier) to enter the premises to view their condition.

The landlord, however, is not liable under the section until he has notice of the disrepair. In addition the section only applies to the demised premises, and not to any common part which the landlord retains — stairs, for example.

Avoiding section 11

It is possible to avoid section 11. Can the parties contract out of the section? The answer is given in section 12 which states that any attempt to contract out of the section is void and of no effect. Similarly, any attempt to avoid the application of the section by imposing a forfeiture, disability of penalty upon the person relying on the section will be void.

Section 11 *may* be excluded, however, if the county court feels that it is reasonable to do so. If the parties consent it can authorise in any lease or collateral agreement, provisions which will have the effect of modifying or excluding the application of section 11.

Ancillary property

Where a landlord lets premises to which access is by a staircase or other area which he retains in his possession and control and the maintenance of the staircase or other area is necessary for the enjoyment of the premises let there is an implied obligation on the part of the landlord that he will take reasonable care that the premises retained by him are kept in reasonable repair.

In *Liverpool City Council v. Irwin* (1977) the Council was held to have discharged this obligation, having expended large sums of money to repair lifts and stairs in a block of multi-storey flats, the subsequent, almost immediate disrepair being due to vandalism.

Furnished lettings

Where furnished houses, flats or rooms are let, the landlord incurs an implied obligation that the premises will be fit for occupation at the time when the tenancy begins.

It should be noted that the effect of this implied covenant is basic to the tenancy in the sense that if the premises are not fit for occupation when the tenancy begins the lessee is perfectly entitled to rescind the contract and quit the premises. The obligation is, in other words, a condition upon which the contract rests. The fact that it is a condition can be seen from the result that follows where the landlord puts the premises into a proper condition under his obligations, but does so only on the day *after* the date on which the tenancy begins. In such a case the tenant can refuse to take the premises, and will not be liable to the landlord in an action for rent, or use and occupation.

The extent of this common law obligation should be noted, however:

(a) if the premises are fit for human habitation *when let,* this is the sum total of the landlord's obligation — the covenant imposes no obligation to *keep* the premises in this condition;

(b) the implied undertaking does not extend to unfurnished premises;

(c) if the landlord is in residence, there is no obligation to inform the tenant that the premises have become insanitary.

Illustration of defects which have been held to render a house unfit for habitation appear in *Smith v. Marrable* (1843) (infested with bugs); *Wilson v. Finch Hatton* (1877) (defective drains); *Collins v. Hopkins* (1923) (recent occupation by a person suffering from pulmonary tuberculosis). This last case shows that the test to decide whether or not the premises are habitable will be whether there is an actual or appreciable risk to the tenant, his family or his household.

Low rental houses

Section 8 Landlord and Tenant Act 1985 provides that if a house is let at a relatively low rent there is an implied condition that the hosue is fit for human habitation at the beginning of the tenancy. There is also an implied undertaking by the landlord that he will *keep* it in this condition throughout the tenancy, unlike the situation discussed above.

This undertaking cannot be avoided: a stipulation in the contract which affects to exclude the provisions of the Act will be void.

The section applies to a house let for human habitation:

(1) Where the contract of letting was made between July 31, 1923, and July 6, 1957, and the annual rent was not more than £40 for a house in the administrative county of London and not more than £26 for a house elsewhere.

(2) Where the contract of letting was made between July 6, 1957, and April 1, 1965, and the annual rent was not more than £80 for a house in London and not more than £52 for a house elesewhere.

What is meant by rent in this section? It means the gross rent actually paid to the landlord, without deduction for rates or any other outgoings for which the landlord is liable.

The provision does not apply to tenancies of houses for at least three years, which are not determinable by option within three years, and which provide that the lessee is to put the house into a condition reasonably fit for human habitation.

The obligation of the landlord is confined, like that under the Section 11, to defects of which he has notice: the tenant must give the landlord notice of the defects and the landlord may then, on giving twenty-four hours' notice in writing to the occupier, enter to view the condition of the premises.

Statutory standard

Small defects can amount to a breach of the statute: the test is not so much how difficult it is to repair the defect, but whether the state of the house is such that by ordinary user the occupier might be injured in limb or in health.

A standard is in fact laid down by statute. Regard must be paid to the condition of the house in respect of:

(a) repair;
(b) stability;
(c) freedom from damp;
(d) internal arrangement;
(e) natural lighting;
(f) ventilation;
(g) water supply;
(h) drainage and sanitary conveniences;
(i) facilities for preparation and cooking of food and disposal of waste water.

As far as application of the Act is concerned, in *Summers v. Salford Corporation* (1943) it was held that a broken sash cord in the only window of one bedroom was a breach of the undertaking; as was a fall of plastic from the ceiling in *Walker v. Hobbs* (1889). In *Stanton v. Southwick* (1920), on the other hand, the invasion of the house by rats was held not to be breach of the implied covenant, though if they had habitually occupied and bred in the house the decision might have been different.

It should be noted that the common law test of unfitness is different from this statutory standard — see, for example *Smith v. Marrable* (1843).

The statutory dut operates as does the duty under Section II by way of an implied contract so it makes the landlord liable in contract only to the tenant personally. As we shall see later, there may well be liability to others, however, under the Occupiers' Liability Act 1957 or the Defective Premises Act 1972.

Where the local authority is satisfied that any dwelling-house is in any respect unfit for human habitation they must, unless they are satisfied that it is not capable of being rendered fit for habitation at a reasonable expense, serve on the person in control a notice in the prescribed form. This will require that the works specified in the notice be executed. If the notice is not complied with, the local authority may, subject to certain specified conditions, do the work themselves, and then recover the expenses from the person in control. Where the dwelling-house cannot at reasonable expense be made fit for human habitation a local authority may order its demolition, and if the order is not obeyed they may themselves demolish it and recover the expenses from the person in control.

Agricultural workmen

The same condition and undertaking that the house is and will be kept, fit is implied by the Act as part of the contract of employment of an agricultural workman where part of the remuneration consists of the use of a house or part of a house.

Agricultural tenancies

By statutory instrument made under section 7 of the Agricultural Holdings Act 1986 the rights and liabilities of the landlord and tenant under a letting of an agricultural holding are specified. These provisions are subject to the actual agreement.

Implied obligations of the tenant

The main implied obligation of the tenant is that he shall use the property in a tenant-like manner. This obligation has already been referred to but from the point of view of repairs it may be noted that:

(a) the tenant must not commit voluntary waste (this is dealt with later, (see p. 102);

(b) the tenant must repair damage caused by himself, his family, or his guests;

(c) the tenant from year to year may have to keep the premises "wind- and water-tight" (though this has been doubtful and in any case probably means little more than tenant-like user).

The situation is, therefore, that if there is no express covenant or agreement by the tenant to do repairs he is not bound to carry our any substantial repairs not make good ordinary wear and tear. He is under a continuing obligation to use the premises in a tenant-like manner however, doing the little jobs that a reasonable tenant would do and, unless prevented from doing so by an act of God, to deliver them up at the end of the tenancy in a tenant-like condition. As we shall see, he is also under a duty to repair damage caused by acts amounting to voluntary waste so that if he delivers up the premises with structural alterations which have changed their character he is liable to an action for damages for breach of this obligation, or alternatively, for waste.

if the demised property is of an agricultural nature the tenant is bound to cultivate according to the rules of good husbandry.

It should be noted that when furnished accommodation is taken there is no implied obligation or warranty that the tenant is a fit and proper person to occupy the premises, not that he is not suffering from an infectious disease. On the other hand, in *Shaw v. Anthony* (1939) it was held that the introduction of bugs and fleas in large quantities into the premises by the tenant amounted to untenant-like user and a breach of his implied obligation.

THE DOCTRINE OF WASTE

Waste may be defined as a spoiling or destroying of houses, gardens, trees or other corporeal hereditaments, whereby the reversion of the landlord is injured. Waste falls into several categories and is separate from any express or implied covenant to repair.

(1) Voluntary waste

This is actual, deliberate waste such as felling timber trees, pulling down houses, opening mines or pits or changing the course of husbandry; breaking or carrying away windows, or removing floors, is also voluntary waste.

(2) Permissive waste

Permissive waste is omission rather than commission; it is the failure to do what should have been done, such as the non-repair of buildings, or sea or river walls. The mere non-cultivation of land does not amount to permissive waste, however.

(3) Ameliorating waste

This is such voluntary waste as *improves* the property; it will not therefore be prevented by the courts unless the landlord can show that he has suffered substantial damage by the act.

(4) Equitable waste

This consists of acts of gross damage such as the cutting down of ornamental timber by a tenant "without impeachment of waste" (*i.e.*, not normally liable for waste), It has little relevance to the landlord and tenant relationship since contracts of tenancy are never made without impeachment of waste.

Liability for waste

Under a yearly or other periodic tenancy the tenant must use the premises in a tenant-like manner. As Denning L.J., put it in *Warren v. Keen* (1953):

"He must, if he is going away for the winter, turn off the water and empty the boiler. He must clean the chimney's, when necessary, and also the windows. He must mend the electic light when it fuses. He must unstop the sink when it is blocked . . . But apart from such things, if the house falls into disrepair through fair wear and tear or lapse of time, or for any reason not caused by him, then the tenant is not liable to repair it".

He is, however, liable for voluntary waste and he must not alter the character of the property, such as by converting the premises into a shop when it was let as a dwelling-house. In *Marsden v. Heys* (1972) it was stated "A tenant who takes a dwelling-house cannot at the end of the tenancy yield up a storehouse, or a stable, or a cowhouse, however elaborately constructed". In *Manchester Developments v. Garmanson* (1986) it was held that a tenant who removed his fixtures and fittings without reinstating the premises afterwards committed an act of waste. On the other hand a periodic tenant is free from liability for permissive waste.

A tenant at will is not liable for permissive waste either but if he commits voluntary waste his tenancy is at once terminated by his act.

A tenant for years is liable for waste, both voluntarily and permissive, but will not be liable under this doctrine to rebuild premises which are destroyed "by using the property demised in what was apparently a reasonable and proper manner, having regard to its character and to the purposes for which it was intended to be used", thus, in *Manchester Bonded Warehouses Co. v. Carr* (1880) the tenant of a warehouse was not liable for the fall of its floors where he was making a reasonable use of the property for the purposes for which it was let. Nor will it be waste to make alterations which are compatible with the user of the premises which is permissible under the lease.

It is the reversioner upon the lease who can claim damages against the tenant for waste.

MEASURE OF DAMAGES

Before the Landlord and Tenant Act 1927 came into operation the measure of damages in an action brought by the landlord for breach of a covenant to repair was:

(i) during the period of tenancy, the damage to the reversion;

(ii) after the termination of the tenancy, the cost of putting the premises in the condition in which the tenant should have left them.

But, by section 18 of the Landlord and Tenant Act 1927 it is provided that damages for a breach of a covenant or agreement to keep or put or leave the premises in repair shall in no case exceed the amount by which the value of the reversion (whether immediate or not) in the premises is diminished by the breach. In particular, no damages can be recovered for a breach of any covenant or agreement to leave premises in repair at the temination of the lease, if it is shown that the premises, in whatever state of repair they might be, would, at or shortly after the temination of the lease, have been or be pulled down, or such structural alterations made upon them as would render valueless the repairs covered by the covenant or agreement.

Three points may be noted as following on from this:

(a) the section will apply whether the covenant is express or implied;

(b) the mere fact that repairs are necessary may at least be taken as prima facie evidence of damage to the reversion, particularly where the landlord has had, or intends to have, the repairs carried out. If, however, there is little or no likelihood that the landlord will repair, evidence must be given of an *actual* diminishing of value in the premises otherwise only nominal damages will be awarded. Where the breach is of a covenant in a sub-lease the sub-lessors liability to his own landlord must be taken into account.

If the landlord recovers damages, he is not bound to expend them in repairing the premises but he will continue to have the benefit of the covenant. As a breach of covenant to repair is a continuing breach he can sue on the covenant again and will be able to obtain damages anew, except that credit will be given for any damages he had earlier received for breaches of the covenant.

Where the premises have been acquired compulsorily the measure of damages will be the difference between the price a willing buyer would have paid for the premises as they were immediately before the compulsory acquisition, and the price he would have paid had the covenant been performed.

If a landlord re-enters for breach of covenant so that the reversion is accelerated the measure of damages will be the difference between the value of the property as it stands, and the value which it would have had if the tenant had fulfilled his obligation: *Hanson v. Newman* (1934).

Breach of the landlord's covenant

Section 18 would seem, from its wording, not to cover a breach of a landlord's covenant to repair. The measure of damages in such a case is probably:

(i) the difference in value to the tenant between the house unrepaired and the house in the condition it would be had the landlord fulfilled his obligations after proper notice, the time running from the date of the request to repair; and

(ii) any damage to the property of the tenant during that period, caused by the default of the landlord.

Leasehold Property (Repairs) Act 1938

The action for non-repair can be maintained by the landlord at any time during the term of the lease as well as after the term expires. Statutory restrictions have been placed upon the bringing of such actions in many instances, however, and by the Leasehold Property (Repairs) Act 1938, as extended by the Landlord and Tenant Act 1954 (s. 51), the leave of the court is required before action can be instituted.

The situation, as extended, now is as follows:

Application

The restrictions apply where:

(a) the tenancy was granted for a term of years certain of not less than seven years;

(b) of which three years or more remain unexpired at the date of service of the notice of dilapidations, or at the date of commencement of action for damages; and

(c) the property is not an agricultural holding as defined by the Agricultural Holdings Act 1986.

The Act was passed to protect tenants of small houses under long lease from having to pay heavy bills of dilapidations under the threat of forfeiture for breach of covenant. The situation previously was that speculators could buy the reversion of a dilapidated house property at a low price, then enforce forfeiture of the lease because of the non-repair. Thus, the speculator would obtain the remainder of the term without paying anything for it.

The restrictions

Where the Act applies, the landlord may not sue for damages, nor may he enforce forfeiture for failure to repair unless he first serves on the tenant a notice under section 146 of the Law of Property Act 1925.

This notice must:

(i) specify the breach complained of; and
(ii) require it to be remedied, if this is possible; and
(iii) require the tenant to make compensation in money for the breach, if the landlord requires such compensation.

The notice under section 146 must also state that the tenant can serve a counter-notice under the 1938 Act; in *Sidnell v. Wilson* (1966) the landlord omitted such a statement but later served a further notice containing such a statement; it was held that the two together constituted a good notice.

Reasonable details of the breach must be given, and the notice must be served in writing at his last known abode or business address or be left for him at the demised premises. It will be sufficient service to send it by registered letter or recorded delivery to his last known abode or business address provided it is not returned as undelivered.

One month must then elapse after service before the landlord can proceed, and within twenty-eight days after service of the notice the tenant can serve a counter-notice claiming the benefit of the Act.

The result of this procedure? It is simply that the landlord cannot proceed further without leave of the court. This will be given only for reasons specified in the Act such as that in *Phillips v. Price* (1959) — that immediate repair is necessary because the cost would be small compared with the cost of future repair. Another reason for an order would be that immediate repair is necessary because compliance with a by-law relating to the safety or repair of houses is required. In *Sidnell v. Wilson* (1966) it was stated that leave of the court may be given only on establishing at least a prima facie or arguable case. In granting or refusing leave the court may impose such terms and conditions on the lessor or lessee as it thinks fit.

INDEMNITY COVENANTS

On an assignment of a lease the question arises as to the protection of the outgoing tenant or lessee whom we call the assignor and whom we have seen remains liable in contract for the continuing performance of the obligations arising out of the lease. Before 1926 the assignee would give a covenant in favour of the assignor that he, the assignee, would continue to perform the obligtions — the exact width of his liability depended on the phrasing used in such a covenant — known as a covenant by way of indemnity. Since 1925 the position is simpler — in all assignments for value (other than by way of mortgage) such a covenant by way of indemnity is implied by virtue of section 77 of the Law of Property Act 1925, the effect of which is that the assignee or his successors in title keeps fully indemnified from the date of the assignment of all other obligations arising under the lease.

STATUTORY DUTIES OF CARE

To date we have been dealing with the liabilities of the landlord and tenant as to repairs arising under the express terms of the lease or by implication of law.

Formerly, where the landlord was under no express or implied liability to repair he was not liable for accidents which happened during the tenancy to poeple who came on the premises — though he might be liable if he installed some dangerous article upon the premises and an accident occurred because of his failure to take proper precautions.

Basically, the situation is that a duty of care is placed upon the *occupier* of premises to ensure that no defects exist which might cause injury to persons lawfully using or upon the premises. Failure to comply with this duty of care will result in liability in damages. However, the Occupiers' Liability Act 1957 and the Defective Presmises Act 1972 have imposed statutory duties of care in certain circumstances.

Occupiers' Liability Act 1957

Under this Act, the *occupier* of the premises owes a common duty of care to all persons (classified as licensees and invitees) who are lawfully upon the premises. This duty is defined as: "a duty to take such care as in all the circumstances of the case is reasonable to see that the visitor will be reasonably safe in using the premises for the purposes for which he is invited or permitted by the occupier to be there" (s. 2).

It will be noted that the liability is placed upon the *occupier.* Thus, where premises fall into disrepair liability may arise not only under the covenant to repair but, as far as the occupier is concerned, in respect of any injuries suffered by individuals who are lawfully on the premises, provided those injuries arose out of the defective state of the premises.

The occupier of demised premises will be the tenant, but the landlord will be the occupier of part of premises not demised. The defect may be in relation to the staircase, for instance, which the landlord has retained in his possession but which is used by the tenant. As far as his liability towards the tenant is concerned, the landlord can cut down his liability by agreement, but with respect to his duty under the Act towards third persons he cannot cut down his liability.

The common duty of care will in fact normally be fulfilled, according to the circumstances, by the occupier's giving adequate warning of the danger, by providing adequate lighting, or by fencing the dangerous structure. It is possible that merely carrying out repairs will be enough to satisfy the duty imposed by the Act, but such cases are likely to be rare.

Defective Premises Act 1972

Section 4 of this Act imposes upon a landlord who, under the terms of a tenancy has an obligation to repair premises, a duty to take reasonable care that anyone who might reasonably be affected by defects in the premises is reasonably safe from personal injury or damage to property because of a defect. The duty is also owed where the landlord has merely an express or implied *right* to repair, although the tenant cannot sue if the defect is a breach of his covenant to repair.

TREES AND TIMBER

"Timber" means trees fit to be used in building and repairing houses, *i.e.*, oak, ash, elm and other trees which are classified as timber according to the custom of the area — such as beech in Buckinghamshire.

The implied rights in trees are that the property in them is vested in the owner of the inheritance in which they grow — the landlord; the property in bushes, in the tenant. Windfalls of sound timber trees belong to the landlord, but windfalls of non-timber trees, or decayed timber, belong to the tenant, subject to the tenancy agreement.

Cutting down, detroying or topping all trees classiffied as timber amounts to waste, as does the commission of any act which has the effect of causing a decay of the wood. The cutting of other trees which afford a defence or shelter for the house will also be waste.

The relationship of landlord and tenant also imposes on the tenant an obligation to preserve the boundaries and not to allow them to be destroyed. The actual occupier has the duty of repairing fences, and to do this he may take sufficient wood including timber. Apart from any express covenant on his part, the landlord is under no liability to repair fences.

VALUATION OF DILAPIDATIONS

The landlord has no legal right to enter the demised premises during the term to view their condition, or the dilapidations or want of repair, unless (1) this power is given to him in the lease or agreement, or (2) he has the written consent of the tenant, or (3) the power to enter is implied to enable him to perform his own covenant. We have already seen that he might have this implied power under section 11 of the Landlord and Tenant Act 1985 whereby the tenant is obliged to permit the landlord, at all reasonable times on twenty-four hours' notice in writing by the landlord to the occupiers, to enter the dwelling-house to view its condition.

Indeed, near the end of the term a surveyor or architect is often employed by both parties to carry out a survey, to discover what defects or want of repair exist and what should be put right under the covenants or stipulations in the lease or agreement. The position of the surveyor here should be one of an arbitrator; armed with the lease or agreement he should be able to tell the parties what needs to be done and how much it should cost. Usually, when this is done, the tenant will pay the cost of the repairs to the landlord, rather than carry out the repairs himself. A similar valuation can be made between incoming and outgoing tenants as opposed to landlord and tenant.

In advising a landlord whether to accept the cost of carrying out the repairs in cash or to opt that the repairs themselves by carried out, a surveyor should make a detailed valuation of the property as a whole considering its future use. This will enable him to discover whether it is preferable for the landlord to accept the money rather than have the repairs carried out, if, for example, the property has a limited life in the future.

INSANITARY HOUSES AND DANGEROUS STRUCTURES

It has already been noted that local authorities have certain powers of ordering the repair or demolition of houses which are deemed unfit for human habitation. These powers are contained in the Housing Act 1985.

The local authority in such cases will serve a notice upon the person in control of the house calling upon him to carry out the necessary work within a reasonable time (not less than twenty-one days). A similar notice may be served where the house is not unfit for human habitation but is not suitable for occupation by the number of people living there where the house is let in lodgings.

If the notice is not complied with, the authority may do the work and recover the expenses as a civil debt from the person having control of the house. The tenant who incurs expenditure in complying with the notice can recover from his landlord such part (if any) of the expenditure as has been agreed upon by them. If there is no agreement, the county court judge may decide what the proportions shall be, having regard:

(i) to their respective obligations under the tenancy as far as repairs are concerned;
(ii) to the length of unexpected term;
(iii) to the rent; and
(iv) to other relevant circumstances.

Demolition orders

If the local authority is satisfied that the house in question cannot be made fit for occupation at reasonable expense, it may serve a notice on the persons interested as to the time and place at which the condition of the house, and undertakings in respect of it, will be considered. The authority may thereafter make a demolition order in respect of the house if no undertaking is given to make the house fit, or such undertaking is given but not fulfilled. In similar proceedings, the local authority may make a closing order prohibiting the use of any room or part of the house for any purpose other than a purpose approved by the local authority. Such approval must not be unreasonably withheld.

If the authority feels that the house could provide accommodation which would be adequate for the time being by the rendering of works, they may purchase the house instead of making one of the above orders. Compensation payable will be at cleared site value with a well-maintained allowance if earned.

If a demolition order has been made, the house-owner must demolish it within the time limited by the order; otherwise the authority may demolish it and sell the materials with any further expenses being recoverable from the owner.

What is meant by "owner"? By section 322 of the Housing Act 1985 he is defined as anyone, other than a mortgagee not in possession, who is for the time being entitled to dispose of the fee simple. It includes a person entitled to or holding the rents and profits under a lease or agreement of which the unexpired term is more than three years.

Appeal against such order lies to the county court, with a further appeal on a point of law to the Court of Appeal.

Dangerous structures

If it appears to a local authority that a building or structure is in a dangerous condition that may make application under section 58 of the Public Health Act 1936 to the magistrates' court, and that court may order the owner either to execute the necessary work or demolish the building. This section deals with situations where there is a danger to persons in the premises; section 24 (1) of the Public Health Act 1961 extends the provision to persons in the street also. Section 25 of the 1961 Act confers emergency powers on local authorities to deal with dangerous structures, and section 27 deals with powers regarding ruinous or dilapidated buildings.

Nuisances

By section 92 of the Public Health Act 1936 a statutory nuisance includes premises in such a state as to be prejudicial to health or a nuisance, and by section 93 the local authority must in such circumstances serve an abatement notice on the owner of the premises, or the occupier, if the person who is responsible for the nuisance cannot be found. The notice will call upon the person in question to abate the nuisance and execute such works and take such steps as may be necessary for that purpose. No instructions as to the methods to be used are necessary.

If the nuisance arises from a structure defect, the notice must be served on the *owner.*

Upon default a nuisance order may be made by the court or summary jurisdiction and if this is not complied with the local authority can abate the nuisance, recovering the expenses from the person against whom the order was made.

It should be noted also that a *private person* can obtain a nuisance order, not only against another individual but also against the local authority if they fail to carry out their duty in this respect, or if they themselves cause the nuisance.

Overcrowding

By the Housing Act 1985 ss. 324 to 328 local authorities can, by a control order, obtain possession of property in extreme cases of overcrowding. This can be done only where the authority is satisfied that no other remedy is possible.

The order is valid for five years but may be revoked by the county court or by the High Court on appeal.

How does such an order affect the residents? It is as though the local authority becomes the proprietor, and the local authority can create new licences or tenancies, but on not more than a monthly basis (unless written consent of the owners is obtained). When the order ends, the landlord/tenant relationship between tenant and owner is resumed.

CHAPTER TEN

EASEMENTS

The common law recognised a limited number of rights which could be enjoyed by one person over the land of another, and one of these rights is the easement.

The term has a limited application: it applies only to those particular rights which conform to certain essentials. Briefly, the essentials are that:

(a) there must be land over which the easement is enjoyed, and land for whose benefit the easement exists (in legal terms, there must be a dominant and a servient tenement);

(b) the easement must be for the benefit of the dominant tenement (the right enjoyed in *Hill v. Tupper* (1863), discussed on p. 15, could not exist as an easement as it was a purely commercial advantage);

(c) the two properties concerned must not be owned and occupied by the same person; and

(d) the easement must be capable of forming the subject matter of a grant (though as we have seen, the list of easements is not closed: see *Ward v. Kirkland* (1966), p. 44).

From these rules it is apparent that a distinction is to be drawn between, on the one hand the easement, and on the other hand analogous rights such as:

(i) natural rights *e.g.* to support of land or to receive a flow of water — these exist automatically and need not be acquired like the easement;

(ii) public rights (which are exercised by members of the public, whereas the easement is enjoyed in connection with a particular piece of land);

(iii) licences (see p. 11);

(iv) customary rights (which again exist independently of the ownership of land); and

(v) rights arising from the rule against the vendor or landlord derogating from the grant that he has made. In *Aldin v. Latimer Clark* (1894) a lease was granted to a timber merchant who required a free flow of air to his stacks of drying timber and it was held that no building could be erected upon the lessor's adjoining land so as to obstruct the ventilation required — but this could not be an easement, since the flow of air is too vague a right to exist as an easement. However, a right acquired under this rule might amount to an easement.

The easement should also be distinguished from the *profit à prendre:* the profit involves taking something from another's property, such as fish; the easement involves only the using of another's property.

ACQUISITION OF EASEMENTS

An easement can exist as a legal interest in land only if it is held for an interest equivalent to a fee simple absolute in possession, or a term of years absolute, and it must have been created either by statute, or by deed of grant, or by prescription.

If a grant of an easement is made by a document which is not under seal but which was made for value, an *equitable* easement may be created, as it may in the case of an oral agreement for value of which there is a note in writing or part performance.

The simplest way to create an easement is obviously by express grant by deed, but it can also be created by implied reservation or grant, as in the case of the easement of necessity, and as we have seen, it may arise under section 62 of the Law of Property Act 1925 (see p. 43). An easement may also be created by prescription, but perhaps the situation may be most clearly illustrated by reference to specific kinds of easements. The right of way may be used to illustrate the general type of easement, and reference must be made to the right of light since it enjoys a special status in the law of easements.

It should perhaps be noted first of all that the relationship of landlord and tenant will generally preclude the acquisition of an easement: the tenant may show that he has had the use of the premises for thirty years or more, but he will be taken to enjoy this right under his *lease,* and so he will obtain no easement over the land.

On the other hand, in *Morgan v. Fear* (1907) it was held that a tenant can acquire a right of light against another tenant of his own landlord, and therefore a right of light against the landlord himself. But this is an exception applying only to light and arising under the Prescription Act 1832; if the landlord leases two plots of land to two tenants the general position is that one tenant cannot acquire by prescription an easement against the other, nor, it was held in *Gayford v. Moffat* (1868), can a tenant prescribe for an easement against his landlord's adjacent land.

Private rights of way and public ways

Before proceeding further, however, it would be wise to clear up one point that occasionally confuses the student — the distinction between public ways and private rights of way. The distinction has been stated already in discussing the nature of the easement but it will bear reiteration here.

The private right of way is an easement over the soil of another. The methods by which it may be acquired will be dealt with shortly, but such a right may be a footway only, or a carriageway, and it may exist for specific purposes only, depending upon the terms of the grant.

The public way on the other hand is enjoyed by the public in general and is not restricted to the ownership of land which is benefited. It is created by a dedication by the landowner and an acceptance by the public — such dedication and acceptance may be express, or it may be presumed from the public in fact using the way without interruption. The question of acquisition was somewhat simplified by the Rights of Way Act 1932 which provides that a right of way can be established by twenty years' enjoyment of way over land by the public as of right and without physical interruption unless the land-owner can show that during the period in question there was no intention to dedicate a way. He can show such absence of intention by, for instance,

(a) closing the way for one day each year; or

(b) exhibiting a notice visible to those using the way (and if the land is leased the landlord is entitled to enter to erect such a notice); or

(c) depositing a map with the local authorities with a statment of what ways he admits to be highways, and lodging statutory declarations at intervals of not more than six years stating whether any other ways have been dedicated.

Moreover, as we shall see, while a private right of way may be extinguished by obstruction this does not apply in the case of the public way — "once a highway always a highway".

Methods by which private rights of way are acquired

The methods by which a right of way may be acquired are as follows.

(1) *Express grant*

A deed granting an easement may be entered into by a landlord and his tenant, where the right granted is defined and the dominant and serviant tenements clearly identified. The question may arise however, as to whether the use of the right of way has been reasable. In *Callard v. Beeney* (1930) the right of way was expressed in the deed of conveyance of a farm to be over a certain field to a particular field which was part of the farm; it was held that this gave the grantee a right of passage to and from *any* part of the farm as being a reasonable use of such a way. The matter of excessive use is really to be determined by construction of the words in the grant. There may also be an express *reservation* of an easement by a landlord who grants a lease, of course, *e.g.*, "To pass and repass with or without animals at all times and for all purposes along the path A-B" — the path being part of the demised premises.

(2) *Implied grant*

The general rule is that no easements will be implied in favour of the grantor but there are two exceptions: easements of necessity, and intended easements.

An easement of necessity will arise for example where a staircase in the occupation of one party is the only access to premises in the occupation of the other party, and in *Devine v. London Housing Society* (1950) it was held that the landlord is under no obligation to use reasonable care to keep the staircase for the use of the tenant.

It should be noted, however, that there must be a necessity in all cases, not merely a need for convenience.

An example of an easement of necessity arose in *Wong v. Beaumont Property Trust* (1964): a basement was let as a restaurant and the tenant covenanted to comply with the Public Health regulations, one of which required adequate ventilation. The tenant argued that he was entitled to a ventilation duct from the basement to the roof and the court held that there was an easement of necessity even though neither party realised the necessity at the time of the grant.

Implied grant under Wheeldon v. Burrows and section 62. A right of way could be implied also under what was known as the *Rule in Wheeldon v. Burrows* (1879) whereby a grant of part of a tenement passes all "quasi-easements" that are continuous and apparent, or are necesary for the reasonable enjoyment of the land granted, and are being used at the time of the grant. This rule has been added to by the provisions of section 62 of the Law of Property Act 1925 (noted in detail on p. 43). The importance of the section is shown in *International Tea Stores v. Hobbs* (1903). The tenant was allowed to use a roadway leading into the landlord's yard and his subsequent purchase of the reversion converted his use into an easement. Again, in *Goldberge v. Edwards* (1950) the landlord let the tenant into possession before granting the lease and allowed him the use of a passage through his own property: the subsequent grant of the lease converted what had been a revocable licence to use the passageway into an irrevocable easement.

It should be noted that *Wheeldon v. Burrows* applies to a contract for a lease but section 62 does not. On the other hand there is no requirement of necessity for reasonable enjoyment in section 62.

(3) *Prescription*

The basis of prescription is that if a right has been enjoyed for a long period of time the court will uphold it by presuming the use had a legal origin and is in fee simple. There are in fact three methods of prescription: common law prescription (user since time immemorial, 1189), prescription by lost modern grant, and prescription under the Prescription Act 1832. The first two need not concern us here.

Prescription Act 1832. The provisions tht are relevant to the right of way are as follows:

(a) an easement enjoyed for twenty years as of right and without interruption cannot be defeated by proof that user began after 1189 (which was the stumbling block in prescription at common law);

(b) an easement enjoyed for forty years as of right and without interruption is deemed absolute and indefeasible unless enjoyed by written consent;

(c) the period of enjoyment is that period next before the suit or action in which the claim is brought into question;

(d) no act amounts to an "interruption" until it has been submitted to or acquiesced in for one year after notice both of the interruption and the person making it.

The words "as of right" mean not by violence, or secretly, or by the land-owner's permission. It is this requirement that prevents a tenant acquiring a right of way against his landlord.

"interruption" means some hostile obstruction, even though it has been made by some third person. Mere non-user of the way will not amount to interruption — though it may mean that there has not been sufficient enjoyment to support a claim in the first place.

These provisions noted above are to be found in sections 1 and 2 of the Prescription Act 1832. An easement by prescription, acquired by a tenant, is acquired as agent of his landlord because prescription must be in fee simple. Thus one tenant cannot prescribe for an easement over land of another tenent of the same landlord — a landlord cannot prescribe against himself. Similarly no-one else can acquire an easement over land occupied by a tenant unless the prescription period began when the landlord occupied.

THE ACQUISITION OF A RIGHT TO LIGHT

There is no natural right to light; this means that one man may build on his land and so obstruct the light flowing to his neighbour's windows. If that neighbour obtains the easement of light, however, he can restrain interference with his light in this way. (In practice a landlord who demises part of his land will invariably place a clause in the lease stipulating that the tenant or his successor in title shall not acquire by any means a right of light or any other easement that would prevent the landlord from using his adjoining land in the future in any manner he pleases).

The easement can exist only in respect of a window or some other opening such as a skylight.

The amount of light to which the occupier is entitled in enjoyment of the easement is as much as is required for ordinary purposes of living there or carrying on business there. There is no "forty-five degree" rule of law (whereby interference is actionable only if the obstruction rises above a 45° angled line drawn from the centre of the window), though it is useful for evidentiary purposes, and in considering the amount of light account is taken of other sources of light available.

The methods by which the right to light may be acquired are similar to those already described but the provision of the Prescription Act 1832 differ somewhat in respect of the right to light.

Prescription Act and the right to light

The Act rendered the right to light perhaps the easiest right to acquire.

Section 3 of the Act states that the actual enjoyment of the access of light to a dwelling-house, workshop or other building for *twenty years* without interruption shall make the right absolute and indefeasible, unless enjoyed by written consent or agreement. In other words, where it generally takes forty years' enjoyment to obtain an absolute right to an easement, it takes only twenty years' enjoyment in the case of the easement of light.

Moreover:

(i) enjoyment itself is enough, and there is not mention of its being "as of right" (though written, but not oral, consent will destroy it);

(ii) the mere payment of rent for the use of light does not defeat prescription.

It is because the use need not be as of right that a tenant can acquire a right to light against his own landlord, or against another tenant of his landlord, but in *Willoughby v. Eckstein* (1936) it was held that if the landlord reserves in the lease the right to rebuild the adjoining property this may amount to a sufficient consent in writing to defeat the claim of the tenant to the right to light, however: light must be acquired, if at all, in fee simple, even though it may be against a tenant.

To prove a right under the Prescription Act, continuous uninterrupted user in each year for the twenty years next before the action must be shown; interruption may be by physical obstruction or by the registration of a notice of obstruction in the local land charges register under section 2 of the Right of Light Act 1959. This Act removed the necessity for physical obstruction of a window for the effect of registration of such a notice is precisely the same — it amounts to an interruption. The notice lasts for one year, or otherwise until cancellation of the registration.

Where an action for obstruction of the right to light is brought, either the tenant in possession or the reversioner may sue.

REMEDIES FOR INFRINGEMENT OF EASEMENTS

The right of way and the right to light are not the only easements that may exist, of course: other examples are seen in rights of water, rights of air, rights of support for buildings and various miscellaneous easements such as the right to use a wall for nailing trees thereto, the right to use a coal shed (*Wright v. Macadam* (1949), p. 51) and the right to enter premises to effect repairs to a wall (*Ward v. Kirkland* (1966), p. 44) — even the right to use a lavatory was held, in *Miller v. Emcer Products Ltd.* (1956), to amount to a right capable of existing as an easement.

But what remedies are available if any of these easements are infringed?

(1) *Abatement*

The owner may abate any obstruction to his easement such as by breaking open a locked gate which closes his right of way, or taking down a board which obstructs his right to light. He must use no more force than is reasonably necessary, however, and as a general rule the law does not look upon this remedy with favour.

(2) *Action*

The owner of the easement may sue in a court of law for damages, or he might seek an injunction to stop the interference with his easement, or he might ask for a declaration that he is entitled to an easement, or he may ask for any combination of these. If the interference is trivial or temporary, he will get no injunction, however, and in an action for infringement the owner of the easement must prove his title, even against third parties.

EXTINGUISHMENT OF EASEMENTS

The right to an easement may come to an end in one of several ways.

(1) By statute

An Act of Parliament may extinguish an easement expressly, or by implication.

(2) By release

Express release must be by deed to be effective at law, but in equity an informal release will be sufficient provided it would be inequitable for the owner to insist that the easement still exists after the release.

A release may also be *implied* by reason of abandonment — mere non-user is not normally enough — but the intention to abandon is a question of fact. The bricking up of a door for over thirty year has been held not to amount to an abandonment; the demolition of a house to which a right of light is attached would be an implied release, but not if the intention were that the house should be replaced by another building, for it is not necessary that the windows should be in the same position as the old provided they will receive substantially the same light.

(3) By unity of ownership and possession

If the dominant and servient tenements are owned and occupied by the same person in the same capacity any easement is extinguished. If they are both held under a lease the assignment of both leases to T or both reversions to L would not extinguish the easement, but if the leases and the reversions became vested in X, extinguishment would take place. It was held in Simper v. Foley (1862) that if the fee simple owner of one tenement takes a lease of the other the right is not extinguished, but merely suspended during the period of the lease.

PROFITS A PRENDRE

Finally, a note on *profits à prendre* may be added.

It will be remembered that a *profit* involves the taking of something from the property, rather than the mere use of the property: thus, if A has the right to take fish from B's stream, or gravel from his land, or turf from his fields he enjoys a *profit à prendre* — though if he has the right to take water, this is classified as an *easement* (since water on or under land is normally incapable of ownership. Unlike the easement, however, the profit can be enjoyed "in gross", *i.e.*, independent of the ownership of the land and can therefore be acquired by a tenant as a personal right against his landlord.

The profit can be granted by deed, but a landlord may reserve the right to take, for instance, game, merely by a writing without seal, or even by words alone.

Many agricultural leases contain reservation of the game to the lessor but sporting rights of this nature are often granted to third persons and this should be done by deed. If a person has a specifically enforceable contract for the grant of such a profit, however, and he enters into possession of it, he can bring an action of trespass against anyone who then interferes with his right over the land.

Profits can be acquired by prescription, of course: the rules are the same as those that apply to easements other than the easement of light, except that the periods of prescription are not twenty and forty years, but thirty and sixty years respectively.

The remedies for interference with profits are the same as those already discussed in relation to easements, as are rules as to extinguishment.

CHAPTER ELEVEN

ASSIGNMENTS AND SUB-LEASES

A landlord who transfers his reversion, or a tenant who transfers his term of years may be described as an "assignor". An assignment is a transfer of some term or reversion, or some estate, right, title or interest: the person who makes the transfer is the assignor; the person to whom the transfer or conveyance is made is called the assignee.

Not *all* interests are assignable. A tenant on sufferance cannot assign the interest that he holds. If a lease contains an absolute covenant against assignment it can be assigned but the breach will entitle the landlord to exercise his remedies against the assignee. A tenancy at will can, it appears, be assigned but the tenancy is determined as soon as the landlord has notice of the assignment.

FORMAL REQUIREMENTS

An assignment may be effected by act of parties or by operation of law — such as on the bankruptcy or death of the lessee. Operation of law will be dealt with briefly later. But what are the formal requirements for an assignment by act of parties?

By section 52 of the Law of Property Act 1925 a conveyance of land or or any interest in land will be void for the purposes of conveying or creating a legal estate unless it has been made by deed.

A distinction must be drawn between a contract for assignment and an assignment proper.

CONTRACT FOR ASSIGNMENT

If no assignment has yet been made, but a contract for assignment has been entered into, the position will be governed by section 40 of the Law of Property Act 1925 which, it will be remembered, demands for evidentiary purposes a written note or memorandum of the terms of an oral agreement. Failure to comply with the section will mean that the contract is unenforceable, subject to the equitable doctrine of part performance (see p. 34). Contracts to assign are registerable as estate contracts (Class C) in the register of land charges.

The reversion

If the contract is to transfer property which is subject to a lease, then the lease if legal will bind the purchaser of the reversion irrespective of whether the purchaser knew of the lease or not, or whether the tenant is in possession or not. If the tenant merely has an equitable lease, it will not bind the assignee whether or not the tenant is in possession unless it is registered as a land charge.

The term

A contract to assign the term must satisfy the requirements of section 40 even though the term was created orally; these requirements have already been discussed.

In *Buttermere v. Hayes* (1839) the tenant agreed to give up his tenancy and allow X to take possession and become tenant for the rest of the term in consideration of X's paying a sum of money towards the completion of particular repairs to the premises. Was this a contract to assign a lease within section 40? The court held that it was, being an agreement for the sale of an interest in land within the statute.

In *Kelly v. Webster* (1852) A held a seven years' lease under a parol agreement. He verbally agreed to allow B to enter into possession as tenant. In return, B agreed to pay A £100. A gave up possession and B was accepted as a tenant from year to year at a rent different from A's by the landlord. B paid A £51 but no more and A then sued for the balance. The court held that since A could provide no written note or memorandum as demanded by the statute he could not recover the balance claimed; the contract was for the sale of an interest in land.

Covenants

We have already seen that covenants in a lease which touch and concern the land bind a purchaser of that lease and that negative covenants may bind a sub-lease (see p. 79).

Title of the vendor

By section 44 (2) of the Law of Property Act 1925 the intended lessee or assignee cannot call for the title to the freehold where there is a contract to grant a lease or to assign a term of years. This applies in the case of terms to be granted out of freehold or leasehold land. Subsection (3) of the same section denies the intended assign the right to call for the title to the leasehold reversion. Either sub-section is, of course, subject to contrary provision in the contract itself.

The result is that an assignee of a lease under an open contract is entitled to inspect only the lease that he is purchasing and is deemed to have notice of the covenants in it, even though he does not in fact inspect it. A sub-lessee has a right to inspect the head lease out of which the sub-lease is being granted, but an assignee of that sub-lease can only see the sub-lease and not the head-lease.

By section 45 of the Act the purchaser must assume unless the contrary appears that covenants have been performed, provided the receipt for the last rent due is produced.

ASSIGNMENT

This matter may conveniently be dealt with by examining the position where the reversion is assigned, and then where the term itself is assigned.

Assignment of the reversion

This must be done by deed. By section 141 of the Law of Property Act 1925 the rent reserved by the lease and the benefit of every covenant and provision contained in the lease is annexed to the reversion. The person who from time to time is entitled to the income of the whole or part, as the case requires, of the leased land can enforce such rents, covenants or provisions. The word "lease" includes underleases and other tenancies and probably covers oral tenancies also, provided they conform to the rule in *Walsh v. Lonsdale* (1882).

What is the situation with relation to the rights and liabilities of the original parties after the assgnment has been made? We have noted this matter earlier: the lessor will remain liable in contract to the original tenant on the express covenants in the lease. In other words, the assignment does not affect his liability and this is so even though the lessee or his assignee has a remedy against the lessor's assignee.

By the Law of Property Act 1925, s. 77, there is, in all assignments for valuable consideration made after 1925, an implied covenant by the assignee that he will

(a) at all times pay all rent becoming due under the lease, and

(b) perform and observe all the covenants in the lease, and

(c) keep the assignor indemnified against any omission to pay the rent and any breach of covenant.

Upon the failure of an assignee to pay rent the landlord may claim rent from the original tenant. In *Centrovincial Estates plc v. Bulk Storage* (1983) an original tenant was held liable to pay the whole new rent which had been raised since the assignment under a rent revision clause in the lease, even though the original tenant had not consented to the rent revision.

Covenants running with the land

When a reversion is assigned, privity of estate is created between the assignee and the lessee; similarly, when a lease is assigned, privity of estate is created between the assignee and the reversioner. In each case all covenants which touch and concern the land can be enforced by the assignee and are binding upon him. In *Spencer's Case* (1583) it was said: "A covenant is said to run with the land when either the liability to perform it or the right to take advantage of it passes to the assignee of that land.

A covenant is said to run with the reversion when either the liability to perform it or the right to take advantage of it passes to the assignee of that reversion".

It was decided in *Spencer's Case* that the benefit of such covenants by the lessor and the burden of such covenants by the lessee are annexed to the demised premises. If the covenant by a lessee related to something not in existence, however, the burden would not run with the land to the assignees unless he had expressly covenanted for himself and his assigns. An example would be a covenant to build a wall upon the demised premises. Now, by section 79 of the Law of Property Act 1925, where such a covenant is made after 1925, the assigns are bound unless a contrary intention is expressed.

Law of Property Act 1925, ss. 141, 142. The benefit of covenants running with the land and made by the lessee and the burden of covenants running with the reversion and made by the lessor are annexed by statute to the reversion. This rule appears in sections 141 and 142 of the Law of Property Act 1925 which provide that:

(a) The benefit of every covenant in a lease "having reference to the subject-matter thereof" and on the lessee's part to be observed and performed shall be annexed to and shall go with the reversionary estate in the land.

(b) The obligation of any covenant entered into by a lessor "with reference to the subject-matter of the lease" shall, if and so far as the lessor has power to bind the reversionary estate expectant on the term granted by the lease, be annexed to and shall go with that reversionary estate.

These sections apply to an oral tenancy and probably, also, to an enforceable contract for a lease.

Sections 141 and 142 apply if the covenants touch and concern the land (or in the Act's language — "have reference to the subject-matter" of the lease). Thus, they apply only to covenants which affect the nature, quality or value of the land or the mode of using and enjoying it. They do not apply to merely collateral covenants for the personal benefit of the covenantee. As we have already seen, the test is whether the covenant affects the landlord as a landlord or the tenant as a tenant: if the answer is affirmative the covenant runs with the land. Examples falling on either side of the line have already been noted (see p. 78).

Benefit of the covenant. In some cases a person can take the benefit of a covenant even where the benefit does not run with the land or reversion, as the case may be. By section 56 of the Law of Property Act 1925:

a person may take an immediate or other interest in land or other property, or the benefit of any condition, right of entry, covenant or agreement over or respecting land or other property, although he may not be named as a party to the conveyance or other instrument.

To take advantage of this section a person must, however, be "within the benefit of the covenant" according to its true construction — the instrument must be made directly for his benefit in such circumstances that it was intended to be enforceable by him: *Beswick v. Beswick* (1966).

The position in equity. The postion with regard to the burden of covenants restricting the use of demised premises passing in equity has already been discussed (see p. 76).

Assignment of the term

A tenant can assign his term unless the contract of tenancy expressly prohibits this. By section 52 (1) of the Law of Property Act 1925 the assignment must be by deed to pass the legal estate of the assignor. Equity may enforce equitable assignments, of course.

The assignment is usually made by the word "assign" but sometimes the words "grant, assign and convey" are used. No particular words are necessary, however, as long as the parties' intention to assign appears. Covenants for title are implied under section 76 of the Law of Property Act 1925 in every assignment for valuable consideration where the assignor conveys as "benefitial owner".

Although there is no obligation upon assignor or assignee to give notice to the lessor of the assignment, leases often contain a covenant that notice shall be given.

COVENANTS AGAINST ASSIGNMENT

Absolute and conditional covenants

If the lease contains no prohibition against assignment the tenant can assign freely; because of this, leases often contain a covenant against assignment, underletting or parting with possession.

Such a covenant does not invalidate an assignment; it means simply that an assignment is a breach of covenant. If the covenant is reinforced by a forfeiture clause the breach could then result in the determination of the lease. In any case, the landlord can sue for damages.

It was shown in *Field v. Barkworth* (1986) that a covenant prohibiting the assignment or underletting of any part restrains assignment or underletting of the whole.

The covenant may be absolute. If it is, the landlord can waive it, but if he insists that it is followed to the letter he cannot be compelled to waive it even if his attitude is shown to be entirely unreasonable.

The covenant will often be qualified, i.e. one against assigning "without licence or consent", and there is an important distinction to be drawn between this and the absolute covenant; the Landlord and Tenant Act 1927 states that the qualified covenant is subject to a proviso that the licence or consent is not to be unreasonably withheld. This provision may now be dealt with in detail.

Landlord and Tenant Act 1927, s. 19 (1)

Section 19 (1) of the Landlord and Tenant Act 1927 states that in any lease, made before or after the commencement of the Act, covenants, conditions or agreements against assigning, underletting, charging or parting with the possession of the demised premises or any part of them without the licence or consent of the lessor will be subject to a proviso.

This proviso is to the effect that the licence or consent must not be unreasonably withheld — though the landlord has the right to demand payment of a reasonable sum in respect of expenses incurred in connection with the licence or consent. Moreover, if the lease is a building lease the consent itself may not be necessary, for the same section states that if a lease is one for more than forty years, made in consideration of the erection or improvement of buildings, there is a proviso that in the case of an assignment effected more than seven years before the end of the term no consent or licence is required if notice in writing of the transaction is given to the lessor within six months after the transaction is effected. This proviso has application only if the lessor is not a government department, local or public authority, statutory or public utility company.

Section 19 (1) does not apply to leases of agricultural holdings within the Agricultural Holdings Act 1986 (See also p. 76).

Law of Property Act 1925, s. 144

A further proviso in respect of covenants against assignment is to be found in section 144 of the Law of Property Act 1925. This section states that all leases that contain covenants, conditions or agreements against assignment without licence or consent shall be deemed to be subject to a proviso that no fine shall be payable for such licence or consent. This section applies as long as the lease contains no express provision to the contrary and it is any case without prejudice to the landlord's right to demand payment of a reasonable sum to cover the expense incurred in relation to such licence or consent.

Unreasonable refusal of consent

When will a refusal of consent be unreasonable? A guide (which does not amount to a rigid doctrine to be followed on all occasions) is that a refusal of consent to an assignment will generally be considered unreasonable if it is made on a ground that has no reference either to the personality of the proposed assignee, or to the effect of the proposed assignment on the user and occupation of the demised premises or kindred matter during or after the tenancy.

In other words, it is the motives of convenience and interest which affect the landlord that are to be considered. Reasonableness as such is not, therefore, confined *only* to matters touching both parties to the lease. In *Re Town Investments' Underlease* (1954), it was held that the landlord is not acting unreasonably in refusing consent if a reasonable man, in his position, might regard the proposed transaction as damaging to his property interests. In such a case the landlord's view cannot be said to be without foundation, even though some persons might take a different view, and so he is not acting "unreasonably". But in *Bromley Park Estates v. Moss* (1982) the landlord's reason, his intent to relet the building as a whole to another single tenant was held to be unreasonable because it was extranneous to the intentions of the contracting parties. *International Drilling Fluids v. Lousiville Investments (Uxbridge)* (1986) showed that where the reason for refusal was that technically the assignment would be to the detriment of the reversion, because the reversion was in fact unaffected, the refusal was unreasonable.

Remedy for refusal

If the landlord does unreasonably refuse consent it is open to the tenant either to complete the assignment without the consent, or make application to the court (which by section 53 of the Landlord and Tenant Act 1954 may be the county court) for a declaration that the consent has been unreasonably refused. In proceedings the burden of proving that the action as unreasonable will lie upon the tenant.

Examples of reasonable and unreasonable refusals

The tenant must show that the withholding of consent is unreasonable. This is a question of fact. The decided cases are numerous but it might be useful to give some examples of reasonable and unreasonable refusals in reported instances.

Reasonable refusals

Refusal has been held to be reasonable where the reason was:

(a) that the references of the proposed assignee were not satisfactory: *Shanley v. Ward* (1913);

(b) that the property would be used by the proposed assignee for trade competition detrimental to the landlord's other property; *Premier Confectionery, etc. v. London Commercial, etc.* (1933);

(c) that the proposed assignee would acquire a statutory right that the assignor could not claim: *Bickel v. Duke of Westminster* (1976);

(d) that the tenant was in serious breach of a covenant to repair the property; *Goldstein v. Sanders* (1915).

Unreasonable refusals

A refusal was held to be unreasonably withheld where:

(a) the landlord's motive was merely that he wished to recover the property for himself: *Bates v. Donaldson* (1896);

(b) the landlord refused permission unless the proposed sub-tenant covenanted with the head landlord to pay him the rent: *Balfour v. Kensington Gardens Mansions Ltd.* (1932);

(c) the proposed assignee was also the tenant of the landlord, and on assignment would vacate the other house, which would be difficult to re-let: *Houlder Brothers & Co. v. Gibbs* (1925).

Breaches of covenant

Even where a landlord has no grounds for refusing consent, it is a breach of the covenant if the tenant does not apply to him for consent before assigning. But to amount to a breach there must in general be some voluntary dealing with the property — a bequest of the lease, for instance, would not amount to a breach any more than would a compulsory sale of the lease under statutory provisions.

Having requested consent however, the tenant must give the landlord reasonable time to consider the application: *Wilson v. Fynn* (1948).

The strict application of the covenant can be seen in the fact that a covenant not to sub-let the premises would not prevent the sub-letting of *part* of the premises if the words "or any part thereof" do not appear in the covenant, not would such a covenant be broken by an assingment. Similarly, a covenant against parting with possession does not exclude the grant of a licence, at all events if the licensee is not given exclusive possession.

SUB-LEASES

An Assignment of a lease is a transfer by a lessee (including an assignee of the lessee) of the whole or part of the premises for the whole of the term or the entire residue of the term created by the lease.

A sub-lease (or underlease) on the other hand is a grant by the lessee of the whole or part of the premises comprised in the lease for a *part* of his whole term. It creates neither privity of contract not privity of estate between the head lessor and the sub-lessee. It follows, therefore, that the sub-lessee is unable to enforce against the head lessor any covenants in the head lease. Nor can the head lessor enforce against the sub-lessee any covenants by the lessee in the head lease — apart from restrictive covenants of which the sub-lessee has notice (see p. 79).

Any grant of a period less than the whole residue of the term takes effect as an underlease; conversely, any grant purporting to be an underlease, which comprises the whole or the entire residue of the term, takes effect as an assignment.

The right to sub-let

Every lessee, no matter how short his term, has the right to sub-let, unless his contract of tenancy restrains him from doing so, either absolutely, or on condition that the landlord's consent must be obtained. If the lease is silent the subletting can be made without the landlord's consent *Leith Properties v. Byrne* (1983).

We have already seen that there is no privity between the lessor and the sub-lessee but even so it is still open to the lessor to obtain an injunction to prevent a sub-lessee from committing a breach of a restrictive covenant which runs with the land in equity. In practice, a sub-lease usually contains an express covenant by the sub-lessee to observe and perform all the covenants and conditions in the original lease, other than those which he is exempted from performing. A covenant to perform the covenants of the head lease will imply an indemnity.

In *Ayling v. Wade* (1961) the defendant held the premises under a lease that contained covenants to repair. He underlet them to an undertenant and covenanted to observe the covenants in the lease and to indemnify the undertenant against them. The plaintiff was the undertenant's successor in title. He succeeded in an action on the covenant when the defendant failed to repair a skylight and thus allowed flooding of the premises.

What is the situation if the lessee surrenders his lease? Where will this leave the sub-lease? The answer is that a sub-lessee is not affected by the voluntary surrender of the lease by the sub-lessor to the superior landlord.

ASSIGNMENT BY OPERATION OF LAW

Bankruptcy of the lessor

There will be an assignment by operation of law of the reversion on a lease if the landlord becomes bankrupt. By the Insolvency Act 1986 the trustee in bankruptcy is empowered to bring or defend any action, or other legal proceeding, in respect of the property of the bankrupt. The trustee takes the revision subject to such equities as affected it while under the bankrupt's control.

Bankruptcy of the lessee

It is common to insert in a lease a proviso for re-entry by the lessor when the lessee becomes bankrupt, though it is not one of the "usual" covenants. The lease will vest in his trustee in bankruptcy when the lessee is adjudged bankrupt, subject to the trustee's right to disclaim and the right to re-enter.

Death of the lessor

Under the Administration of Estates Act 1925, the reversion devolves on the personal representatives of the lessor. Where he has died intestate or without having appointed an executor of his will, until the grant of letters of administration, real and personal estate vests in the President of the Probate Division. If the lessor has appointed an executor, the reversion vests in the executor immediately on the death.

Death of the lessee

When a lessee dies his lease devolves similarly to the lessor's reversion.

Statutory vesting of coal

On January 1, 1947, all interests in unworked coal or mines of coal vested automatically in the National Coal Board. This includes leases and reversions in coal and coal mines, whether owned by colliery concerns or by the Coal Commission under the Coal Act 1938.

ASSIGNMENT BY MORTGAGE

If a mortgage of the reversion is created subsequently to the grant of a lease, it operates as a grant of the reversion and carries with it a right to the rent and the benefit of the landlord's remedies for recovery of the rent. But what if the rent is paid to the mortgagor without notice of the mortgage? This payment is valid, but a voluntary payment in advance if the tenant has notice when the rent is actually due does not fall within this rule.

Since January 1, 1926, a mortgage of a lease must be by sub-demise or by charge by way of legal mortgage; an assignment of the term by way of mortgage operates a sub-lease to the mortgagee, for a term (in the case of a first mortgage) ten days less than the term stated to be assigned.

CHAPTER TWELVE

THE RIGHT OF DISTRESS

Distress is the taking, where no legal process is involved, of chattels as a pledge. It is a remedy used to compel the other party to satisfy a demand, or perform some duty, or compensate for some injury. If the rent is in arrear the landlord may distain for that rent at common law.

The levying of distress in the case of protected or statutory tenancies is restricted by the Rent Acts and therefore this remedy is of less importance than it used to be.

CONDITIONS FOR DISTRESS

Distraint can be made only where the following conditions are satisfied:

(i) The relationship of landlord and tenant must have been created, either expressly by a lease or by an agreement for a lease, or by implication of law such as where rent is paid and is regarded as an admission of the existence of a tenancy (see p. 22). Thus, in *Hancock v. Austin* (1863), where the owner of a factory let standings for looms and supplied power for working them at a weekly payment, it was held that he could not distrain for the weekly payments since there was no demise merely a licence.

(ii) The relationship of landlord and tenant must exist at the time of the distraint. In *Bridges v. Smyth* (1829) the landlord elected to determine the lease upon a forfeiture being incurred. It was held that after commencing proceedings for ejectment he could not subsequently distrain for rent since his right of distress had ended.

(iii) The reversion must be in the person exercising the distress.

(iv) The rent must be certain, both in its amount and in the terms of payment.

(v) The rent must be in arrear. We have already seen that rent is not in arrear until midnight of the day when it is due. If the rent is payable in advance, however, it is in arrear as soon as the period for which it is payable commences. In *London & Westminster Loan Co. v. L.N.W.R.* (1893) it was provided that the rent should be payable in advance only if required by the landlord: it was held that a demand for payment by the landlord was necessary before distraint could be made for advance rent. Rent may lawfully be made payable on a Sunday.

The general rule at common law is that all goods found on the demised premises can be taken, whether they belong to the tenant or to some other person. This is subject to modification as we shall see in the next section when we talk of things privileged from distress. In discussing the nature of distress it should be pointed out that although the right is incident to rent-service, it is not so inseparable that it cannot be postponed. Even though the rent is in arrear the landlord may agree that he will not distrain for a period. Such an agreement, if it is supported by consideration (or if the *High Trees* principle of equitable estoppel applies) will be enforceable. Distress for rent may even be made upon other lands of the lessee where there is an agreement to this effect. But it would be convenient now to turn to the question of what goods are subject to the right of distress.

ABSOLUTE PRIVILEGE

Distress was originally in the nature of a pledge and it was not until 1689 that goods so taken could be sold. The general rule is that everything on the property demised can be taken where the rent is in arrear. In fact however this general rule is subject to many exceptions — we may first deal with those things which are absolutely privileged from distress. They are:

(a) Fixtures and other things which cannot be returned in the same condition as they were taken. The law relating to fixtures will be dealt with later (see p. 159).

(b) Animals *ferae naturae* (wild by nature) which have not been reduced into possession.

(c) Things in actual use.

(d) Things delivered to a person exercising a public trade, to be carried, wrought or worked up or managed in the pursuit of his trade.

(e) Things in the custody of the law.

(f) Things belonging to the Crown.

(g) Money, unless it is in a sealed bag or other receptacle so as to be indentifiable.

(h) Beasts that stray on the land through the fault of the tenant or the landlord until they have been *levant* and *couchant* on the land (in other words, lying down and rising up on the premises for a night and a day without pursuit made by their owner).

All these things are, at common law, absolutely privileged from distress.

Other types of goods which are also absolutely privileged by statute include:

(i) Gas, water and electric fittings and apparatus supplied to the tenant by "statutory undertakers" (Gas Act 1948, Water Act 1945, Electric Lighting Acts 1882 and 1909).

(ii) Wearing apparel and bedding of the tenant and his family, and the tools and implements of his trade to the value (in all) of £50. The Lord Chancellor has power from time to time to prescribe a larger amount (Administration of Justice Act 1956). In *Lavell v. Richings* (1906) it was held that if the only article on the premises is worth more than the stipulated figure it cannot be seized under the right of distress.

(iii) On agricultural holdings within the Agricultural Holdings Act 1986, agricultural or other machinery not belonging to the tenant and being on the holding under an agreement with him for the hire or use thereof in his business, and livestock not belonging to the tenant and being on the holding solely for breeding purposes.

(iv) The goods of an undertenant, lodger, or other person not being a tenant of the premises, subject to the provision of the Law of Distress Amendment Act 1908 (see below).

CONDITIONAL PRIVILEGE

There are other types of goods which are conditionally privileged. This means that they *can* be taken in distress, but only if there is an insufficiency of other goods available to satisfy the distress.

Things conditionally privileged are:

1. *At common law,* the tools of a man's trade or profession, even though they are not in actual use, beasts of the plough and sheep and instruments of husbandry.

2. *By statute,* on agricultural holdings within the Agricultural Holdings Act 1986 livestock belonging to another person and taken in to be fed at a fair price or on the premises solely for breeding (Section 18).

LAW OF DISTRESS AMENDMENT ACT 1908

The effect of this Act is, with certain exceptions, to protect from distress the goods of persons other than the tenant.

By section 1 of the Act, if a superior landlord (which by section 9 includes a landlord if the goods seized are not those of an under-tenant or lodger) distrains any furniture, goods or chattels belonging to specified persons for arrears or rent due to the distraining landlord by his immediate tenant, the person concerned can serve a written declaration upon that landlord or his bailiff. The declaration must have a correct signed inventory of the goods annexed to it and state that the immediate tenant has no property or beneficial interest in the goods; that the goods are the property or are in the lawful possession of the declarant and are not goods or livestock to which the Act is expressed not to apply. It must also confirm, in the cases where the declarant is an undertenant or lodger, the amount of any rent due from him to his immediate landlord and the times at which future instalments will become due and their amount, and undertake to pay the superior landlord all the rent so due or to become due until the arrears distrained for are paid off. Where the landlord is a company the signature of its authorised agent is sufficient for the declaration under Section 1 *Lawrence Chemical Co. v. Rubenstein* (1982).

Persons protected

But who are these persons specified in the Act as being protected by the Act and enabled to serve the declaration on the distraining landlord? They are detailed by section 1 as:

(1) any undertenant liable to pay by equal instalments not less often than every actual or customary quarter of a year a rent which would return in any whole year the full annnual value of the premises comprised in his undertenancy; or

(2) any lodger (the Act does not define the word "lodger" but does say that the word "tenant" or "undertenant" does not include a loder); or

(3) any other person who is not a tenant of the premises or any part thereof, and who has no beneficial interest in any tenancy of the premises or part of the premises.

Thus, if the goods of any of these persons are distrained he may serve the written declaration noted above upon the distraining landlord or his bailiff. But what if the distress is proceeded with even after the declaration has been served?

Disregard of the declaration

If the landlord, or his bailiff or employee, proceeds with the distress after service of the declaration in writing and the inventory and (in the case of an undertenant or lordger) payment or tender of any rent then due, he will be guilty of an illegal distress and can be sued for damages. The undertenant, lodger or other person protected by the Act can also make an application to a stipendiary magistrate or two justices of the peace who shall make such order for recovery of the goods or otherwise as seems just, after inquiry into the truth of the declaration and inventory.

As far as the declaration is concerned, it may be noted that this need not be a statutory declaration and may be made for a firm by one partner signing his own name. It should also be noted that by section 5 of the Perjury Act 1911 to make a knowingly untrue statement in the signed declaration and inventory is a misdemeanour.

It was held in *Lowe v. Dorling & Son* (1905) that the bailiff, as well as the landlord, can be sued for an illegal distress.

Non-application of the Act

The Act of 1908 has no application in the case of:

(1) goods belonging to the husband or the wife of the tenant whose rent is in arrear;

(2) goods comprised in any bill of sale, hire-purchase agreement or settlement made by such tenant;

(3) goods in the possession, order or disposition of the tenant whose rent is in arrear by consent of an permission of the true owner, under such circumstance that the tenant is the reputed owner of those goods — in *Chappell & Co. Ltd. v. Harrison* (1910), for instance, it was held that a

piano lent to a tenant under a hire-purchase agreement is in his reputed ownership, even though it is in a theatre where such hiring would be common practice;

(4) any livestock to which section 18 of the Agricultural Holdings Act 1986 apply;

(5) goods of a partner of the immediate tenant;

(6) goods (other than the goods of a lodger) upon premises where any trade or business is carried on in which both the immediate tenant and the undertenant have an interest;

(7) goods (other than those belonging to a lodger) on premises used as offices or warehouses where the owner of the goods neglects for one calendar month after notice to remove the goods and vacate the premises;

(8) goods belonging to and in the offices of any company or corporation on premises of which the immediate tenant is a director or officer, or in the employment of such company or corporation;

(9) goods belonging to any undertenant where the undertenancy has been created in breach of any covenant or agreement in writing between the landlord and his immediate tenant.

Notice by the landlord

Section 6 of the Act provides that where the rent of the tenant of the superior landlord is in arrear the superior landlord may serve a notice upon the undertenant or lodger. It must

(a) state the amount of arrears of rent;

(b) require all future payments of rent, whether already due or not, to be made direct to him by the undertenant or lodger until such arrears have been paid.

The notice will then operate to transfer to the superior landlord the right to recover, receive and give a discharge for such rent.

By section 3 of the Act, for the purposes of the recovery of any sums payable by the undertenant or lodger, either under the undertaking given under section 1 or the notice given by the landlord, the undertenant, or lodger will be deemed to be the tenant of the superior landlord. By the same section the sum payable is deemed to be rent and may, when paid, be deducted by the undertenant or lodger from the rent due to his immediate landlord.

PROCEEDINGS IN DISTRESS

Time for distress

At common law the right of distress was available to the landlord only during the continuance of the tenancy, and applied only in respect of goods actually upon the premises. But, by sections 6 and 7 of the Landlord and Tenant Act 1709, a landlord can distrain for rent after the determination of the lease, provided:

(a) his title still continues; and

(b) the tenant is still in possession; and

(c) he makes the distress witin six calendar months after the determination of the tenancy.

Moreover, by sections 1 to 3 of the Distress for Rent Act 1737, if the tenant "fraudulently or clandestinely" removes his goods from the premises after the rent has become due, in order that he might prevent the landlord from distraining, the landlord may within thirty days follow and distrain the goods. This applies wherever the goods might have been taken but the landlord loses this right if the goods have been sold in good faith and for valuable consideration to a purchaser without notice.

Under the provisions of the 1737 Act the landlord can follow and distrain goods only when, if the goods had not been removed, he might have distressed them either under the common law or under the Landlord and Tenant Act 1709. Thus, he cannot follow and distrain goods if the tenancy has come to an end and the tenant is no longer in possession. In addition only the tenant's goods can be followed and not those of another.

Personal representatives

In the case of deceased landlord, section 26 (4) of the Administration of Estates Act 1925 allows a personal representative to distrain in the same way as the deceased might have done had he been alive, and to distrain after the termination of the lease or tenancy, provided it is done:

(i) within six months after termination of the tenancy;

(ii) during the continuance of the possession of the lessee or tenant from whom the arrears of rent were due.

Method of distress

Distress can be made only by a landlord in person, or by a bailiff holding a certificate under the Law of Distress Amendment Act 1888.

The distress must be made between sunrise and sunset and must be made by *legal* entry upon the premises. The means that the landlord or bailiff may not break open the outer door of the house or any building or open a window that is closed even if it is not fastened. He may, of course, use the normal methods of entry so that if the door is on the latch he is not making an illegal entry if he lifts the latch in order to enter. If a window is *open,* he may effect an entry at that point and the fact that he has to open the window *wider* does not make his entry illegal.

Moreover, it should be noted that the rules as to closed doors apply to *outer* doors. Thus, if the landlord or bailiff effects a legal entry through the outer door, he does not act illegally if he breaks open an inner door. It would, of course, amount to trespass if other persons were to climb over the wall of the yard, but the landlord or bailiff effecting an entry in this manner in order to exercise the right of distress does not commit trespass thereby.

If the landlord does make an unlawful entry, such as by breaking open a window, or putting his hand through a hole in the door to draw back the bolt, his subsequent distress is illegal. The reason for this is that he has initially committed a treapass and the distress is them void *ab initio* (from the beginning).

In such as case he can abandon the distress, and then make a second, legal entry, because he has not lost the right of distress by his unlawful action. Generally speaking, however, a second distress for the same rent cannot be made where the first has been abandoned.

If the distrainer is ejected after lawful entry, he may use force to re-enter provided there was not abandonment of the distress. He may similarly use force to re-enter if, having lawfully entered the premises, he leaves them and is then refused re-entry by the tenant. He must not, of course, have abandoned the distress by leaving the premises. By section 7 of the Distress for Rent Act 1737, where goods have been fraudulently or clandestinely removed the distrainer may break open any house or building in which the goods are suspected to be hidden. But he can do this only

(a) in the presence of a constable, and

(b) if a dwelling house is involved, after he has made oath before a justice of the peace that he has reasonable ground for believing that the goods are concealed on the premises in question.

Seizure

After lawful entry has been made it is necessary to seize the goods. Seizure may be actual by laying hands on the goods or it may be constructive. A constructive seizure will occur where the distrainer states that he intends to prevent the removal of the goods from the premises.

After the goods have been seized an inventory of them should be made. A copy of the inventory, together with a written notice of the distress and its cause, must be left at the premises before the goods can be sold. The notice should inform the tenant, or person whose goods have been seized, of precisely what goods have been taken and the amount of arrears of rent. If the notice specifies certain articles and then continues "and any other goods, chattels and effects on the premises, or in and about the premises" this will be a sufficient notice. In *Kerby v. Harding* (1851), however, it was held that a notice which continued "and all other goods upon the premises (unless specially exempt) sufficient to satisfy the amount of this distress" was not valid.

If a proper notice is not left on the premises the distress itself is not thereby rendered invalid; it will, however, make a sale of the goods irregular.

Impounding

After the goods have been seized the next step is to *impound* the goods. The effect of impounding is to place the goods distrained upon in the custody of the law. It used to be the case that impounding could take place only by depositing the goods in a proper pound but now, by section 10 of the Distress for Rent Act 1737, they may be impounded upon the premises, and in some cases they must be impounded on the premises. When this is done the impounding is complete when notice of the distress with an inventory of the goods has been delivered. It is not necessary that the landlord or his bailiff should remain in possession. When *must* the impounding be carried out on the premises? By section 8 of the 1737 Act and section 2 of the Distress Act 1689, impounding on the premises is compulsory in the case of corn, straw and hay and growing crops made distrainable by those section, unless, in the case of growing crops, there is no convenient barn upon the premises in which to store them when cut.

Right to sell

The *right to sell* goods which have been distrained is given by section 2 of the Distress Act 1689. This section states that if the tenant fails to replevy the goods (i.e. provide security and bring an action for recovery) within five days after notice of distress, the "person distraining shall and may . . . lawfully sell the goods and chattels so distrained for the best price that can be gotten for the same, towards satisfaction of the rent". By section 6 of the Law of Distress Amendment Act 1888, the period of five days within which the tenant can replevy is extended to fifteen days, provided that the tenant or owner of the goods makes a written request to the landlord to that effect, and gives security for any additional costs thereby occasioned.

Can the landlord himself buy the goods distrained? In *Moore Nettlefold & Co. v. Singer Manufacturing Co.* (1904) it was held that a purchase by the landlord himself, even at an auction, is invalid and passes no property in the goods to him where the goods belong to a third person, and the position is the same where the goods belong to the tenant.

PREFERENTIAL CLAIMS

The amount for which a landlord may ordinarily distrain is six years' arrears of rent. In the case of agricultural holdings falling within the Agricutural Holdings Act 1986, however, he can distrain only for one year's rent before the making of the distress (section 16 of the 1986 Act). If the ordinary custom between the landlord and the tenant has been to defer payment of rent until a quarter or half year after it became due, then the rent, for purposes of distress, is deemed to have become due at the expiration of the quarter or half year, and not at the date when legally it became due.

The right of distress may, however, be affected by the fact that the goods have been taken in execution of a judgment debt, or that the tenant has become bankrupt. Similarly, where the tenant is a company, the right of distress may be affected by the fact that the company is in the process of being wound up.

It is beyond the scope of this book to attempt more than an outline of the position in these cases but it must be noted that if the goods have been seized in execution they are in the custody of the law and so distrain upon them is, at common law, impossible. By statute, however, goods seized in execution cannot be removed by the creditor until he pays arrears of the tenant's rent up to:

(a) four weeks' rent in the case of a weekly tenancy;

(b) two terms of payment in the case of executions issuing under a county court warrent where the tenancy is for any other term less than a year (and four terms of payment in other cases);

(c) one year's rent in the case of any other tenancy.

Bankruptcy of the tenant

If the tenant becomes bankrupt the provisions of The Insolvency Act 1986 apply. The landlord can distrain at any time the goods of the bankrupt, either before or after the commencement of the bankruptcy. The bankruptcy commences when the bankruptcy order is made by the court.

If the distress is levied after the commencement of bankruptcy, however, it is available only for six months' rent accrued prior to the order. It is open to the landlord to prove in the bankruptcy as an ordinary creditor for any surplus for which distress is available. The effect of this provision is that he has a *preferential* claim only in respect of six month's rent: the rest he can claim for, and will rank, as an ordinary unsecured creditor.

The Insolvency Act 1986 also provides that where goods are taken in execution the preferential claim of the landlord under (b) or (c) above extends only to six months' rent unless notice of the claim was served on the sheriff before the commencement of the bankruptcy.

Company winding up

If the tenant is a limited company which is in the process of being wound up by the court, or is subject to the supervision of the court, any distress put in force against the effects of the company after the winding up commences is void, except by leave of the court.

Preferred debts

Certain preferential claims are a first charge on goods distrained or the proceeds thereof. These arise where the landlord distrains upon the good of

(a) a person who is bankrupt or becomes bankrupt within three months: or

(b) a limited company which is being wound up, or is wound up within three months; or

(c) a tenant who dies insolvent within three months.

In respect of any money paid under any such charge the landlord will have the same rights of priority as the persons to whom the payment is made.

These preferred debts are laid out in similar form in the Insolvency Act 1986, Schedule 6, and the Companies Act 1985, to apply to the bankrupt tenant and the tenant who is a limited company being wound up, respectively. The preferred debts are a follows:

(a) all debts due to the Inland Revenue for the period of 12 months prior to the date of the bankruptcy order

(b) all debts due to the Customs and Excise for the period of 6 months prior to the bankruptcy order

(c) Social Security contributions which come under the Social Security Act 1975 for the periods of

(i) 12 months before the bankruptcy order for clause 1 or 2 contributions or

(ii) contributions assessed to the 5th April next after the date of the bankruptcy order for class 4 contributions.

(d) contributions to occupational pension schemes which fall within S3 Social Security Act 1975 and

(e) remuneration for employees for the period of 4 months prior to the bankruptcy order and not exceeding the prescribed sum at that date and holiday pay accrued up to the date of the bankruptcy order.

LOSS OF THE RIGHT TO DISTRAIN

The right of distress may be lost in one of several ways. It may be barred:

(i) by agreement; or by estoppel;

(ii) by payment or tender of the rent or by the recovery of judgment for the rent — though it would not be barred by judgment upon a collateral security;

(iii) by acceptance by the landlord of something in satisfaction of the rent;

(iv) by a previous distraint upon the same goods for the same rent.

WRONGFUL DISTRESS

A distress will be regarded as wrongful where it is:

(i) *Excessive.*

(ii) *Irregular.* Here, although the right to distrain does in fact exist, some wrongful act is committed after the seizure has been made. There may be, for instance, some irregularity in the selling of the goods distrained.

Formerly, the situation was that any such act rendered the landlord a trespasser *ab initio.* By section 19 of the Distress for Rent Act 1737 it is provided, however, that "where any distress shall be made for any kind of rent justly due, and any irregularity or unlawful act shall be afterwards done by the party ... distraining ... the distress itself shall not be therefore deemed to be unlawful, nor the party making it be deemed a trespasser ... *ab initio;* but the party ... aggrieved ... shall or may recover full satisfaction for the special damage he ... shall have sustained thereby; and no more".

(iii) *Illegal.* Here there will be no right to distrain in the first place, because, for instance, there is no rent in arrear, for the goods seized are classified as goods privileged from distress.

But what remedies are available if a wrongful distress is made?

Remedies for wrongful distress

The first and perhaps most obvious remedy that might be noted is an action for damages; the tenant can sue the landlord for damages for the loss that he has sustained. But there are other remedies; he may, where no rent was due, bring an action under section 4 of the Distress for Rent Act 1689, by which he can claim the double value of any goods sold. In the case of illegal distress he may also bring an action of replevin (to recover the goods) and certain summary remedies are available to him.

Should the wrongful distress be merely threatened the tenant may, of course, obtain an injunction to prevent the unlawful act.

CHAPTER THIRTEEN

DETERMINATION OF THE TENANCY

There are several ways in which a lease or tenancy may be determined:
(1) by expiry,
(2) by surrender,
(3) by merger,
(4) by enlargement,
(5) by disclaimer,
(6) by notice to quit,
(7) by forfeiture.

TERMINATION BY EXPIRY

The rule at common law is that a lease or tenancy for a fixed period will automatically end when the fixed period has run its course. There are certain exceptions to the rule, however, which have been created by statute, whereby the tenancy is prolonged automatically with provision for the grant of a new tenancy. These provision, together with those whereby the tenant may be entitled to remain indefinitely in possession as a statutory tenant, have already been touched upon and will be dealt with in more detail later.

A lease will also expire where it is made determinable upon the happening of a certain event and that event occurs, provided the lease is limited to last only until the condition is fulfilled.

TERMINATION BY SURRENDER

Surrender is the yeilding up of the term to the person who has the immediate estate in reversion. Such surrender may be made expressly, or it may arise by operation of law.

Express surrender

An express surrender must be made by deed to be effective except in the case of leases which are for terms not exceeding three years at the best rent that can be obtained without taking a fine. A lease of this nature may be surrendered by writing signed by the person surrendering or his agent lawfully authorised in writing.

It should be noted that an agreement by a tenant to offer the surrender of his lease before he makes any proposed assignment of it is void (*Allnatt London Properties v. Newton* 1983). A letter (not a deed) releasing a tenant from arrears of rent in return for a surrender of the lease was held to be unenforceable by the landlord (*Tarjami v. Panther Securities* 1983).

Surrender by operation of law

Surrender arises by operation of law where the person involved is estopped by his conduct from denying that a surrender has taken place — even though an express surrender has not been made by deed. Thus, a surrender by operation of law takes place:

(i) if the tenant accepts a new tenancy during the currency of his existing tenancy. In *Re Savile Settled Estates* (1931) it was held that the alteration of an existing lease by extending the term operates as a surrender of the lease and the grant of a new lease. There is no surrender if the new tenancy is void or voidable, however.

(ii) if the landlord accepts possession from the tenant with the intention of allowing the tenancy to determine. Thus, in *Boynton-Wood v. Trueman* (1961), where the landlord accepted the key of a cottage forming part of an agricultural hereditament in order to carry out repairs it was held that there had been no surrender of the lease: the necessary intention had not been present.

(iii) if there is a grant of a new tenancy to a stranger, with the assent of the tenant and change of possesison at or about the time of the grant of new tenancy.

Mere abandonment of the premises will not amount to a surrender of itself (though the landlord may apply to the court under section 54 of the Landlord and Tenant Act 1954 for an order to determine the lease). The landlord may wish the liability of the tenant under the lease to continue in such circumstances. The mere delivery of the key of the premises to the landlord is not enough nor acceptance of the key nor the landlord charging the locks unless it is shown that there was an intention to determine the tenancy. Again, a contract by the tenant to purchase the reversion will not of itself amount to a surrender. In other words, to bring about a surrender by operation of law the parties must do something which shows an *intention* to terminate the lease, in circumstances such that it would not be equitable for them to rely on the lack of a deed of surrender.

In *Preston Borough Council v. Fairclough* (1982) it was held that the mere fact that a tenant vacated premises owing rent did not invoke an inference of surrender. To show this evidence must be given that the absence was for a substantial time owing substantial rent.

Operation of the surrender

A lessee cannot prejudice the rights of his sub-lessee by surrendering his lease. The surrender will destroy his own reversion on the underlease but by section 139 of the Law of Property Act 1925 the estate of the head lessor is deemed to be the reversion on the underlease in order to preserve the incidents and obligations of the under-lease.

Moreover, by section 150 of the same Act, if a lessee, with a view to acceptance of a new lease, surrenders a lease out of which an underlease has been granted, the position of the head lessor, the lessee and underlessee remains the same after the grant of the new lease as if no surrender had taken place.

Surrender of a lease does not release the tenant from liability for breach of covenant before the surrender — even if the landlord had no legal title for the tenant is estopped from denying the landlord's title: *Industrial Properties (Barton Hill) Ltd. v. Associated Electrical Industries Ltd.* (1977).

TERMINATION BY MERGER

A merger occurs where a tenant acquires the reversion on his lease, or when a third party acquires both lease and reversion. The lease in both cases merges with the reversion and disappears.

The tenant must hold the lease and the reversion in the same capacity, of course: thus, if he holds the lease in a personal capacity and the reversion as an executor or administrator there will be not merger.

TERMINATION BY ENLARGEMENT

Termination by enlargement is not common. A lease may be enlarged into a fee simple by execution by the tenant of a deed of enlargement under section 153 of the Law of Property Act 1925 where he has a term of at least two hundred years at no rent or a rent of no money value.

TERMINATION BY DISCLAIMER

If a lessee becomes bankrupt his trustee in bankruptcy will normally take the lease and hold it, or deal with it generally for the benefit of creditor. Alternatively, if the lease consists of onerous property within the meaning of the Insolvency Act 1986, by Section 317 the trustee may, with the leave of the court, disclaim the lease. It should be noted, however, that a statutory tenancy under the Rent Acts will not pass to the trustee in bankruptcy and so cannot be disclaimed: *Sutton v. Dorf* (1932).

The effect of disclaimer is that all the rights, liabilities and interests of the bankrupt under the lease determine from the date of the disclaimer and the trustee is released from all personal liability. the disclaimer does not otherwise affect the rights and liabilities of any other person, however.

The landlord, and any other person injured by the operation of the disclaimer, is deemed to be a creditor to the extent of his injury and he may prove in the bankruptcy.

The disclaimer must be made within twelve months from the appointment of the trustee, unless the property does not come to the notice of the trustee within one month of his appointment. In such circumstances he has twelve months from the time at which he becomes aware of the property, in which to disclaim.

The trustee can lose the right to disclaim, however. If the landlord makes an application in writing to the trustee to decide whether or not he will disclaim and the trustee does not then disclaim within twenty-eight days or such further time as may be allowed by the court, he cannot thereafter disclaim.

In the winding up of a limited company the liquidator, by Sections 618 and 619 of the Companies Act 1985, has a similar power of disclaimer with the leave of the court.

It may also be noted that, by the Landlord and Tenant (War Damage) Act 1939, the provisions of which are lengthy and now of little importance, a tenant whose land or buildings have been rendered unfit for use by war damage (as defined by the Act) is given the right either to disclaim his tenancy or retain it on terms specified in the Act. Further, by the Landlord and Tenant (Requisitioned Land) Act 1942, the tenant is given the right, in the conditions mentioned in the Act, to disclaim his lease or tenancy when his residential or business premises have been requisitioned. Similarly, under the Housing Act 1985 the lessor or lessee can apply to the court for an order to determine a tenancy of property subject to a demolition or closing order.

TERMINATION BY NOTICE TO QUIT

A landlord or tenant, or the assignees or representatives of either, to determine a periodic tenancy without the consent of the other, must give notice.

An interesting reflection of the nature of the notice to quit arose in *Chapman v. Honig* (1963). The tenant gave evidence in a case against the landlord in court and in order to victimise the tenant the landlord then gave him notice to quit. It was held that the service of this notice was in contempt of court but the tenant himself had no right to sue for damages. The object of the court's jurisdiction to punish the landlord for contempt of court was to protect the administration of justice, and not to protect the rights of individual citizens.

Fixed term

Unless there is an express agreement to the contrary, a lease or a tenancy for a fixed period cannot be ended by notice: a tenant for a fixed term is not generally entitled to receive not bound to give notice to quit; his term ends automatically.

There are important statutory exceptions to this rule, however: in the case of business tenancies, under the Landlord and Tenant Act 1954; and in the case of certain agricultural tenancies, under the Agricultural Holdings Act 1986. These provisions will be dealt with in detail later.

A fixed term may be determinable by notice under an express "break clause", in the lease. Such notice is subject to the same rules as notice to quit under periodic tenancies.

Notice in periodic tenancies

In the case of periodic tenancies the question of notice to quit is regulated by (i) common law, (ii) agreement and (iii) statute.

Common law

At common law, in the absence of an express stipulation, a tenant from year to year is entitled to, and must give, a half-year's notice to quit, expiring at the end of a current year of the tenancy. If the tenancy begins on one of the usual quarter days a customary half-year's notice is sufficient — *i.e.*, notice given on or before one quarter day for the second succeeding quarter day. If it begins on any other day the notice must be a full half-year's notice of 182 days, excluding the day on which it is given and including the day on which it expires.

Where there is an express tenancy for a fraction of a year and a year or period of years, and the tenancy is continued from year to year by holding over, the notice must expire on the anniversary of the termination of the original tenancy and not on that of its commencement.

If a periodic tenancy is less than a yearly tenancy the notice should correspond with the period of tenancy. Thus, it should be a month's notice in a monthly tenancy, and a week's notice in a weekly tenancy, and should terminate at the end of a periodic month or week or on the first day of a period.

In *Bathavon R.D.C. v. Carlile* (1958) it was held that a notice to quit "by noon" on the proper day or on the following day is bad. Where, for instance, the proper day is Friday, a notice to quit for the Saturday is ordinarily treated as good only because it is capable of referring to the very first moment of that day. If, however, some specific time on that day is mentioned, it is not possible to draw this inference and so the notice must be regarded as bad.

Problems can be avoided by the use of a formula such as a notice to expire on a given date "or on such other date as the period of your tenancy would expire being not less than twenty-eight days from the date of the service upn you of this notice". It should be noted also that by section 61 of the Law of Property Act 1925 the term "month" in all deeds, contracts and other instruments made or coming into operation after December 31, 1925, means, unless the contract otherwise requires, a calendar month and not a lunar one.

Agreement

The landlord and tenant may modify the common law rules with regard to notice to quit by agreement. But the length of the notice to quit agreed upon must not be greater than that of the tenancy contemplated. Moreover, in the case of a yearly or other periodic tenancy the stipulation must not be repugnant to the nature of the tenancy. In *Breams Property Investment Co. v. Stroulger*(1948) it was held that a promise not to serve notice to quit within the first three years of the tenancy is not repugnant to the nature of a quarterly tenancy. There may be a stipulation for three months' notice to quit at any time in a tenancy from year to year, or terminable at the will of the lessor, or on the occurrence of a particular event. But where there is a *yearly* tenancy a stipulation that it may *at any time* be determined by three months' notice will not enable it to be determined by a notice expiring before the end of the first year.

Statute

Details of the statutory provisions relating to notice will be dealt with later in this book, but it may be noted here that they cover residential premises, agricultural holdings and business premises.

Dwelling-houses

By section 15 of the Protection from Eviction Act 1977 no notice by a landlord or a tenant to quit any premises let as a dwelling is valid unless it is in writing, contains any information prescribed by the Sectretary of State and is given not less than four weeks before the date on which it is to take effect. "Not less than four weeks" was held, in *Schnabel v. Allard* (1966) to mean "inclusive of the date of service and exclusive of the day of expiry".

Section 5 applies only where the real relationship of landlord and tenant exists: it does not apply, therefore, where notice is given under an attornment clause in a mortgage deed, and in *Crane v. Morris* (1965) it was held to have no application to a tenancy at will.

Form of the notice to quit

No particular form is required at common law for a notice to quit. Oral notice could terminate an oral tenancy. It must however be a "clear, distinct and unambiguous notice" of the determination of the party giving it, to bring the existing tenancy to an end at a certain time. In *Scholl Manufacturing Co. v. Clifton (Slim-Line)* (1966) landlords of business premises, let on lease with a break clause allowing them to terminate the tenancy by six months' notice, sent the tenants a notice under section 25 of the Landlord and Tenant Act 1954 with a covering letter saying it was their intention to terminate the tenancy. The court held that notice and letter together amounted to a sufficient notice to quit within the break clause.

The burden of proving that a notice to quit is valid lies upon the landlord, but the court may impute to the tenant knowledge which renders clear that which without the knowledge would be neither clear not unambiguous. Thus, in the case of a yearly tenant, a notice to quit on a named date or "at the expiration of the year of your tenancy which shall expire next after the end of one half-year from the date of this notice" was held to be valid in *Phipps & Co. v. Rogers* (1925), because the date of the expiration of the tenancy is a question of fact which the tenant knows or can properly be deemed to know.

Similarly, the *Dagger v. Shepherd* (1946), it was held that a notice to quit "on or before" a specified date is valid, because it takes effect as an irrevocable notice to determine the tenancy on that date coupled with an offer to accept a determination on any earlier date of the tenant's choice. A notice to quit "by" a certain date is equivalent to "on or before" that date.

The court will lean in favour of reading the notice in such a way as to give it validity and where it is otherwise clear and specific but inaccurate in an obvious way, the court may cure the inaccuracy. An example is seen in *Carradine Properties v. Aslam* (1976) where notice is given in September 1975 to quit by September "1975" was held valid as both parties knew that "1976" was intended.

Notice must be unconditional

A notice to quit must not be conditional. It is therefore invalid if it is expressed to take effect upon some contingency such as the tenant continuing to commit a breach of covenant. It must not be optional: for instance, if it is expressed to take effect unless the tenant agrees to pay an increased rent, it is invalid. It is not invalid merely because the landlord adds an offer for a *new* tenancy at an increased rent, however; in such a case the fact that the tenant remains in possession may be evidence of his agreement to pay the increased rent, entitling him to remain in possession unless he has a statutory right to do so.

Part of the premises

At common law a notice to quit part of the premises held on a single tenancy is invalid. Section 140 of the Law of Property Act 1925 provides, however, that were the reversionary estate in any land comprised in a lease is severed (as, for instance, where a landlord sells in two lots to two different purchasers land that is let on a single tenancy) every condition or right of re-entry shall be apportioned and shall remain annexed to the severed parts of the reversionary estate. The "conditions" will include a right to determine the lease by notice to quit or otherwise.

Where a notice to quit is served by a person entitled to a severed part of the reversion, so that it extends to part only of the land demised the lessee may within one month determine the lease in regard to the rest of the land by giving to the owner of the reversionary estate therein a counter-notice expiring at the same time as the original notice.

Special provisions exist in relation to agricultural holdings.

Waiver of notice

It has been said that waiver is an inaccurate expression: the question really is whether the parties intended by their conduct to create a new tenancy. Nevertheless, the term is a useful one and it may be used in stating the rule that a notice to quit may be withdrawn during the course of the tenancy, or may be "waived" after its expiration. The effect in either case will be to create a new tenancy commencing at the expiration of the old tenancy. To avoid such an inference, after service of the notice to quit the safest course is to stipulate to the tenant that all payments made thereafter by him are received by the landlord as mesne profits.

A new tenancy may be implied from any conduct that indicates that both parties recognise the existence of a tenancy in spite of the determination of the original term by a valid notice to quit. In *Keith Prowse & Co. v. National Telephone Co.* (1894) it was held that the payment and acceptance of rent for a period subsequent to the determination of the tenancy will usually justify this inference but *Davies v. Bristowe* (1920) illustrates that the inference cannot be drawn where the premises are subject to the Rent Act. The matter is entirely a question of the intention of the parties, as can be seen from *Clarke v. Grant* (1950) (where the rent was accepted by mistake — no new agreement) and *Marcroft Wagons v. Smith* (1951) (where the rent was accepted from a person with an ostensible claim to protection under the Rent Act — no new agreement).

The service of a second notice to quit is of no effect unless by its terms it is the basis for inferring an intention to create a new tenancy after the expiration of the first notice.

TERMINATION BY FORFEITURE

It is possible that the landlord may become entitled to re-take the premises and thus put an end to the lease. He may have this right under the terms of the lease itself, or he may have it by operation of law. It will be convenient here, however, to deal with the matter of forfieture under two separate heads: first, where the forfeiture arises otherwise than for non-payment of rent, and second, forfeiture for non-payment of rent.

(1) Forfeiture otherwise than for non-payment of rent

In these circumstances, forfeiture may arise by disclaimer by the tenant of his landlord's title, by breach of a condition subsequent, or by breach of a covenant by the lessee.

Disclaimer

When the tenant disclaims his landlord's title he is in effect repudiating the relationship of landlord and tenant. He may do this by claiming to hold possession upon a ground that is inconsistent with the existence of the relationship of landlord and tenant, or by impuging the title of his landlord such as where he delivers possession to a third person who claims by a title adverse to that of the landlord.

The action of the tenant in asserting a title in himself, or allowing a third person to set up a title adverse to that of the landlord must be deliberate, however, it is a question of fact as to what intention underlies the words or actions of the tenant.

Breach of a condition subsequent

The estate of the tenant may be qualified by a condition that it shall be defeated upon the occurrence of some particular event. In such a case the landlord will have a right of re-entry upon the event happening whether or not there is an express stipulation to that effect in the lease.

It should be noted, however, that a condition must be distinguished from a conditional limitation. The latter arises where the grant is made *until* a certain contingency happens. Where there is a conditional limitation there is nothing to carry the estate beyond the happening of the contingency, upon which it immediately determines.

Breach of covenant by the lessee

Nearly every lease contains a recital of things that the tenant can or cannot do. Usually these are drawn up as covenants, though they may be framed as conditions. Where the landlord and tenant have entered into covenants a proviso is usually inserted that on breach by the tenant of some or any of his covenants the landlord will have a right of re-entry. If the obligations of the tenant are framed as conditions the lease becomes liable to forfeiture if the condition is broken, even if there is no forfeiture clause, since the continuance of the lease is conditional upon performance of the obligations. The lease then becomes voidable at the landlord's option (but not void).

It is more usual to insert the obligations as covenants, however, supported by a proviso for re-entry on breach. The landlord will then have a right of re-entry on the stipulated events occurring, but if there is a breach of covenant not within that proviso he will have merely the right to maintain an action for damages, or for an injunction to restrain the breach or possibly specific performance *Jeune v. Queens Cross Properties, Ltd.* (1973).

The landlord must do some "final and positive" act indicating his intention to determine the lease either by making peaceable entry or by issuing a writ for possession. The former remedy is normally inadvisable since if any force is used in the re-entry he may be criminally liable, while in the case of residential property the landlord must always seek the court's assistance.

Waiver of the breach. The landlord may show that he is treating the lease as forfeited, but he may even then lose the right to proceed if he waives the breach. Waiver can be express, of course, but it may be implied where

(a) the landlord has knowledge of the acts or omissions of the tenant which make the lease liable to forfeiture, and

(b) he does some unequivocal act which recognises the continued existence of the lease.

Thus, the law *presumes* the intention to waive a known breach from acceptance or demand of rent, no matter what the actual intention might have been. This is so even if the landlord attempts to preserve his right by accepting rent "without prejudice". However, his common law right to recover damages for the breach is not affected by waiver of the right to forfeit.

Conversely, the issue and service of a writ in ejectment is such a final election by the landlord to determine the tenancy that a subsequent receipt of rent cannot amount to a waiver of the forfeiture.

If rent is payable in advance a demand for, or acceptance of, the rent operates as a waiver of past and continuing breaches, but only in respect of those known to the landlord at the time, and for such period that he knows they will continue. In *Segal Securities v. Thoseby* (1963) it was held that it does not operate as a waiver of breaches subsequent to demand or acceptance.

Relief against forfeiture

The courts tend to lean against forfeiture and both equity and statutes have allowed tenants to be freed from liability to forfeiture in particular instances. Equity has jurisdiction to relieve against forfeiture but has exercised this jurisdiction narrowly, following its general rule that relief will be given only where a covenant to pay money is broken (usually non-payment of rent) or where the landlord is guilty of fraud or other conduct which disentitles him from insisting on his legal rights, or if the breach has been due to some accident or mistake, not being the result of any negligence or misconduct on the part of the tenant. It appears that these heads do not exhaust the courts' discretion, however.

Law of Property Act 1925, s. 146. The question of enforcing a forfeiture is now generally governed by section 146 of the Law of Property Act 1925 although this section does not detract from the equitable jurisdiction of the court. This section provides that the landlord must serve a statutory notice on the tenant before he can proceed to enforce the forfeiture by action or re-entry. The notice must:

(a) specify the breach of covenant; and

(b) demand that it be remedied, if it is a breach capable of remedy; and

(c) require the tenant to pay monetary compensation for the breach, if the landlord requires such compensation.

The notice may be served by written notice at the tenant's last known abode or business address, or by being left on the demised premises, and it is sufficient to send the notice by registered post or recorded delivery to the last known abode or business address provided it is not returned undelivered. A lease may provide for a procedure as to services of notice and in such cases that procedure must be followed insofar as it is consistent with the Act.

The landlord must allow the tenant a reasonable time in which to comply with the notice — what is reasonable, depends upon the circumstances. Even where the breach cannot be remedied reasonable notice must be given to allow him time to consider the position and while in such cases two days would be inadequate, forteen days has sufficed.

If the notice is not complied with during the reasonable time given, the landlord may proceed with enforcement of the forfeiture, either personally or by action. Section 146 also provides that where the landlord is "proceeding" to enforce such a right of re-entry or forfeiture the tenant may, in the lessor's action, if any, or in any action brought by himself, apply to the court for relief. The court may refuse or grant relief as it thinks fit and will have regard to the conduct of the parties and the circumstances of the case in doing so. If relief is granted it will be on such terms as the court thinks fit with regard to costs, damages, compensation or the grant of an injunction to retrain any like breach in the future. The court will not normally exercise its discretion in favour of tenants who allow the premises to be used for immoral purposes.

The general rule is that the breach must be remedied or, at the least, an undertaking given to remedy it,, before relief is given. It is within the court's discretion however, in appropriate circumstances, to grant relief even though the breach is not remedied.

In *Di Palma v. Victoria Square Property Co.* (1985) it was held that where a County Court had granted relief against forfeiture on the basis that the tenant should pay his rent arrears, the High Court had no jurisdiction to grant relief when the tenant failed to pay his arrears.

It should be emphasised that the foregoing applies only where the landlord is proceeding to enforce his right, not where he has actually re-entered before the tenant has commenced poroceedings for relief. Where there are joint lessees relief against forfeiture cannot be granted on the application of only one of them.

By section 146 (3) the landlord may recover from the lessee all reasonable costs and expenses incurred by him in reference to any breach giving rise to a right of entry or forfeiture which, at the request of the lessee, is waived by him, or from which the lessee is relieved under the Act.

Non-application of section 146. Sub-sections (8) and (9) provide that the section does not extend.

(i) in the case of a mining lease, to a covenant or condition for allowing the lessor to have access to or inspect books, accounts, records, weighing machines or other things, or to enter or inspect the mine or the workings thereof;

(ii) to a condition for forfeiture on the bankruptcy of the lessee, or on taking in execution of the lessee's interests if contained in a lease of

(a) agricultural or pastoral land;

(b) mines or minerals;

(c) a house used or intended to be used as a public house or beer shop;

(d) a house let as a dwelling-house, with the use of any furniture, books, works of art, or other chattels not being in the nature of fixtures;

(e) any property with respect to which the personal qualifications of the tenant are of importance for the preservation of the value or character of the property, or on the ground of neighbourhood to the lessor, or to any person holding under him.

Where, however, a condition of forfeiture on the bankruptcy of the lessee or on the taking in execution of the lessee's interest is contained in a lease *other than* the classes mentioned above them:

(i) if the lessee's interest is sold within one year of the bankruptcy or taking in execution, section 146 will apply to the condition;

(ii) if the lessee's interest is not sold before the expiration of that year, section 146 then ceases to apply.

Sub-section (11) provides that the section does not apply to non-payment of rent.

Relief to underleases. Section 146 also provides relief to underleases: where the lessor is proceeding by action or otherwise to enforce the right of re-entry or forfeiture under any covenant, proviso or stipulation in a lease, or *for non-payment of rent.* The court may make an order on the application of a person claiming as *underlessee.* The court may do this in the lessor's action or in any action brought by the underlessee. The order will vest the property concerned for the whole term or less in any person entitled as underlessee upon such conditions as to the execution of any deed or other document, payment of rent, costs, expenses, damages, compensation, giving security or otherwise, as the court thinks fit. But in no case will any underlessee be entitled to require a lease to be granted to him for a term longer than that which he had under his original sub-lease.

It should be noted that the provision as to the grant of relief to underleases are not affected by anything in section 146 (8), (9) and (11), detailed above. Thus, an underlessee can obtain relief in cases where relief would not be granted to a lessee.

A mortgagee by way of legal charge is entitled to relief under section 146 (4) in the same way as if he were an underlessee. In *Re Good's Lease* (1954) it was held that a guarantor with a right to call for a proper legal charge or mortgage was similarly covered.

There can be no contracting out of the provisions of section 146: the section has effect in spite of any agreement to the contrary.

Relief in respect of particular covenants

Dilapidations. By section 18 (2) of the Landlord and Tenant Act 1927 a right of re-entry or forfeiture for breach of a covenant or agreement to keep or put premises in repair during the currency of a lease is not enforceable, by action or otherwise, unless the lessor proves knowledge of the service of the notice required by section 146 (1) of the Law of Property Act 1925. He must show that the fact that the notice was served on the lessee was known either to the

(i) lessee; or

(ii) underlessee holding under an underlease which reserved only a nominal reversion to the lessee; or

(iii) person who last paid the rent due under the lease either on his own behalf or as agent for the lessee or underlessee.

He must also show that a time, reasonably sufficient for the repairs to be executed, has elapsed since the time when the fact of service of the notice came to the knowledge of the relevant person. It may be noted here that under section 196 of the Law of Property Act 1925 in a case of forfeiture other than for dilapidations it is enough to serve the section 146 notice by leaving it at or affixing it to the premises, but in the case of forfeiture for dilapidations it is still necessary to prove that the fact of service has come to the *knowledge* of one of the persons mentioned above.

Decorative repairs. By section 147 of the Law of Property Act 1925, after a notice is served on a lessee relating to internal decorative repairs, he may apply to the court for relief. If the court is satisfied, having regard to the circumstances of the case (and in particular the length of the lessee's term of interest remaining unexpired) that the notice is unreasonable, it may order complete or partial relief from liability for the repairs in question.

Section 147 does not apply, however,

(i) where the liability arises under an express covenant or agreement to put the property in a decorative state of repair and the covenant or agreement has never been performed;

(ii) to any matter necessary for putting or keeping the property in a sanitary condition, or for the maintenance or preservation of the structure;

(iii) to any statutory liability to keep a house in all respects reasonably fit for human habitation;

(iv) to any covenant or stipulation to the contrary, and the term "lease" in this section includes an underlease and an agreement for a lease. The term lessee has a corresponding meaning and includes any person liable to effect the repairs.

Repairing covenants. Where the repairing covenant is contained in a lease for a term of years certain of not less than seven years, restrictions are placed upon its enforcement by the Leasehold Property (Repairs) Act 1938.

By section 1 (1) (as amended by the Landlord and Tenant Act 1954, s. 54) where a lessor serves notice under section 146 on a lessee holding under such a lease, relating to breach of a repairing covenant or agreement in respect of property other than an agricultural holding, the lessee may within twenty-eight days from that date serve counter-notice on the lessor claiming the benefit of the Act. At the date of service of the lessor's notice three years or more of the term of the lease must remain unexpired for the section to apply.

Similarly, the lessor's right to damages for the breach is not enforceable by action unless notice under section 146 has been served and the lessee has twenty-eight days within which to serve counter-notice claiming the benefit of the Act.

If the counter-notice is served by the lessee, leave of the court is necessary before proceeedings can be taken by the lessor to enforce a right of re-entry or forfeiture can be taken by the lessor to enforce a right of re-entry or forfeiture for breach of the covenant or agreement in question, or for damages for the breach. Leave of the court is not necessary, however, if the lessee gives no counter-notice and this is so even if another person, such as a mortgagee who need not have been served gives a counter-notice. A counter-notice by the lessee will, however, protect his assignee.

Notice served by the lessor is invalid unless it contains a statement, in characters as conspicuous as those used in other parts of the notice, that the lessee is entitled to serve a counter-notice, and a similarly conspicuous statement specifying the time and manner in which a counter-notice can be served, and the name and address for service of the lessor.

What is the situation if the leave of the court is asked for? By section 1 (5) leave will not be given unless the lessor proves at least one of the following matters:

(a) that the immediate remedying of the breach in question is necessary to prevent substantial diminution in the value of his reversion, or that its value has been substantially diminished by the breach:

(b) that the immediate remedying of the breach is necessary for giving effect to any enactment, or any by-law or other provision relating to the safety, repair, maintenance or sanitary condition of houses or for giving effect to any court order or requirement of any authority under any such enactment by-law or provision;

(c) that the immediate remedying of the breach is necessary in the interests of the occupier of the whole or part of the premises where the lessee is not in occupation of the whole;

(d) that the breach can be immediately remedied at relatively small expense in comparison with the greater expense that would probably be occasioned by postponement of the necessary work; or

(e) special circumstances which render it just and equitable in the court's opinion that leave should be given.

Where section 1 (5) is satisfied the court has a *discretion* to allow the landlord to sue for breach of covenant and the landlord should be given leave unless the court is clearly convinced that the application should be refused.

In granting or refusing leave the court may impose such terms and conditions on lessor or lessee as it thinks fit.

By section 2 of the 1938 Act the landlord who has been served with a counter-notice cannot recover from the lessee costs and expenses incurred in references to the breach unless he applies for leave as above and the court can direct whether and to what extent the landlord is so entitled.

The Leasehold Property Repairs Act 1938 does not apply to a breach of covenant or agreement in so far as it imposes an obligation on the lessee to put premises in repair on his taking possession or within a reasonable time thereafter.

The Act applies to the Crown.

(2) Forfeiture for non-payment of rent

The landlord's right to re-enter for non-payment of rent arises only where payment is a condition of the lease or there is an express proviso for re-entry in the lease or tenancy agreement, *e.g.*, a proviso giving him a right of re-entry if the rent or any part thereof shall be in arrear and unpaid for thirty days after it is due.

Enforcement at common law

A common law, to take advantage of the right the landlord must make a formal demand.

(i) at the place, if any, specified for payment of the rent or, if no place is specified, on the land itself;

(ii) of the exact rent due;

(iii) at a convenient time before sunset of the last day for payment, the demand being continued until sunset.

The common law rule is usually nullified by an express proviso giving the landlord a right of re-entry for non-payment of rent "whether legally demanded or not".

Common Law Procedure Act 1852

By section 210 of the Common Law Procedure Act 1852 the landlord can serve a writ for recovery of the demised premises without formal demand or re-entry provided that half a year's rent is in arrear and he has a right to re-enter for non-payment. If these two facts are established at the trial and it is also shown that no sufficient distress is to be found on the demised premises, the landlord can recover judgment and execution in the same manner as if the rent had been legally demanded and a re-entry made.

At common law a distress operates as a waiver of forfeiture incurred by non-payment of rent but this rule does not appear to apply to cases within section 210 of the Common Law Procedure Act 1852 under which distress must be attempted by the landlord in order to complete the right given him by the Act.

By section 212 of the Act all proceedings must be stayed if the tenant, at any time before trial, tenders to the landlord or pays into court all the arrears together with costs. The section applies only where six months' rent is in arrears however; so, in *Standard Pattern Co. v. Ivey* (1962) the tenant could not compel a stay of proceedings where only one quarter's rent was unpaid though it was held that equitable relief could be granted.

Relief against forfeiture

Sections 210 and 211 of the Common Law Procedure Act 1852 which apply where rent is half a year in arrears provide that relief in equity is obtainable in the High Court within six months after judgment for possession upon payment of all arrears of rent and the costs of the action. Section 46 of the Judicature Act 1925 provides that equitable relief is obtainable even where the rent is not half a year in arrears, but it appears that application must still be made within six months after execution. In *Belgravia Insurance v. Meah* (1964) it was held that relief under the 1925 Act could be granted not only to lessees but also to underlessees and mortgagees by assignment.

No relief can be obtained by a sqatter. In *Tickner v. Buzzacott* (1965) a squatter paid rent to the landlords after her friend, the tenant, had died, unknown to the landlords. In 1962 the landlords peaceably re-entered for non-payment of rent. The court held that the squatter could not get relief against forfeiture — the acceptance of rent did not create a yearly tenancy as no intention to so so could be inferred.

CHAPTER FOURTEEN

RIGHTS ON DETERMINATION

We have already seen that certain rights and obligations arise under the lease itself. Having dealt with the circumstances in which a lease can be determined, we may now examine the rights that arise on the termination of the tenancy.

RIGHTS OF THE LANDLORD ON TERMINATION

Right to possession

As a general rule the landlord has at the termination of the tenancy the right to quiet possession of the demised premises together with everything annexed to those premises, including the profits of sub-leases and intermediate mortgages. It was shown in *Official Custodian for Charities v. Mackay* (1984) that this is so even when the landlord forfeits the lease for the tenant's breach despite the fact that there is an appeal pending which may return the interest to the tenant. The law as to fixtures will be dealt with shortly but we may note here that the landlord's right to possession is subject to any express stipulation to the contrary in the tenancy, and there is also a common law exception to the rule.

Emblements

The common law exception is seen in the tenant's right to emblements. Where a tenant holds for a periodic term such as from year to year, and his interest is determined otherwise than in consequence of his own act he is entitled to emblements. This means that he is entitled to take any growing crop of a species which ordinarily repays the labour by which it is produced within the lunar (*i.e.,* not calendar) year in which that labour is carried out. The tenant may enter upon the land after the termination of his tenancy to take the crops.

A tenant at sufferance has no right to emblements but at common law a tenant at will, a yearly tenant, or a tenant for years determinable with lives is entitled. The importance of the rule was much undermined by statute, however, and now by section 21 of the Agricultural Holdings Act 1986, a tenant under tenancy at a rack rent (*i.e.,* "the full anual value") has no right to emblements. Instead, he has the right to remain in occupation until the expiration of a twelve months' notice expiring at the end of a year of the tenancy.

A tenant for a fixed term has no right to emblements, but in the case of agricultural land the rights of a tenant are widely extended by local customs. The parties are deemed to contract with reference to these local customs the general object and effect of which vary in different localities. The basic principle of them is, however, that the tenant should be given the benefit of work done by him during the last year of his tenancy by allowing him to enter after termination of the lease and take growing crops, or by giving him compensation for unexhausted improvements.

Remedies of the landlord

If the tenant fails to deliver up quiet possession the landlord has the following remedies unless the tenant holds over under a statutory right:

(1) He might bring an action for recovery of the land and for mesne profits and any special damage that he has suffered through being out of possession.

Thus, where a tenant sub-let part of the premises in *Henderson v. Squire* (1869) and at determination of the tenancy the sub-tenant held over, the landlord could recover damages from the tenant, based on the value of the premises for the time that he was kept out of possession, as well as the costs of ejecting the sub-tenant.

(2) If the tenancy ends through notice to quit by the tenant he may bring an action for double the rent or he may distrain for double rent.

The action for possession may be brought in the county court if the net annual value for rating of the premises does not exceed £1000, otherwise it must be brought in the High Court.

(3) If the landlord had given a written demand for possession at termination of a *tenancy for years* and the tenant wilfully holds over, the landlord may bring an action for double the *yearly* value of the land but cannot distrain for it. The term "wilfully" applies only where the tenant holds over contumaciously, and not where he does so in mistaken but honest belief that the notice to quit is invalid, as in *French v. Elliott* (1960).

(4) He may re-enter and take possession and eject the ex-tenant. If he enters forcibly he commits an offence which renders him liable to criminal proceedings but not civil proceedings by the tenant, unless more force is used than is necessary to evict the tenant, or there was any want of proper care in the removal of his goods. The general inadvisability of making a re-entry in person can be gathered from R. v. Hussey (1924) where the tenant was held not guilty of the crime of unlawful wounding when he shot his landlady who tried to forcibly evict him under an invalid notice to quit. The provision of the Protection from Eviction Act 1977 (see p. 181) should also be noted.

Derlict land

It may be that the tenant of the premises cannot be found, or it may be difficult or even impossible to serve upon him a notice to quit. This type of situation is covered by section 54 of the Landlord and Tenant Act 1954.

This section enables a landlord with power to determine a tenancy by notice to quit, to apply to the county court for an order to determine the tenancy. An order will not be given unless the landlord can satisfy the court:

(a) that he has taken all reasonable steps to communicate with the person last known by him to be tenant, and has failed to do so;

(b) that during the six months ending with the date of the application neither the tenant, nor anyone claiming under him, has been in occupation of the property comprised in the tenancy or any part of it; and

(c) that during this period of six months no rent was payable by the tenant, or alternatively rent was payable but has not been paid.

If the court thinks fit it may then order termination of the tenancy from the date of the order.

A further right is given to the landlord as far as entry into possession is concerned by section 16 of the Distress for Rent Act 1737 (as amended by the Deserted Tenements Act 1817). He is given a summary remedy, by which two or more justices, or a stipendiary magistrate, may grant him possession if:

(i) the tenancy is at a rack rent or at three-fourths of the yearly value of the premises;

(ii) half a year's rent is in arrear;

(iii) the tenant has deserted the premises and left them uncultivated or unoccupied;

(iv) there is no sufficient distress to meet the arrears of rent.

An appeal from the justices lies to the Crown Court.

RIGHTS OF THE TENANT ON TERMINATION

We have already discussed one right that the tenant may possess on termination of his tenancy — the right to emblements. There are others, however. Some of these have already been discussed on earlier pages — for instance, he may be entitled to exercise an option for renewal of the lease, or an option to purchase the reversion (see p. 52). Other statutory rights possessed by the tenant will be discussed later in detail.

FIXTURES

We have already seen that the term "land" comprises corporeal and incorporeal hereditaments; ti also covers fixtures.

What is meant by the term "fixtures"? They are articles which have become affixed to the land and are therefore legally incorporated into it. Objects are classified as chattels but when attached to the land they may become classified as fixtures, having become part of the land. Indeed, this is the general rule: whatever is attached to the land becomes part of it. However, when does an article become a fixture, or, to put it another way, when does a chattel become "affixed" to the land so as to become part of it?

Tests of annexation

The question here posed is of obvious importance for the tenant. While in possession of the land he may have erected something on the land. Does this thing become a fixture, or not? If it is a fixture it will belong to the landlord, even though as a chattel it belonged to the tenant. If it is not a fixture, ownership of the article still vests in the tenant.

In many cases the answer will be fairly easy. If a building is erected on the land so as to be placed there permanently then it will obviously be a fixture. But there are many cases, as we shall see in a moment, where the answer is not so easily obtainable. How then is the line to be drawn? There are in fact two tests to apply: (a) what is the degree of annexation? (b) what is the purpose of annexation?

Degree of annexation

This has long been regarded as the main test; indeed, at common law it was originally regarded as the only test. The principle was that if the article was fixed to the land in some substantial way it would classify as a fixture. If the article merely rested on the ground by its own weight, so that it was removable, it would not be a fixture, the degree of annexation being too slight.

Thus, in *Culling v. Tufnal* (1694) a Dutch barn standing in sockets let into the ground was regarded prima facie as not a fixture; in *Buckland v. Butterfield* (1820) it was said that such things as fireplaces, panelling, wainscoting and conservatory on a brick foundation would be fixtures.

Purpose of annexation

The problem raised by the degree test was that it was unduly restrictive: it might be relatively easy to remove the article but if the method of annexation used was "substantial", such as by nails or screws, the article would still classify as a fixture. Exceptions came to be considered and finally the second test was evolved, namely, what is the purpose of annexation? Is the article affixed in order that it may be better enjoyed as a chattel? Or is it affixed in order that it may become part of the land?

Thus, this test suggests that if the pupose of annexation is merely to enjoy the article better as a chattel, a chattel it will remain; otherwise, it becomes a fixture.

The leading case is *Leigh v. Taylor* (1902). The tenant for life placed valuable tapestries on the manison house walls. He fixed them with tacks to a wooden framework which he nailed to the wall. He surrounded the framework with a mouldong which was also nailed to the wall. When he died, the question arose as to whether the tapestries should be classified as fixtures or chattels. The House of Lords held that the tapestries were chattels, not fixtures. The attaching of the articles to the wall was no more than was necessary for their better enjoyment as articles of personal property. Similarly, in *Viscount Hill v. Bullock* (1897) a collection of stuffed birds in cases nailed to the walls was held to be chattels, not fixtures.

The importance of this test, and the decline of the test of degree of annexation, can be seen in *D'Eyncourt v. Gregory* (1866) where statues and stone garden seats were held to be fixtures under the "purpose" test even though they stood on the land only by their own weight — they were part of an overll garden design. The lines of demarcation are not clearly drawn however, and we are left with cases such as *Webb v. Frank Bevis Ltd.* (1940) where a corrugated iron shed bolted to metal straps fixed in concrete was held to be a fixture, while in *Billing v. Phill* (1954) an army hut fixed in substantially the same way was held to be a chattel being essentially a temporary structure on a permanent base.

The statement of Blackburn J. in *Holland v. Hodgson* (1872) is regarded as the principle to follow. This runs:

"Perhaps the true rule is, that articles not otherwise attached to the land that by their own weight are not to be considered as part of the land, *unless the circumstances are such as to show that they were intended to be part of the land* ... and that ... an article which is affixed to the land even slightly is to be considered as part of the land, *unless the circumstances are such as to show that it was intended all along to continue a chattel*". (Italics supplied).

The removal of fixtures

It has already been noted that if the article is classified as a fixture, the general rule is that it belongs to the landlord, not to the tenant. This, indeed, is the prima facie case: all fixtures attached to the land by the tenant will be regarded as belonging to the landlord as part of the land and must therefore be left for him at the termination of the tenancy.

There are exceptions to this rule, however. In some cases, although the object has become a fixture, the tenant has the power to sever it and reconvert it into a chattel during the tenancy, and thus reclaim legal title to it. A periodic tenant may also exercise this right within a reasonable time after termination of the tenancy. It was held in the *New Zealand Property Corporation case* (1982) that a tenant retains the rights to his fixtures if he remains in possession after the expiry of the lease whether it expired by effluxion of time or by surrender followed by the granting of a new lease. It was previously thought in the latter case a tenant lost all right to the fixtures.

The fixtures over which the tenant possesses this power are known as tenant's fixtures. There is no right to remove them if the removal would cause substantial injury to the land.

Tenant's fixtures

Tenant's fixtures are classified as of three kinds: trade fixtures, ornamental and domestic fixtures, and agriculural fixtures. The first two classifications are creations of the common law; the last was largely the creature of statute.

Trade fixtures. If the tenant attaches fixtures to the premises for purposes of trade or business he can remove them. Examples from decided cases include public house fittings, vats, shrubs planted by a market gardener and petrol pumps.

Ornamental and domestic fixtures. Examples include ornamental chimney pieces, window blinds, stoves, grates and kitchen ranges. A conservatory on brick foundation has been held not to be removable under this exception, however.

Agricultural fixtures. The situation is not governed by the Agricultural Holdings Act 1986. By section 10 the tenant of an agricultural holding who has attached fixtures to the land can remove them before or within two months after the end of his term. But he must:

(a) give one month's written notice to the landlord;

(b) pay all rent due and satisfy all his obligations under the tenancy;

(c) ensure that no available damage is done in removal and make good and damage done;

(d) allow the landlord to retain the fixtures if the landlord serves a counter-notice in writing and pays the tenant what would be their fair value in an incoming tenant.

Moreover, it may be noted that although the general rule is that tenant's fixtures belong to the landlord until the tenant exercises his power of removal, in the case of agricultural fixtures the Act specifically states that they are the property of the *tenant,* as long as he has the right to remove them.

COMPENSATION

In some cases it is possible for the tenant of business premises or an agricultural holding to make a claim against the landlord in respect of compensation for disturbance, and compensation for improvements made to the premises which increase the value of the letting. These matters will be considered in more detail when such tenancies are discussed later.

PART THREE

PARTICULAR STATUTORY PROVISIONS

We may now proceed to an examination of certain statutory provisions applicable to the relationship and to the rights of landlord and tenant. To some extent these provisions have already been touched upon and will not be completely unfamiliar. This point is emphasised, for it would be a mistake to assume that the topics here dealt with can be divorced from the rest of this book. This chapter is really concernced with an amplification of some of the points already mentioned.

CHAPTER FIFTEEN

THE RENT ACTS

At the end of the First World War residential accommodation was in considerable demand and it became apparent that this demand could not be met by the available dwellings. To prevent undue exploitation of this situation the government of the day introduced the Increase of Rent and Mortgage Interest (Restriction) Act 1920. The purpose of the Act was to deflate artificially the rent chargeable for dwelling-houses and to restrict the landlord's right to recovery of possession. In addition to this, subsequent Acts also dealt with the condition and repair of the particuar dwelling-house.

The original legislation was not intended to be an all time remedy to the housing shortage — it was, however, a convenient and effective one at the time. Over the years, between the wars, other amending and enlarging Acts emerged and because of the complexity of the subject-matter, many cases arose in the courts concerning the interpretation and scope of the various Acts.

By 1939 some houses that had been controlled were no longer so but in that year further Rent Act legislation took place and most rented houses were brought into the net. The result was that two controls arose — one imposed by the pre-1939 legislation and the other by the 1939 legislation.

After the Second World War yet again Parliament's remedy for the housing shortage was further Rent Act legislation. Even then no attempt was made to consolidate what had become by now a morass of legislation on the subject through which landlord and tenant alike had to plough.

In 1957 an attempt was made to abandon rent control, that is, an artificially low rent imposed on certain premises coupled with security of tenure. It was provided in the Rent Act 1957 that no new tenancies were to be subject to control (this became known as "creeping decontrol") while certain premises were, overnight, freed from legislative control.

Eight years later, after a charge of government and metropolitan slum rapidly expanding, rent control was again introduced, by the Rent Act 1965, though in a slightly different form from that before 1957. The life of the 1965 Act, as an entity, proved short, most of it being repealed by the Rent Act 1968, a consolidating statute. Furnished lettings, which were excluded from the 1920 Act and had remained outside the full protection of the Rent Acts, were brought into line with unfurnished lettings by the Rent Act 1974. The Rent (Agriculture) Act 1976 was then passed to give protection to agricultural workers in tied cotages. Other service occupants remain unprotected.

THE RENT ACT 1977

The Rent Act 1977 is a consolidation of the Rent Acts of 1968 and 1974 in part amended by the Housing Act 1980, and the Landlord and Tenant Act 1985. The main provision of the Act apply to a "protected" tenancy (i.e. a contractural "controlled" or "regulated" tenancy) and a "statutory' tenancy. From a specified date most controlled tenancies will be convertible into regulated tenancies: s. 62 (1) Housing Act 1980.

Application of the Act

The Act protects a tenancy (not a licence) under which a dwelling-house is let as a separate dwelling, provided the rateable value of the dwelling-house on the appropriate day did not exceed the relevant rateable value. The tenant must be an individual not a company. The Act will not apply if the Tenant is a company but the occupier is an Individual *First Cross v. East West (Export/Import)* (1980).

The dwelling-house can be part of a house and could, in fact, be one room in a building provided it is a separate part, of which the tenant has exclusive possession. The dwelling must not be only partly used however (*Kavanagh v. Lyraudias* 1984), although it is possible to occupy two houses as residences which come within the Act as shown by the House of Lords in *Hampstead Way Investments v. Lewis Weave* (1985). The occupation must extend to all activities necessary to characterise the premises as a complete home.

The "appropriate day" means 23rd March, 1965 or such later date on which a rateable value for the dwelling-house was first shown in the valuation list. However, because of government policy to extend the statutory protection of the Rent Act and a general revision of rating assessment which came into effect on 1st April, 1973, a tenancy can now be protected even though the rateable value of the dwelling-house originally exceeded the relevant rateable value. By section 4 of the 1977 Act, a tenancy is now protected unless the rateable value of the dwelling-house exceeded £200 (£400 if situate in Greater London area) on 23rd March, 1965 and £300 (£600 in Greater London) on 22nd March, 1973 *and* £750 (£1,500 in Greater London) on 1st April, 1973 or such later date as a value was first shown. Of course, if a value was not shown until after 1st April, 1973 then only the £750 (£1,500) limit is relevant, there being no rateable value on 23rd March, 1965 or 22nd March, 1973. Similar reasoning applies where the dwelling-house was first shown in the valuation list on a date from 22nd March, 1973 up to 31st March, 1973.

Having established that a tenancy does not fall outside the protection of the Act because of the rateable value of the dwelling-house it is still necessary to decide, however, whether that tenancy is a regulated tenancy or a controlled tenancy, as the rent provisions and the grounds for possession in the Act differ for the different types of tenancy. A protected tenancy will be a controlled tenancy only if:

(a) the tenancy was originally created by a lease or agreement coming into operation before 6th July, 1957 or, if created after that date, was granted to a person who immediately before the grant was the tenant under a controlled tenancy of the same, or part of the same, premises; and

(b) the rateble value of the dwelling-house on 7th November, 1956 did not exceed £30 (£40 in London); and

(c) the dwelling-house is not one which was erected or produced by conversion of premises after 29th August, 1954 (but where an improvement grant was payable for the work the tenancy could be controlled); and

(d) the tenancy although originally controlled has not been converted to a regulated tenancy either because the rateable value of the dwelling-house on 31st March, 1972 exceeded £34 (£69 in Greater London) or because of certification by the local authority that the dwelling-house has the standard amenities and is in a good state of repair. By the Housing Act 1980, s. 64, all controlled tenancies will be abolished.

Excluded Tenancies

Certain types of tenancy which are within the relevant rateable values (above) are excluded by the Act from being protected. A tenancy is not protected if:

(a) no rent is payable, or the rent payable is less than two-thirds of the rateable value of the appropriate day, (unless the rent payable is not less than two-thirds of the 1939 rateable value of the dwelling-house in which case the tenancy can be controlled); or

(b) the rent includes payments for board or attendance and the value of the tenant of any attendance forms a substantial part of the whole rent; or

(c) the dwelling-house is let together with other land which is agricultural land exceeding two acres; or

(d) if the tenant is a student at a specified educational institution and the landlord is a specified educational institution ("specified" means designated by the Secretary of State); or

(e) it is a letting for a holiday; or

(f) the dwelling-house is comprised in an agricultural holding and occupied by the person responsible for the control of the farming; or

(g) the dwelling-house includes on-licensed premises; or

(h) the landlord is resident in the building (unless a purpose-built block of flats); or

(i) the landlord is the Crown, a local authority, a housing association, trust or co-operative, or the Housing Corporation or a development corporation of the Commission for the New Towns; or

(j) the dwelling-house is a Church of England parsonage (such property is governed by the Pluralities Act 1838); or

(k) the premises are business premises and the Landlord and Tenant Act 1954 applies. That Act will apply unless the tenancy satisfies the criteria for a controlled tenancy, when the 1977 Act will apply. A tenancy of a dwelling-house for business purposes can never be a regulated tenancy; or

(l) the tenant shares living accommodation with the landlord so that he does not have exclusive occupation of a separate dwelling. (If the tenant has exclusive occupation of *some* accommodation, sharing other accommodation with another tenant or his own sub-tenant does not exclude the Act. Nor does sharing, with the landlord, accommodation, such as a toilet or bathroom, which is not "living" accommodation). Of the Landlords, one of several joint tenants sharing accommodation with the tenants will satisfy this exception (*Cooper* v. *Tait* 1984).

The court will look to the content not form of the lease to see if it falls within the above categories. In *R.* v. *Camden London Borough Rent Officer ex parte Plant* (1981) it was held a lease described as a holiday let was a sham so the rent was registered under the Act.

Statutory Tenancy

The landlord's right to obtain possession of premises when the tenant's tenancy determines is curtailed if the tenancy is a protected one. The Act provides that after termination of a protected tenancy, the tenant of the dwelling-house shall be the statutory tenant of it, if, and for so long as he occupies it as his residence. The terms of the statutory tenancy will be those of the original tenancy must allow the landlord access to the dwelling-house and reasonable facilities for any repairs which the landlord is entitled to execute.

The statutory tenancy is merely a personal right of the tenant and is not a legal estate in the property. If the tenant wishes to give up possession of the dwelling-house he can do so only on giving to the landlord the notice the landlord could have required under the protected tenancy or, if none was provided for, at least three month's notice. This provision in section 3 (3) is subject to section 5 of the Protection from Eviction Act 1977 which provides that at least four weeks notice is required from the tenant of a dwelling-house.

Change of tenancy

As a statutory tenant has merely a personal right to reside he cannot assign his rights, but a statutory tenancy can pass under the Act either by agreement or on the death of the statutory tenant.

The statutory tenant can agree in writing that an incoming tenant should succeed him as the statutory tenant. The agreement is effective only if the landlord is a party to it and also any superior landlord whose consent would have been required to an assignment of the previous protected tenancy. If the outgoing tenant is a statutory tenant by succession (see below), the incoming tenant becomes a tenant by succession unless the written agreement provides otherwise: Schedule 1, para. 13.

On the death of a protected or statutory tenant, his widow, if she resides with him at the time of his death become the statutory tenant of the dwelling-house. If the deceased tenant leaves no widow or is a woman, the right to become the statutory tenant passes to the widower or other member of the deceased's family residing with the deceased for at lease six months immediately before the death. If there is more than one such person entitled, the county court will decide which one shall take the statutory tenancy if they cannot agree between themselves. It is for the prospective tenants to agree among themselves. The Landlord need not be a party to the agreement (*General Management v. Locke* 1980). A mistress of the tenant has been held to be a member of the family. However it has been held that a homosexual couple cannot be equated with spouses for this purpose in *Harrogate Borough Council v. Simpson* (1985).

Because the right to succeed as statutory tenant is vested in a residing member of the deceased's family, it follows that where a protected tenant dies leaving his leasehold interest in the dwelling-house to some other person, the owner of the lease and the statutory tenant will be different. Only two succession are allowed (Schedule 1 as amended by s. 76 Housing Act 1980).

Security of tenure under the Act

To obtain possession of a dwelling-house which is subject to a protected or statutory tenancy the landlord must obtain an order of the court. However, at any time that a dwelling suitable for the working classes is over-crowded so as to constitute an offence under the Housing Act 1985, the statutory protection is raised and nothing in the Act will prevent the landlord obtaining possession. Other than that, the court will not make an order for possession unless any contractural tenancy has terminated and:

(a) it is satisfied that suitable alternative accommodation is available for the tenant and it is reasonable to order possession; or

(b) the circumstances are as specified in any of the cases in Parts I or II of Schedule 15.

Part I of the Schedule deals with cases where the court *may* give an order for possession if it thinks the order reasonable in all the circumstances. They are:

(1) non-payment of rent or breach of some other obligation of the tenant under the tenancy.

(2) the tenant, his lodger or sub-tenant has caused a nuisance or annoyance to adjoining occupiers or has been convicted of using or allowing the dwelling-house to be used for, immoral or illegal purposes;

(3) the condition of the dwelling-house has deteriorated because of acts of waste by, or neglect or default of, the tenant, his lodger or sub-tenant and, where the tenant is not to blame, he has not taken reasonable steps to temove the person responsible;

(4) the condition of furniture provided under the tenancy has deteriorated owing to ill-treatment by the tenant, his lodger or sub-tenant

and, where the tenant is not to blame, he has not taken reasonable steps to remove the person responsible;

(5) the tenant has given notice to quit and in consequence the landlord has contracted to sell or let the dwelling-house, or has taken other steps so that he would be seriously prejudiced by failure to obtain possession;

(6) the tenant has assigend or sub-let the whole of the dwelling-house without the landlord's consent;

(7) the landlord reasonably requires the dwelling-house as a residence for an employee of himself or his tenant and the dwelling-houe was let to the protected or statutory tenant as an employee of the landlord, that employment having now ceased;

(8) the dwelling-house is reasonably required by the landlord as his residence or that of his adult child, his parent or (if the tenancy is regulated only) his parent-in-law and the landlord did not purchase the dwelling-house after it became subject to the Rent act provisions;

(9) the tenant has sub-let part of the dwelling-house ata rent in excess of that recoverable under the Act.

Part II of Schedule 15 deals with cases where the court *must* order possession and they apply to a *regulated* tenancy only. They are:

(10) the landlord was owner-occupier before the tenancy and he now requires the dwelling-house as a residence of himself, or a member of his family who resided with him when he last resided there; and did not let on a protected tenancy;

(11) the owner bough the hosue as a retirement home and he has now retired and requires the dwelling-house as a residence, or has died, and the dwelling-house is required as a residence for a member of his family residing with him at his death; and it is not a protected tenancy;

(12) the dwelling-house is let for a term certain not exceeding eight months and within the twelve months before the tenancy the dwelling-house was occupied as a holiday home;

(13) the dwelling-house is let for a term certain not exceeding twelve months and within the twelve months before the tenancy the dwelling-house was let as a student residence (see (d), p. 167);

(14) the dwelling-house is held for occupation by a minister of religion for performance of his duties, and is not required for such purpose;

(15) the dwelling-house was occupied at some time by an agricultural employee under the terms of his employment, is now required for an agricultural employee of the landlord, and the tenant was never so employed by the landlord, not is the widow of such a person;

(16) amalgamation for agricultural purposes has been carried out and the dwelling-house was, when the amalgamation was proposed, occupied by a person responsible for the control of the farming of the land and after the amalgamation was let to someone other than such person, his widow or an agricutural employee of the landlord, and the dwelling-house is required for an agricultural employee of the landlord;

(17) the last occupier of the dwelling-house, before the present tenancy, was responsible for the control of the farming of land which together with the dwelling-house formed an agricultural unit, the dwelling-house is required for such a person or an agricultural employee of the landlord and the tenant is neither of those nor the widow of either.

(18) the letting was a protected shorthold tenancy and there was no further grant since its end, proceedings having commenced within 3 months after expiry of the appropriate notice by the landlord;

(19) lettings by servicemen.

Cases (10) - (17), although absolute grounds for possession, require that the landlord must have given notice to the tenant by the date the tenancy commenced that he would require possession on the relevant ground. In the cases 11, 12 and 18 above noted, however, the court can dispense with the notice requirement where it thinks it just and equitable in the circumstances.

Regarding case 11, owner occupation must take place immediately before the letting to the tenant which the landlord is seeking to displace (*Pocock v. Steel* 1985). The landlord can obtain possession for his own use even if his visits are going to be short and very intermittent (*Nash v. Curzon* 1985).

If the court does order possession it can stay or suspend execution of the order or postpone possession on such terms, including payment of arrears of rent, as it thinks fit.

Rent control under the Act

Regulated tenancies

The Act regulates the amount which can be claimed under a regulated tenancy. A "fair" rent can be registered for a dwelling-house under Part IV of the Act and that rent becomes the maximum recoverable for that dwelling-house: Section 44. A sub-lease can reserve rent higher than the registered fair rent but only if the terms of the sub-lease are substantially different from those of the lease as in *Brecker v. Field* (1982) where the sub-tenant did not have to pay rates, whereas the tenant did.

If no rent is registered when a protected tenancy commences the parties are free to agree any rent, but at any time an application can be made to register a rent. If when the rent is registered the protected tenancy is continuing the registered rent becomes the "contractural rent limit" and the tenant, if that limit is lower than the rent agreed, can reduce his payments to that limit. If that limit is higher than the agreed rent the landlord can only demand the agreed rent.

If no rent is registered when a statutory tenancy commences the rent under the protected tenancy will continue to be the maximum rent demandable from the tenant: Section 45. The rent can, however, be increased by service of notice of increase on the tenant to take account of increases in costs to the landlord, since the previous contractural period, because of rates, or provision of services for, or the use of furniture by, the tenant, or because of improvements completed after 7th December, 1965 and after the time the contractural rent was agreed. The landlord may increase the rent by 12½ per cent per annum of the amount expended by him on such improvements but the tenant may apply to the court, within one month of the service of notice of increase, for an order cancelling or reducing the order if the improvement was not necessary or more than necessary was spent on it.

If the landlord's costs for rates, services on furniture should have decreased, the rent for the statutory period is reduced accordingly.

If a rent becomes registered during the statutory period that rent becomes the rent limit. If that limit is lower than the rent being paid the tenant can reduce his payments to that limit. If that limit is higher, the landlord can increase the rent up to that limit by serving notice of increase on the tenant. The landlord can also serve notice of increase during the contractural period and if the date specified in the notice is later than the date on which the tenancy could have been deemed by notice to quit, the notice of increase will determine the contractural tenancy giving rise to a statutory tenancy at the increased rent specified.

Enforcement

Sums paid by the tenant in excess of the recoverable rent can be recovered from the landlord within two years, either by suing or by deduction from future rent. It is an offence to enter in a rent book that a tenant is in arrear in respect of any sum which is irrecoverable and a rent book can be rectified by the court.

Regulation of rent under a regulated tenancy

The rent officer for the registration area (commensurate with the local authority area) prepares and keeps a reigster of rents, containing the specification of each dwelling-house for which a rent is registered and the particulars of each tenancy.

An application to register a rent can be made by the landlord (who can also apply for a certification of fair rent as a preliminary to letting the dwelling-house), or by the tenant, or by them both, jointly, or by the local authority. The fair rent determined by the rent officer, or (on appeal against his decision) by a rent assessment committee, is then registered and becomes the rent limit. The registered rent is the net rent, and rates borne by the landlord can be added to that figure.

No one person (but the landlord and tenant, jointly, may) can apply to alter the registered rent within two[1] years of its registration unless there has been a change in the condition of the dwelling-house, the terms of the tenancy, the furniture provided, or other circumstances so that the rent is no longer a fair rent.

1.The period of delay was formerly three years. This continues to apply to rents registered before the date of commencement of the Housing Act 1980; Housing Act 1980, s. 60 (2).

In determining a fair rent of a dwelling-house, the rent officer must have regard to, in particular;

(a) its age, character and locality; and

(b) its state of repair and the quality, quantity and condition of furniture provided; and, generally,

(c) all the circumstances other than personal ones.

On the other hand, the following matters must be disregarded:

(1) its want of repair due to the tenant's breach of obligation;

(2) any improvements by the tenant, otherwise than under the terms of the tenancy;

(3) any improvement to, or deterioration in, furniture provided, such improvement or deterioration being due to the tenant; and

(4) any scarcity value of dwelling-houses of similar type in the locality, available on the same terms as the regulated tenancy.

Rent Agreement

The landlord and tenant may enter in writing into a rent agreement (under section 51) to increase the rent payable under a protected regulated tenancy. If a rent is not already registered, the agreement must inform the tenant of his rights as to security of tenure and registration of a fair rent. If the agreement is made after the conversion of a controlled tenancy to a regulated tenancy (see p. 166) with the person who was tenant at the time of the conversion, the landlord must, at least 28 days before the agreement is to take effect, give to the local authority a document in the prescribed form signed by the landlord and the tenant containing particulars of the agreement and the dwelling-house and a statement as to the tenant's security of tenure and the right of either party to apply to register a fair rent. The local authority may then wish to apply to have a rent registered for the dwelling-house to which the rent agreement relates.

It is permissible to re-negotiate rent levels without using the rent officer, but where a tenancy has become regulated following conversion from a controlled Tenancy, s. 68 (2) Housing Act 1980 effectively re-imposes the rent freeze originally abolished in 1973.

Cancellation of registration of rent

Where a "rent agreement" has been entered into taking effect more than 3 years after registration of a rent, an application can be made by the landlord and tenant, jointly, (under section 73) for cancellation of the registration provided the tenancy agreement cannot be brought to an end earlier than 12 months after the application, except for the tenant's breach. If the rent officer is satisfied that the highest rent payable under the rent agreement does not exceed a fair rent for the dwelling-house, he must cancel the registration, to take effect from the date the rent agrement takes effect.

After cancellation either party may again apply to register a fair rent.

Rent limit under a controlled tenancy

Section 27 states that the rent limit for a controlled tenancy shall not exceed an annual rent of:

(a) the 1956 gross value of the dwelling multiplied by the appropriate factor; plus

(b) the annual amount of rates borne by the landlord; plus

(c) any annual amount agreed, in writing, or determined by the court, to be a reasonable charge for services or for furniture; plus

(d) 12½ per cent per annum of the costs of improvements or repairs by the landlord. (The tenant has the same right to challenge the cost of improvements as has the tenant under a regulated tenancy).

The appropriate factor is 2⅓ decreasing to 1⅓ inversely with the tenant's liability to repair the premises. If the landlord is totally responsible the factor is 2⅓.

As under a regulated tenancy the rent limit is a maximum and the rent payable may be lower. Similarly, however, by service of notice of increase the landlord can increase the rent during the statutory period up to the limit and a notice of increase served during the contractural period may operate to terminate the contactural period and increase the rent for the statutory period.

Premiums

Part IX of the Act deals with premiums. It is an offence under section 119 for any person to require or receive a premium or a loan for the grant, renewal, continuance or assignment of a protected tenancy. Where an excessive price is asked for furniture included in the tenancy the excess over a reasonable price is to be regarded as a premium.

There are exceptions to the basic rule about premiums:

(1) the assignor of a protected tenancy can require or receive a payment for outgoings paid by him and relating to the period after assignment, or for expenditure in structurally altering the dwelling house or for the provision or improvement of fixtures, or for good-will of a business transferred to the assignee.

(2) where a premium was lawfully paid on the grant, renewal continuance or assignment of a tenancy (because the dwelling-house was at the time of the transaction outside the rateable value limits for the statutory provisions to apply (see p. 166)) a premium may be lawfully required on an assignment of the protected tenancy. Schedule 18 gives formulae for calculating the premium which the assignor may require.

(3) where the protected tenancy is a long tenancy (i.e. exceeding 21 years), the basic prohibition in section 119 against premiums does not apply, provided the tenancy is not terminable within the first 20 years, nor rent variable within that period and the tenancy can be assigned or sub-let without payment to the landlord. If those provisos do not apply a restricted premium only can be required, calculated in accordance with

Part II of Schedule 18.

A statutory tenancy cannot of course be granted, or renewed but we have seen (p. 167) that such a tenancy can be transmitted or given up. Part II of Schedule 1 to the Act provides that it is an offence to ask for or receive a payment from anyone other than the landlord as a condition of giving up possession of the dwelling-house, except for a reasonable sum for furniture. Similarly, where the statutory tenant is changed by agreement it is an offence to require a payment as a requirement to entering into the agreement other than for those items allowed to a protected tenant on an assignment (see (1) above).

Restricted Contracts

Although, as has been stated, the main provision of the Rent Act 1977 apply to a "protected tenancy", a certain measure of protection is given to the owner of a "restricted contract" by Parts V and VII of the Act. A restricted contract is, under Section 19, a contract whereby one person (the "lessor") grants to another (the "lessee") the right to occupy a dwelling as a residence in consideration of a rent which includes payment for the use of furniture or for services. Although the Act uses the terms "lessor" and "lessee" (as will be done here) the contract need not be a tenancy — a licence is within the definition; as is a contract where the lessee has exclusive possession of only part of a house.

In two instances the requirement of the definition as to furniture or services need not be satisfied:

(1) where a tenancy is precluded from being a protected tenancy only because there is a resident landlord in the building (see p. 167) that tenancy is to be treated as a restricted contract without the above requirement; and

(2) where a tenancy is precluded from being a protected tenancy only because the tenant shares accommodation with the landlord (see p. 167), the contract is a restricted contract, without the requirement.

"Services" is defined as including attendance, the provision of heating or lighting, the supply of hot water and any other privilege of facility for a dwelling, other than the access, cold water supply or sanitary accommodation.

Excluded contracts

Certain types of contracts within the basic definition are excluded from being restricted contacts. They are:

(a) if the contract creates a regulated tenancy;

(b) if the lessor is the Crown, a government department, a housing association or trust, or local authority;

(c) if the rent includes payment for board and the value of the board to the lessee forms a substantial proportion of the whole rent;

(d) if the Rent (Agriculture) Act applies (see p. 178);

(e) if the dwelling is a holiday home

(f) if the rateable value of the dwelling on the appropriate day, exceeds the limits for the main provisions of the act to apply (see p. 166).

Registration of rent of restricted contract

Under section 77 the lessor or the lessee under a restricted contract, or the local authority, may refer the contract to the rent tribunal* for the district. The tribunal can then require the lessee to supply information and after making such inquiry as it thinks fit (often an inspection of the relevant premises) the tribunal may after hearing the parties, approve the rent payable under the contract, reduce or increase it to such sum as it thinks reasonable, or dismiss the reference. It must notify the parties of its decision, and the local authority. The authority has a duty to prepare and keep a register of rents containing particulars of the contract, the specification of the dwelling and the rent as approved, reduced or increased by the rent tribunal. That registered rent becomes the rent limit for the dwelling. Section 81 provides that where the rent payable for any dwelling is registered, it is unlawful to require or receive as rent any payment in excess of that registered rent. Any excess paid can be recovered by the lessee.

If the rates for the dwelling are borne by the lessor, that fact must be noted on the register and the amount of rates can be added to the registered rent.

Once a rent is registered the lessor and lessee, jointly, can, at any time, refer the rent to the rent tribunal for reconsideration. If a reference is made to the tribunal otherwise than by those jointly, the rent tribunal can refuse to entertain the reference if it is made within two years of when the tribunal last considered the rent, unless the registered rent is no longer reasonable because of a change in:

(a) the condition of the dwelling,
(b) the furniture or services provided,
(c) the terms of the contract, or
(d) any other circumstances taken into consideration with the rent was last considered.

Security

Because the lessor under a restricted contract may be aggrieved by a lessor's application to a rent tribunal to register a rent, a certain measure of security is given to the lessee. The courts are given a special jurisdiction to decide such cases under Rent Act 1977, s. 106A (introduced by Housing Act 1980, s. 69 (2):

106A.—(1) This section applies to any dwelling-house which is the subject of a restricted contract entered into after the commencement of section 69 of the Housing act 1980.

(2) On the making of an order for possession of such a dwelling-house, or at any time before the execution of such an order, the court may—

* The rent assessment committee.

(*a*) stay or suspend execution of the order, or
(*b*) postpone the date of possession
for such period or periods as, subject to subsection (3) below, the court thinks fit.

(3) Where a court makes an order for possession of such a dwelling-house, giving up of possession shall not be postponed (whether by the order of any variation, suspension or stay of execution) to a date later than 3 months after the making of the order.

Shorthold tenancies are created by Housing Act 1980:

52.—(1) A protected shorthold tenancy is a protected tenancy granted after the commencement of this section which is granted for a term certain of not less than one year nor more than five years and satisfies the following conditions, that is to say,—

(*a*) it cannot be brought to an end by the landlord before the expiry of the term, except in pursuance of a provision for re-entry or forfeiture for non-payment of rent or breach of any other obligation of the tenancy; and
(*b*) not later than the beginning of the term the landlord has given the tenant a valid notice stating that the tenancy is to be protected shorthold tenancy; and
(*c*) either a rent for the dwelling-house is registered at the time the tenancy is granted or (i) a certificate of fair rent has, before the grant, been issued under section 69 of the 1977 Act in respect of the dwelling-house and the rent payable under the tenancy, for any period before a rent is registered for the dwelling-house, does not exceed the rent specified in the certificate; and (ii) an application for the registration of a rent for the dwelling-house is made not later than 28 days after the beginning of the term and is not withdrawn.

(2) A tenancy of a dwelling-house is not a protected shorthold tenancy if it is granted to a person who immediately before it was granted, was a protected or statutory tenant of that dwelling-house.

Housing Association Tenancy

We have seen that where the landlord is a public body a tenancy can be neither a protected tenancy nor a registered contract. However Part VI of the 1977 Act provides for registration of the rent of a "housing association tenancy", i.e. where the landlord is a housing association or trust or the Housing Corporation and the tenancy would otherwise be a protected tenancy (section 86).

The Act provides that a part of the register kept by the rent officer for registration of the rent of a dwelling-house subject to a regulated tenancy should be kept for the rent of a dwelling-house subject to, or available for letting under, a housing association tenancy. A rent registered in that part then becomes the rent-limit for the dwelling-house in the same way as with a dwelling-house subject to a regulared tenancy.

RENT (AGRICULTURE) ACT 1976

This Act provides agricultural employees in tied cottages from eviction when the agricultural employment ends. We have already seen that the full protection of the Rent Act 1977 is only given to tenants, and agricultural employees will normally occupy premises under a licence rather than a tenancy. In addition a ground for possession under the 1977 Act, is that the tenant's employment with the landlord has ended and the premises are required for another employee.

Application of the Act

The Act protects an occupancy by an agricultural worker of a dwelling-house under a relvant licence or tenancy if the dwelling-house is owned by his employer or by some-one with whom the employer has an arrangement that it be used to house agricultural employees.

The worker must be a whole-time agricultural employee or one who has worked in agriculture for 91 out of the previous 104 weeks (seasonal workers are therefore excluded).

Relevant licence or tenancy

This means that the occupier has exclusive possession of a separate dwelling and:

(a) The Rent act 1977 would protect the occupancy but for the fact that it may be a licence and that rent may not be payable; and

(b) it is not a term of the occupancy that the employer will provide board or attendance (meals provided merely in the course of the employment are not "board", and "attendance" which is not substantial regarding its value to the occupier is ignored); and

(c) neither the Landlord and Tenant Act 1954 nor the Agricultural Holdings Act 1986 applies to the occupancy.

An occupancy to which the Act applies is called a "protected occupancy".

Statutory tenancy

After termination of a protected occupancy, the protected occupier becomes, if, and for so long as, he occupies the dwelling-house as his residence, the statutory tenant of it on the terms of the original agreement, supplemented, if need be, by Schedule 5 to the Act. Thus the tenant will have a right to quiet enjoyment and the benefit of section 11 of the Landlord and Tenant Act 1985 even though the original agreement was only a licence, and he must allow the landlord access to repair.

As with a statutory tenancy under the 1977 Act the tenant has merely a personal right and no estate in the land but, again, on the death of either a protected occupier or statutory tenant a spouse of the occupier living with him at his death can succeed him as a statutory tenant . If there is no such spouse, a member of his family living with him for six months preceding the death can succeed. In default of agreement between competing members of the family, the court will decide upon the successor.

This Act makes no distinction (as does the 1977 Act) between a widow or widower succeeding and it only allows one succession instead of two. The succession provisions are contained in sections 3 and 4 of the Act.

Security of tenure under the Act

To obtain possession the landlord must establish one of the statutory grounds for possession and show that the protected occupancy has terminated. The grounds (in Schedule 4) are basically the same as Cases 1-12 for possession of premises subject to a regulated tenancy under the 1977 Act (see p. 169) with the court having the like discretion or obligation to grant an order for possession. These are however two variations to the cases: Case 8 is omitted and Case 9 is extended to cover occupation by the landlord's grand-parents or grand-parent-in-law.

Rent

If no rent was payable under the original agreement, no rent is payable under the statutory tenancy until the landlord and the statutory tenant fix a rent (which cannot exceed 1.5 times the rateable value of the dwelling-house) or an application is made to the rent officers to register a fair rent, in the reigster kept under the 1977 Act, as if the tenancy were a regulated tenancy under the Act. Once a rent is registered, that becomes the maximum recoverable rent and the landlord can, by notice of increase, raise the rent payable up to that maximum. Alternatively if the rent payable is greater, than the registered rent, the excess is irrecoverable from the date of the application to register a rent.

A rent may become registered during the protected occupancy, but the rent under the original agreement cannot be increased during that occupancy and if no rent is payable none becomes payable because of the registration until the protected occupancy is terminated. Any excess payable, over the registered rent, becomes irrecoverable.

Similar provision to those under the 1977 Act apply to notices of increase, recovery of excess rent paid and rectification of rent books. the 1976 Act contains no provisions regarding premiums or the transmission by agreement of a statutory tenancy.

Rehousing by local authority

The court has a discretion to grant an order for possession if alternative accommodation which the housing authority thinks suitable is available for the agricultural worker: Case II in Schedule 4. An occupier of land used for agriculture may make an application to the housing authority for the area, to rehouse a protected occupier or statutory tenant if:

(a) vacant possession of the dwelling-house is needed to house an agricultural employee and his family; and

(b) the applicant is unable to provide suitable, alternative accommodation for the occupier of the dwelling-house; and

(c) the authority ought to provide such accommodation in the interests of efficient agriculture

The authority has a duty to use its best endeavours to provide such accommodation, taking into account the resources at its disposal and competing claims on accommodation and it must notify the applicant of its decision on the application within three months.

LANDLORD AND TENANT ACT 1954 PART I

Where the rent under a tenancy is a low rent (i.e. less than two-thirds of the rateable value of the appropriate day) the tenancy cannot be a protected tenancy within the Rent Act 1977 (see P. 166). Many such tenancies arise, however, under long leases (i.e. granted for a term certain exceeding twenty-one years) and if that is so Part I of the 1954 Act may apply. Section 2 provides that the Act applies to a long tenancy at a low rent which would be protected under the 1977 Act but for the low rent. The rateable value limits and the exclusion provisions of the 1977 Act are therefore relevant.

Many tenancies within the protection of this Act are also within the provisions of the Leasehold Reform Act 1967 (see P. 210) but the qualifying conditions are not identical. For example there is no minimum five years period of residence required under the 1954 Act as there is under the 1967 Act. Because the two Acts do overlap, the importance of the 1954 Act is diminshed.

Security

When a tenancy within the Act would determine at common law, it is automatically continued under section 3 of the Act unless determined in accordance with the Act.

The tenant may determine the tenancy by one month's notice in writing expiring on or after the contractural term date (i.e. when the tenancy would have determined at common law).

The landlord may determine the tenancy by notice in the prescribed form, served on the tenant not less than six nor more than twelve months before the date of termination specified in it. That date cannot, of course, be earlier than the contractural term date. The notice must also invite the tenant to inform the landlord within two months whether he will give up possession of the premises. these provisions apply to a landlord's notice proposing a statutory tenancy or to resume possession.

Notice proposing a statutory tenancy

If the tenant is not residing on the premises on the term date, and has not elected to stay by giving notice to the landlord within two months of the notice proposing a new tenanc, the tenancy will determine on the date specified in the landlord's notice. If, however, either of the conditions is satisfied the contractural tenancy will determine and be replaced by a statutory regulated tenancy under the Rent Act 1977. If the terms of the new tenancy are not agreed between the parties, the landlord must apply to the court for the terms to be established at least two months before his notice is to expire, otherwise the contractural tenancy will continue — that is the landlord's notice to have effect.

Notice to resume possession

This informs the tenant that if he is unwilling to give up possession the landlord intends to apply to the court for possession on one of the grounds in cases (1) - (9) of the grounds that he intends to demolish or reconstruct the premises at termination of the tenancy for the purposes of redevelopment.

If the tenant elects to retain possession the landlord must apply to the county court for an order for possession within two months of the tenant's election, or if no election is made, within four months of the service of the landlord's notice. If the landlord fails to make his application in time or the court refuses an order for possession, the landlord's notice ceases to have effect and the contractural tenancy will continue past its term date if either the tenant has elected to retain possession or is residing in the premises on the term date.

PROTECTION FROM EVICTION ACT 1977

Because of the statutory protections given to "sitting" tenants, there is considerable financial advantage to the landlord if he can persuade the tenant to leave the dwelling. Provisions were introduced in 1965 making it a criminal offence to "harass" or unlawfully evict a "residential occupier". These provisions are now contained in the Protection from Eviction Act 1977 as amended by the Housing act 1980, s. 69 (1) and Schedule 25.

Harassment

Section 1 (2) provides that it is an offence for any person to deprive, or attempt to deprive, a residential occupier of his occupation of the premises unless that person reasonably believed that the occupier has ceased to reside in the premises.

A residential occupier is defined as a person occupying premises as a residence under a contact or by virtue of any enactment or rule of law giving him the right to remain in occupation or restricting the right of law giving him the right to remain in occupation or restricting the right of any person to recover possession of the premises. Section 1 (2) therefore protects licencees, tenants of local authorities and tenants where the rateable value of the premises is outside the Rent Act 1977 limits (see

p. 166).

Section 1 (3) provides that any person commits an offence who does acts calculated to interfere with the peace or comfort of the residential occupier or members of his household, or persistently withdraws or withholds services reasonably required for occupation of the premises as a residence, if those acts are intended to cause the residential occupier to give up his occupation of the premises or any part, or to refrain from exercising any right or pursuing any remedy in respect of the premises. An honest belief that the people are not residential occupiers will be a defence to this charge (*R. v. The Koo* 1981). The act of harrasment need be only calculated to interfere with peace and comfort and need not amount to a breach of the Tenant's contractual rights of occupation (*R. v. Yuthinwittana* 1985).

In *McCall v. Abelsz* (1976) the court held that this subsection gave a tenant no right to bring a civil action against a landlord who harassed him (*cf. Warder v. Cooper,* below). The tenant would have to sue for breach of the covenant for quiet enjoyment (see p. 72).

Restriction on re-entry

Under section 2 of the Act it is unlawful to enforce, otherwise than by proceedings in court, a right of re-entry or forfeiture in a lease of premises let as a dwelling, while any person is lawfully residing in the premises.

The section prevents the landlord re-entering under his contractual right, even if that re-entry were peaceable because that would be an unlawful deprivation under section 1 (1).

Eviction without due process

Eviction without due process of law where a dwelling is *not* subject to a protected tenancy under the Rent Act 1977 is also unlawful. Section 3 prohibits recovery of possession of such premises, except by proceedings in court, if the tenancy has terminated but "the occupier" (i.e. any person lawfully residing in the premises under the terms of his employment) continues to reside in the premises. In *Warder v. Cooper* (1970) it was held that this section gives to the tenant an action in tort for damages. The section also applies to licences created by restricted contract.

Agricultural employees

Special protection is given by section 4 of the Act to an agricultural worker occupying premises as a term of his employment but not protected by the Rent (Agriculture) Act 1976 (see p. 178). an order for possession cannot take effect until six months after termination of the employment unless it is reasonable that it should do so and one of the reasons in section 4 (4) applies.

RENT BOOK AND INFORMATION

The Landlord and Tenant Act 1985 provides for information to be given to a tenant. Section 4 of the Act requires the landlord to supply a rent book or similar document where a person has a contractual of statutory right to occupy premises as a residence at a rent payable weekly, unless that rent includes payment for board and the value of it to the tenant is a substantial part of the rent. The rent book supplied must contain:

(a) the landlord's name and address;

(b) the rent and other matters prescribed by the Secretary of State where the premises are occupied under a restricted contract or a protected tenancy within the Rent Act 1977, or a statutory tenancy within the Rent (Agriculture) Act 1976;

(c) information as to overcrowding prescribed under the Housing Act 1985.

If the landlord is a limited company the name and address of every director and of the secretary of the company must also be supplied to the tenant if requested in writing.

The provisions apply no matter what the status of the landlord (save the Crown) and to a licence to occupy as well as a lease. It is an offence not to comply with the provisions.

The Landlord and Tenant Act 1985 also provides for disclosure of identity and for notification of an assignment of the landlord's interest. Section 1 provides that the tenant of any premises occupied as a dwelling may make a written request for the landlord's name and address to any person who demands, or has received and the last payment of, rent, or to any person acting as the landlord's agent. It is an offence not to supply the information within twenty-one days and, if the information given discloses that the landlord is a corporate body, the tenant can request the names and addresses of every director and the secretary of the body. These must then be supplied within a further twenty-one days. Again it is an offence not to comply with the statutory provisions.

CHAPTER SIXTEEN

LANDLORD AND TENANT ACTS

The tendency of legislation in recent years has been to protect the tenant against the landlord. Business premises were first protected by Part I of the Landlord and Tenant Act 1927 under which the tenant might obtain a new lease if he could not otherwise be adequately compensated for goodwill adhering to the premises. Unfortunately, difficulties of proof and procedure led to many claims failing on technical grounds and so the provisions were replaced by Part II of the Landlord and Tenant Act 1954.

There are three matters which we may look at in relation to business tenancies: security of tenure, compensation for disturbance, and compensation for improvements.

SECURITY OF TENURE

The relevant provisions are to be found in Part II of the Landlord and Tenant Act 1954. They apply to tenancies where the property comprised in the tenancy is or includes premises occupied by the tenant for the purposes of his business. A tenancy fulfilling these qualifications is continued until determined in a way permitted by the Act and the tenant can then apply for a new tenancy.

But what is meant by "business"? The Act defines it as including a trade, profession or employment and any activity carried on by a body of persons, corporate or unincorporate. The word "tenancy" does not include a mortgage term or any interest arising in favour of a mortgagor by his attorning tenant to his mortgages, nor a tenancy at will.

The tenant for the purposes of Part II must actually occupy the premises, occupation by the tenant's company is not sufficient. (*Christina v Seear* 1985).

The landlord for the purposes of Part II may not be the immediate landlord of the relevant tenant but is the owner of an interest in reversion (immediately or not) on the relevant tenancy, being either the fee simple or a tenancy which will not end within fourteen months by effuxion of time or by notice to quit already given by the landlord. Provided that such interst is not itself in reversion on an interest fulfilling these conditions. This means that where there is a chain of tenancies the landlord for Part II purposes is that landlord next above the relevant tenant, whose interest will not terminate within fourteen months. Such landlord is termed the "competent landlord".

Unlawful user

If the business carried on is in breach of a general prohibition in the lease against use for business (either trade, profession or employment) the tenancy does not qualify under the Act unless the immediate landlord has either consented to or acquiesced in the breach or the prohibition extends to only part of the premises.

If the business is carried on in breach of a stipulation against a particular business it *will* qualify, however.

Business purposes

Whether premises are occupied for "business purposes" is a question of fact. In *Bagettes v. G.P. Estates* (1956) it was said that the tenant of a block of flats who had sublet the flats was using the premises for business purposes but, as he did not *occupy* any part, his tenancy was not within the Act.

The continuation provisions

A tenancy to which Part II applies will not come to an end until by effluxion of time or by notice to quit but will continue until determined by:

(i) a notice under section 25 by the landlord;

(ii) a tenant's request for a new tenancy under section 26;

(iii) the tenant giving notice to quit, or a notice under section 27 to the landlord;

(iv) surrender (an agreement to surrender is void unless the tenant has occupied for one month)

(v) forteiture under a proviso for re-entry;

(vi) forfeiture of a superior tenancy.

A continuation tenancy is on the same terms as the original tenancy (called the 'current' tenancy) except those relating to its termination and is a legal estate capable of assignment (subject to contractual restrictions), unlike a statutory tenancy under the Rent Acts.

If the tenancy ceases to be one to which Part II applies, the continuation tenancy will not end, but if the current tenancy was granted for a term of years certain, it is thereafter terminable by not less than three and not more than six months' notice in writing by the competent landlord.

We may now examine the types of notices mentioned above — *i.e.*, notices given under sections 25, 26 and 27.

Section 25 notice

This notice must

(a) specify the date for termination (not earlier than six nor later than twelve months after the notice and not earlier than the tenancy would have terminated by effluxion of time or under a contractual notice to quit);

(b) be in the *prescribed* form and served by the competent landlord;

(c) require the tenant to notify the landlord within two months, in writing, whether or not at the date of termination the tenant is willing to relinquish possession comprised in the tenancy; and

(d) state whether the landlord would oppose an application to the court for the grant of a new tenancy and if so, on which of the grounds mentioned in section 30 of the Act he would do so.

Such notice cannot be served if the tenant has first served a section 26 request.

Section 26 request

A tenant can make a request for a new tenancy if his current tenancy:

(a) is one granted for a term of years certain exceeding one year whether or not continued by section 24; or

(b) is one granted for a term of years certain and thereafter from year to year.

The request must state

(i) the property to be comprised in the new tenancy;

(ii) the date from which the new tenancy is to commence. This date must be not more than twelve or less than six months after the request and not earlier than the date on which the current tenancy would end by effluxion of time, or could be ended by notice to quit given by the tenant (this applies to requests made during the subsistence of an existing contractual tenancy);

(iii) the duration of the term asked for;

(iv) the rent to be payable under the tenancy;

(v) the other terms of the tenancy.

No request can be made once the landlord has served a section 25 notice, nor if the tenant has already given notice to quit, or a section 27 notice, to avoid continuance under the Act.

What happens when a tenant serves a section 26 request?

(a) The current tenancy is brought to an end immediately before the date, specified in the request, for the beginning of the new tenancy.

(b) The landlord is entitled, within two months of the request, to give notice to the tenant that he will oppose an application to the court for the grant of a new tenancy, stating on which of the grounds in section 30 he will oppose the application.

Section 27 notice

A section 27 notice is one by which, in the case of a tenancy granted for a term of years certain under which the tenant has been in occupation for one month at least, the tenant states that he does not want the tenancy to be continued. If the continuation has begun, it states that he wishes it to come to an end on a quarter day at least three months after the giving of the notice.

Application to the court for a new tenancy

We have seen that an application may be made to the court for the grant of a new tenancy where the landlord has served a section 25 notice or the tenant has served a section 26 request. In the former case the tenant must have given, within two months, notice of possession; in the latter case the landlord cannot oppose the application unless within two months he gave notice of opposition stating grounds. An application must be made not less than two nor more than four months after the section 25 notice or section 26 request.

If the rateable value of the holding does not exceed £5,000 the court is the county court; otherwise it is the High Court. The respondent is the competent landlord; the parties may agree to a new tenancy without application being made, and the current tenancy will then continue until the date of commencement of the new tenancy.

Grounds

On what grounds can the landlord appose the application? They are set out in section 30 and are as follows:

(a) that under the current tenancy the tenant has obligation as respects the repair and maintenance of the holding, and the tenant ought not to be granted a new tenancy in view of the state of repair of the holding, resulting from the tenant's failure to comply with his obligations;

(b) that the tenant ought not to be granted a new tenancy because of his persistent delay in paying rent which has become due;

(c) that the tenant ought not to be granted a new tenancy in view of other substantial breaches of his obligations under the current tenancy, or for any other reason connected with his use or management of the holding;

(d) that the landlord has offered, and is willing to provide or secure, provision of alternative accommodation for the tenant, on terms that are reasonable with regard to the current tenancy and other circumstances, and that the accommodation and the time at which it will be available are suitable to the tenant's requirements (including requirement to preserve goodwill) having regard to the nature and class of his business and to the situation and extent of, and facilities afforded by, the holding;

(e) that the current tenancy was created by the sub-letting of part of property comprised in a superior tenancy, the landlord is the owner of an interest in reversion on the termination of that superior tenancy, and the aggregate of the rents reasonably obtainable on separate lettings of the holding and the remainder of that property would be substantially less than the rent reasonably obtainable on a letting of the property as a whole, and on termination of the current tenancy the landlord requires possession of the holding for purposes of letting or otherwise disposing of the property as a whole, and that in view of this the tenant ought not to be granted a new tenancy;

(f) that on termination (i.e. the date specified in the section 25 notice or section 26 request) of the current tenancy the landlord intends to demolish or reconstruct the premises comprised in the holding or a substantial part of those premises, or to carry out substantial work of construction on the holding or part thereof, and that he could not reasonably do so without obtaining possession of the holding. In *Betty's Cafes v. Phillips Furnishing Stores* (1958) it was held that the intention must be proved to exist, as a genuine and fixed intention unlikely to be changed, at the date of the hearing of the application; in *Housleys Ltd. v. Bloomer-Holt Ltd.* (1966) it was held that the landlord can rely on this ground if he shows an intention to demolish all the buildings on the holding even though they cover only a minor part of it — in this case a wooden garage and a boundary wall and to reconstruct by concreting the surface of the site "Possession" under ground (f) means legal rather than physical possession (*Heath v. Drown* (1977)) and under section 31 (a) the court will not give the landlord possession if the tenant under a new lease would allow the landlord access to carry out the work or the tenant will accept a new tenancy of an economically separable part of the holding. Substantial redecoration necessitating possession has been held in *Philipson - Stow v. Trevor Square* (1984) to be a sufficient reason to satisfy this ground;

(g) that on termination of the current tenancy the landlord intends to occupy the holding for the purposes, or partly for the purposes, of a business to be carried on by him therein, or as his residence. It should be noted that by section 30 (2) this ground cannot be relied upon if the landlord's interest was purchased or created within five years before termination of the current tenancy, and at all times since purchase or creation the holding has been comprised in a business tenancy or successive business tenancies. The effect of this is that landlords who have acquired the reversion over the head of the sitting tenant within the last five years, either by purchase or grant of a concurrent leasehold interest, cannot rely on this ground. By section 30(3) the business to be carried on under ground (g) can be that of a company in which the landlord has a controlling interest.

It was emphasised in *Housleys Ltd. v. Bloomer-Holt Ltd.* (1966) that the seven grounds here listed are separate, and if any one is proved the landlord is entitled to possession; moreover, a notice not in terms entirely following the section is sufficient if it is clear to the tenant that one particular ground is relied upon.

It should not noted that grounds (a), (b), (c) and (e) give the court a discretion to decide whether a new tenancy "ought not to be granted". The other grounds, if proven, are absolute grounds and the tenant's application must be refused.

Interim continuation

If the effect of a section 25 notice or section 26 request would be to terminate the tenancy before the expiration of three months from the date of the court's disposal of the application, the tenancy is continued until the end of that three-month period (s. 64). When is an application finally disposed of? By section 64(2), when the matter, including any appeal, has been determined and the time for appealing has expired, or the application is withdrawn or any appeal is abandoned.

When a section 25 notice or a section 26 request has been given or made the landlord can apply to the court under section 24(a) to fix an interim rent to begin on the date of the application, or the date specified in the notice or request, whichever date is later. This is a separate application and may be continued even though the proceedings for a new tenancy are discontinued (*Artoc Bank Trust v. Prudential Assurance Co.* 1984).

Order of the court

If the landlord does not oppose the application, or in opposing fails to establish a ground under section 30, the court must order the grant of a new tenancy. If the landlord does establish a ground, the application will be dismissed, with one exception.

If the landlord fails to establish a section 30 ground but the court is satisfied that a ground relied on by him under (d), (e) or (f) above would have been established if the date specified in the section 26 request or section 25 notice had been such later date as the court may determine, being not more than one year later the court can so declare. The declaration will state as to which of the grounds and as to what date it would have been satisfied. The court will then not make an order for grant of a new tenancy, but the tenant has fourteen days from the making of the declaration in which to ask the court to substitute the date specified by the court for the date specified in the notice under section 26 or 25. The notice or request will then "have effect accordingly" and the new date will be the term date of the tenancy.

Misrepresentation or concealment

If the court refuses a new tenancy but it is later shown that the court was induced to act by misrepresentation or concealment of material facts, the court may order the landlord opposing the application to pay the tenant a sufficient sum as compensation for damage or loss sustained by the tenant as the result of the refusal (s. 55 of the 1954 Act).

Excluded tenancies

It should be noted that certain tenancies are excluded from the operation of the security of tenure provisions. They are detailed in section 43 of the Act as follows:

(1) *Tenancy of an agricultural holding* (see Chapter Seventeen).

(2) *Tenancy created by a mining lease, i.e.* a lease for mining purposes or connected purposes: the definition includes sinking and searching for, winning, working, getting, making merchantable, smelting or otherwise converting or working for manufacture, carrying away and disposing of

mines and minerals in or under land, and the erection of buildings and the execution of engineering and other works suitable for those purposes.

(3) *Tenancy subject to the Rent Act.* The 1854 Act provisions do not apply to a tenancy where the property comprised therein is let under a tenancy which either is a controlled tenancy or would be such a tenancy if it were not a tenancy at a low rent (see Chapter Fifteen).

(4) *Tenancy of on-licence premises.* Public houses are thus excluded: residential inns and hotels and licensed restaurants are not.

(5) *Tenancy by reason of office, appointment or employment.* Part II does not apply to a tenancy granted by reason that the tenant is the holder of an office, appointment or employment from the grantor and continuing only while he holds that position; or terminable by the grantor on the tenant's ceasing to hold it, or coming to an end of a time fixed by reference to the tenant's ceasing to hold it. Such a tenancy granted after October 1, 1954, is excluded only if granted by an instrument in writing expressing the purpose for which the tenancy was granted.

(6) *Tenancy not exceeding six months.* If the tenancy is for a term not exceeding six months Part II will not apply unless the tenancy contains provision for renewal or extension beyond six months from its beginning, or the period of the tenant's occupation in carrying on the business has exceeded twelve months. The occupation of the tenant's predecessors may be counted.

Terms of the new tenancy

Where a new tenancy begins under the provisions of Part Ii upon what terms will it be held?

As far as the property is concerned, in the absence of agreement between landlord and tenant, the court order will designate the property by reference to circumstances existing at the time and will order a new tenancy of the "holding", i.e. the part physically occupied by the tenant unless the tenant has agreed to take an economically separable part under section 31(4) (see p. 188). If the current tenancy comprises property other than the holding the *landlord* can require the new tenancy ordered to include such property, and the court order will apply to the whole. All rights enjoyed by the tenant under the current tenancy "in connection with the holding" are to be included in the tenancy ordered by the court (s. 32(3)).

In default of agreement, the tenancy will be "such as may be determined by the court to be reasonable in all the circumstances." Its duration, if it is a tenancy for a term of years certain, will be for not more than fourteen years from the end of the current tenancy. In determining the duration the court may take into account the length of the old lease, the time the tenant has been holding over at the old rent, and the fact that the landlord intends, in the near future, to demolish and reconstruct premises that are dilapidated and ripe for development. In *McCombie v. Grand Junction*

Co. (1962) it was held that a break clause may be inserted by the court in a new lease allowing the landlord to determine the new tenancy when he is ready to demolish and reconstruct the premises.

The rent, in default of agreement, will be determined by the court with reference to the sum at which the holding might reasonably be expected to be let in the open market by a willing lessor, disregarding;

(a) any effect on rent of the fact that the tenant has (or his predecessors in title have) been in occupation of the holding;

(b) any goodwill attached by reason of the business carried on there;

(c) any effect on rent of improvement carried out, under the current or any previous tenancy, by the tenant (or his predecessor in title) otherwise than under his obligation to the landlord;

(d) if the holding comprises licensed premises, any addition to its value attributable to a licence the benefit of which belongs to the tenant.

In default of agreement in writing other terms may be determined by the court having regard to the current tenancy. The court's discretion is wide enough to allow it to include a term that the tenant should provide a guarantor of his obligations. (*Cairnplace v. CBL (Property Investment) Co.* 1984). It would not be usual for the court to include a term that the tenant pay the landlords costs of preparation of the new lease. The effect of the order is that the landlord is bound to grant and the tenant bound to accept a new tenancy in the terms agreed or determined by the court. However, the tenant, if he does not want to take the new tenancy, can apply within fourteen days of the order to revoke it and the court must then revoke it.

It should be noted that there can be no contracting out of the new tenancy rights: section 38 (1) renders such agreements void. Except that the court, on a joint application to it by both parties, can authorise an agreement excluding the rights in a tenancy to be granted, or in an agreement to surrender an existing tenancy (section 39 (4).

Reversions

Where an inferior tenancy is continued under the Act it may extend potentially beyond the end of the term of the superior tenancy. The superior tenancy, so long as it subsists, is, nevertheless, for all purposes an interest in reversion. If there is an intermediate tenancy, it is deemed to be the interest in reversion immediately expectant upon the termination of the inferior tenancy (s. 65 (1)).

Where the continuation causes the inferior tenancy to in fact extend beyond the termination of the interest immediately in reversion, section 139 of the Law of Property Act 1925 is applied. Thus, that interest drops out and the next superior interest will become the estate or interest in reversion. All the incidents and obligations of the inferior tenancy will continue to have effect and govern the relationship between the continuing tenant and the person who now becomes his immediate landlord.

If a tenancy is continued under the Act beyond the beginning of a reversionary tenancy granted to begin on or after the date when the continuing tenancy would have come to an end but for the Act, the reversionary tenancy will take effect as one granted subject to the continuing tenancy.

Similarly, if a new tenancy is granted under the Act for a period beginning on the same date as, or extending beyond the beginning of, a reversionary tenancy, that reversionary tenancy will take effect as one granted subject to the new tenancy.

Trustees and groups of companies

Sections 41 and 42 of the Act contain special provisions for situations where the landlord or the tenant is a trustee or a member of a group of companies. The beneficiaries under the trust or another member company can be treated as the actual landlord or tenant so that, for example, occupation by a beneficiary is occupation by the tenant trustee.

COMPENSATION FOR DISTURBANCE

By section 37 of the Act the tenant of business premises can claim compensation for disturbance where:

(a) he has applied to the court for grant of a new tenancy;

(b) the application has been dismissed on any of the grounds specified in section 30 (1) *(e), (f)* or *(g)* or only those grounds were specified in a section 25 notice or in notice from the landlord after a section 26 request, and either an application was not made or was withdrawn;

(c) and he has quit the holding.

Proof of these matters is facilitated by the fact that when the tenant applies for a new tenancy which the court cannot grant for the reasons above it will certify to this effect.

Amount of compensation

The amount of compensation that may be claimed is either three times the rateable value of the holding or six times the rateable value. The latter can be claimed where it is shown.

(a) that during the whole of the fourteen years immediately prior to the termination of the current tenancy premises being, or compromised in, the holding have been occupied for the purposes of a business carried on by the occupier or for those and other purposes; and

(b) that, if during those fourteen years there was a change in the occupier of those premises, the new occupier succeeded also to the business of the predecessor.

It was held in *Edicron v. William Whitely* (1984) that the "premises" need not mean the whole holding but may refer to an ascertainable part which has been occupied for those fourteen years.

Contracting out

If the business occupation will have been carried on for less than five years at the date of quitting, the agreement can contain provisions excluding or modifying the right to compensation for disturbance. If there is a minimum of five years' occupation, however, any attempt to contract out of the compensation rights is void. If there has been a change of occupier during the last five years the occupation of the previous occupier will count towards the five years, provided the new occupier succeeded to the business.

Any agreement as to the amount of compensation made *after* the right to compensation has accrued is expressly saved, and an agreement providing for additional compensation over and above the statutory compensation will not be cut down or excluded.

It may be noted that premises are continuously occupied by tenants for the purposes of their business even though for a period they conduct their business from other property while, for instance, as in *Connaught Fur Trimmings Ltd. v. Cramas Properties Ltd.* (1955) decorators are working on the premises provided there is a continuity of business use.

COMPENSATION FOR IMPROVEMENTS

By Part I of the Landlord and Tenant Act 1927 provision is made for compensation for improvements on the termination of tenancies of business premises where the tenant gave notice to the landlord of the proposed improvement.

By sections 1-3 of the Act, as amended by Part II of the Landlord and Tenant Act 1954, a tenant of premises used for a trade, business or profession can recover compensation from his landlord on leaving, if he has carried out improvements to the premises which add to their letting value. He must, however, satisfy certain conditions (below) and in the absence of agreement all questions of compensation must be determined by the court. This will be the county court within whose district the premises are situated where the rateable value does not exceed £5,000; otherwise, it will be the High Court.

Conditions

The claim for compensation must be made within time limits set out in the 1954 Act:

(a) within three months after service of a section 25 notice, or a notice from the landlord after a section 26 request, or notice under Part I of the 1954 Act;

(b) not earlier than six, nor later than three months, before termination where the tenancy ends by effluxion of time;

(c) if a tenancy is determined by forfeiture or re-entry, within the period of three months beginning with the effective date of the order of the court for recovery of possession or, if the tenancy is terminated by re-entry without such an order, the period of three months beginning with the date of re-entry. The effective date of an order is the date when the order is to take effect according to its terms or the date on which it ceases to be subject to appeal, whichever is the later.

If a claim is made in the prescribed manner a tenant of a holding to which this part of the 1927 Act applies is entitled to be paid compensation when he quits the holding at the termination of the tenancy. It will be paid in respect of any improvements (including buildings) on his holding (not being a tenant's fixture which he removes) which adds to the letting value of the holding at the termination of the tenancy. A tenant is not entitled to compensation under this part of the Act for any improvement made before the Act, or less than three years before termiation of the tenancy (unless made on or after October 1, 1954), or made in persuance of a contractual obligation.

Amount of compensation

The compensation must not exceed

(i) the net addition to the value of the holding as a whole as the direct result of the improvement; or

(ii) the reasonable cost of carrying out the improvement at the termination of the tenancy less the cost (if any) to the landlord of putting into reasonable repair the works constituting the improvement.

In determining the amount of net addition regard must be had to any intention to demolish or structurally alter any pat of the premises, or to use them for a different purpose and the length of time likely to elapse between termination of the tenancy and the demolition, alteration or change of use.

The court must take into consideration, in deciding the amount of compensation, any benefits which the tenant or his predecessors in title may have received from the landlord or his predecessors in title in consideration of the improvement.

Notice of intention to execute improvement

The tenant cannot claim compensation for improvements unless he has served this notice, or unless his predecessors in title have done so. What is the situation if the tenant wants to effect improvements to which the landlord objects? When the tenant has served notice on the landlord of his intention to carry out an improvement, with a specification and plan, the landlord has three months in which to serve a notice of objection. If he does so the tenant can apply to the court. If no such objection is made or if the court certifies that the improvement is a proper one the tenant may execute the improvement in spite of anything to the contrary in the lease.

Where the landlord does object, the court can certify the improvement a proper one but must not do so if the landlord proves that he has offered to execute the improvement himself, in consideration of a reasonable increase of rent, or such increase as the court may determine. If it is subsequently proved that the landlord has failed to carry out his undertaking the court can certify the improvement. If the court does certify the improvement the tenant must comply with any conditions imposed and the improvement must be completed within the time agreed between landlord and tenant or fixed by the court.

When the tenant has completed the improvement he may ask the landlord for a certificate to this effect and if the landlord fails to do so the tenant may apply to the court for a certificate of due execution.

Consents

The lease may contain a covenant or other condition or agreement to the effect that no improvement shall be made without licence or consent. In such cases, by section 19 (2) of the 1927 Act, the licence or consent is not to be unreasonably withheld, whatever the agreement may state.

This does not preclude the landlord's right to demand payment of a reasonable sum as a condition of the licence or consent, to cover the cost of damage or diminution in the value of the premises or neighbouring premises belonging to him, and to cover expenses properly incurred in giving the licence or consent. Nor does it preclude his right to require, where reasonable, an undertaking from the tenant that he will reinstate the premises in their former condition, where the improvement does not add to the letting value of the holding.

Section 19 (2) must be read into any lease where there is a covenant prohibiting the making of alterations or additions without licence or consent and will apply even if the proposed alterations or additions will not add to the letting value of the holding.

CHAPTER SEVENTEEN

AGRICULTURAL HOLDINGS

Early legislation, beginning with the Agricultural Holdings (England) Act 1875, was concerned with securing compensation for the tenant of the agricultural holding — in the first instance, in respect of improvements, and by 1923 in respect of termination of tenancies without good cause. Not until 1947, however, did provisions appear concerning protection as to rent, and security of tenure. They culminated in the Agricultural Holdings Act 1948, modified by the Agriculture Act 1958 and the Agricultural Holdings (Notices to Quit) Act 1977 which have been consolidated with amendments in the Agricultural Holdings Act 1986. The effect of the modern legislation is that it covers security of tenure, compensation for improvements made by the tenant and for unreasonable disturbance, damage done to his crops by game, and his right to remove fixtures.

But what is meant by an "agricultural holding"?

In the meaning of the Act of 1986 it covers the aggregate of the agricultural land comprised in a contract of tenancy, not being a contract under which the said land is let to the tenant during his continuance in any office, appointment or employment under the landlord. By "agricultural land" is meant land used for agriculture which is so used for the purposes of trade or business and other land designated by the Minister of Agriculture, Fisheries and Food or agricultural land. "Agriculture" includes horticulture, fruit growing, seed growing, dairy farming, livestock breeding, the use of land as grazing land, meadow land, osier land, market gardens and nursery grounds, and the use of land for woodlands where that use is ancillary to the farming of land for other agricultural purposes.

TERMS OF THE HOLDING

Protection as to rent

When an agricultural tenancy is first granted it is open to the parties to decide upon what rent shall be paid. By section 12 of the Agricultural Holdings Act 1986, however, either party, can call for the amount of rent to be submitted to arbitration by an arbitrator appointed by agreement. If the parties cannot agree, it is the Minister who will make the appointment. The arbitration will be on the basis of the open market rent.

If the arbitrator awards an increase or a decrease in the rent payable, the alteration will take effect as from the next day on which the tenancy could have been determined by a notice to quit given when the reference to arbitration was demanded.

The result of this is that no revision of rent will be possible where there is a tenancy for a fixed term which is not determinable by notice to quit.

By section 13 of the Act the landlord may also by notice increase the rent where he has carried out certain improvements, the increase taking effect from completion of the improvement.

Repairs

It is an implied term of a tenancy of an agricultural holding that the tenant will manage and cultivate the land in a good and husband-like manner according to the custom of the county, *i.e.*, the prevalent course of good husbandry in the neighbourhood.

This implied term can, of course, be excluded by agreement. The Agriculture Act 1947 lays down in section 11 certain rules of good husbandry, which can be incorporated into the tenancy by agreement, and they are relevant to the enforcement of notices to quit and compensation for disturbance.

Section 7 of the Act makes the landlord of an agricultural holding liable for the maintenance and repair of those items of "fixed equipment" (including buildings) which are specified in regulations made under the section (Agriculture (Maintenance, Repair and Insurance of Fixed Equipment) Regulations 1973), except in so far as liability in this respect is by written agreement imposed on the tenant.

The position with respect to distress and fixtures has already been noted, on pages 161 and 189 respectively.

SECURITY OF TENURE

Notice to quit an agricultural holding is invalid if it purports to terminate the tenancy before the expiration of twelve months from the end of the then current year of the tenancy (Section 25, 1986 Act). In *Flather v. Hood* (1928) it was held that this is so even where the notice is given by the tenant.

This section does not extend to a case where a bankruptcy order is made against the tenant, nor in certain other cases such as:

(i) a notice given in pursuance of a provision in the contract of tenancy authorising the resumption of possession of the holding or some part of it for a specified purpose other than agriculture;

(ii) a notice given by a tenant to a sub-tenant;

(iii) a notice where the tenancy is one which by section 149 (6) of the Law of Property Act 1925 has taken effect as a term of ninety years (see p. 19)

A notice to quit will also be invalid if the rent is wrongly stated in the notice as when shown in *Dickinson v. Boucher* (1983).

Under section 2 a tenancy or licence of an agricultural holding for a period of one year certain or less is converted into a tenancy from year to year unless the minister approved the entering into of the agreement. By section 3, for tenancies granted before the 12th July 1984, if an agricultural tenancy is one for two years or upwards, it will not determine at the end of the term but will continue as a tenancy from year to year unless the landlord or tenant, not less than one year or more than two years before the date fixed for its expiration, gives to the other *written* notice of an intention to terminate the tenancy.

This section does not apply to a tenancy granted before January 1, 1921, nor to a ninety year term under section 149 (6) of the Law of Property Act 1925. Where the section does apply, however, it cannot be excluded by any agreement to the contrary.

Because a tenancy under either section 2 or section 3 becomes a periodic tenancy, notice to quit is required to terminate it, and section 25 will apply to such notice. Only a tenancy of more than one year but less than two will expire without notice to quit.

Counter-notice

Apart from these modifications, a landlord's right to serve a notice to quit remains unaffected. The tenant can, however, serve a counter-notice which has the effect of rendering the landlord's notice to quit ineffective unless supported by consent of the Agricultural Land Tribunal. A tenant must serve counter-notice within one month of receiving the original notice to quit.

There are only six cases in which the Tribunal can give its consent to the operation of a landlord's notice to quit, but where it does give consent, the notice will determine not only the tenancy but also the sub-tenancies whether notices have been served on the sub-tenants by the tenant or not.

Restrictions upon counter-notices

A landlord may serve notice to quit; the tenant may serve counter-notice. This is the general position. There are eight cases, however, where the tenant *cannot* serve a counter-notice. They are as follows (s. 26 and Schedule 3).

(a) the land is let as a smallholding to a tenant over 65 who will be deprived of accommodation by the notice to quit, but where there is alternative accommodation available.

(b) where the land is required for non-agricultural use for which planning permission has been given, or is not required;

(c) where the Tribunal is satisfied, on application made within the previous six months, that the tenant is not farming according to rules of good husbandry, and has so certified;

(d) where the tenant has committed a breach of a term of his tenancy and has failed to comply with a written notice from the landlord demanding compliance within two months (for rent) or a reasonable time (in respect of other terms);

(e) where the landlord's interest has been materially prejudiced by an irreparable breach by the tenant of a term of the tenancy in accordance with good husbandry;

(f) where the tenant is bankrupt or has compounded with his creditors;

(g) where the notice is given within three months after the death of the sole (or sole surviving) tenant.

However, the deceased tenant's spouse, brother, sister or child can within three months after the death, apply to the Tribunal for a direction allowing that person to succeed to the holding. A direction from the Tribunal renders the notice to quit ineffective but the landlord can prevent a direction by asking the Tribunal's consent to the notice taking effect on a ground in section 3. The applicant for a direction must have derived his livelihood from the holding for 5 out of 7 years before the death. This requirement need only be satisfied to a material extent however. This was held to mean in *Littlewood v. Rolfe* (1982) that it must be fulfilled substantially in terms of time and value. Only two succession to the holding are allowed.

The act provides for notice of this application to be given to the landlord. However failure to do so is not fatal to the application as it was held in *Kellet Alexander & Kellett v. Cady* (1981) that the requirement in the Act is purely procedural.

(h) where the notice to quit is given to enable the use or disposal of the land for the purpose of amalgamation or reshaping of an agricultural unit and the Minister has so certified.

The landlord who wishes to rely on one of the grounds in section 2, must make it clear which ground he relies on. If the tenant decides to contest the reasons stated in (b), (c) or (d) he must serve notice on the landlord within one month requiring the matter to be settled by arbitration.

Consent of the Tribunal

It was noted that there are only six cases where the Tribunal can give its consent to the operation of the landlord's notice to quit. Even where one of the cases is shown the Tribunal will still not consent if in all the circumstances a fair and reasonable landlord would not insist on possession. The six cases (in section 7) are as follows:

(a) the landlord proposed to end the tenancy for a purpose that is desirable in the interests of good husbandry; or

(b) for a purpose that is desirable in the interests of sound management of the land concerned or the estate of which it forms part; or

(c) for a purpose that is desirable for agricultural research, education, experiment or demonstration, or for the purposes of the statutes concerning smallholdings or allotments; or

(d) the carrying out of a purpose that is desirable for the purposes of the enactments relating to allotments; or

(e) greater hardship would be caused by withholding consent than by granting it; or

(f) the landlord proposes to terminate the tenancy for the purpose of the land being used for some non-actricultural use not falling within case (ii) of the non-counter notice grounds (above).

However where there has been a failure to pay rent, a valid notice has been given and no counter notice served, the court has no discretion to refuse a possession order (*Parrish v. Kinsey* 1983).

Notice to quit part of the holding

By section 31 of the Act, the landlord of an agricultural holding held by a tenant from year to year can give notice to the tenant to quit part of the holding, where he wants to adjust boundaries between agricultural units or to amalgamate agricultural units, or where he wants to carry out certain specified objects. If he does give such notice, however, the tenant will be entitled to a reduction in rent, and also to compensation in respect of any depreciation in the value to him of the residue of the holding caused by the severance, or by the use to be made of the part severed. Moreover, the tenant may accept within twenty-eight days, by counter-notice, the landlord's notice to quit part, as a notice to quit the entire holding.

COMPENSATION

What is the situation as regards compensation if the agricultural tenant quits his holding at the end of the tenancy? At common law he was entitled to nothing unless his entitlement arose by custom or by express agreement. The Act of 1986 gives him certain rights to compensation, however; these fall into four kinds. Compensation for improvements; for increase in the value of the holding due to a special system of farming; for damage done by game, and for unreasonable disturbance.

Each of these may now be dealt with in outline.

Compensation for improvements

At the termination of his tenancy and on qitting his holding a tenant of an agricultural holding can obtain compensation from his landlord in respect of those improvements specified in the Seventh Schedule or in Part I of the Eighth Schedule to the Act. Similarly, the tenant can obtain compensation in respect of the tenant-right matters specified in the Ninth Schedule.

The amount of the compensation for specified improvements in the Seventh Schedule is an amount equal to the increase attributable to the improvement in the value of the agricultural holding as a holding having regard to the character and situation of the holding and the average requirements of tenants reasonably skilled in husbandry (s. 65).

If the improvement is one specified in Part I of the Eighth Schedule or the matter falls within Part II of that Schedule, the amount will be the value thereof to an incoming tenant calculated in accordance with regulations made under the Act (s. 66). The parties may, however, specify their own measure of compensation for Part II matters in a written agreement.

By section 66, the amount of any grant paid from money provided by Parliament in respect of an improvement must be taken into account in assessing the compensation.

The Seventh Schedule

The Seventh Schedule is in two parts.

Part I includes long-term improvements such as the making of osier beds, water meadows, irrigation works, watercress beds and gardens, and the planting of hops and orchards. No compensation is payable under the Act in respect of such improvements unless the landlord gave his written consent to the making of the improvement before it was actually carried out. The landlord's consent may be given unconditionally, or upon terms as to compensation agreed upon in writing between landlord and tenant. In such a case compensation payable under the agreement will be paid, and not compensation under the Act.

Part II of this schedule comprises other long-term improvements including the erection, alteration or enlargement of buildings, the claying of land, the making or improvement of roads, bridges or watercourses, the reclamation of waste land, and land drainage (other than mole drainage and works to secure its efficient functioning), provision or laying on of electric power, and provision of means of sewage disposal.

Part II differs from Part I as far as consents are concerned in one way. If the landlord refuses consent the tenant may apply to the Agricultural Land Tribunal for approval of execution of the improvement, as he may also do if he is unwilling to agree to the terms subject to which the landlord is prepared to consent.

The Tribunal can approve the execution of the improvement either unconditionally, or upon terms it regards just. It can also withhold approval. If it grants approval the effect is as though the landlord had given consent, unless the landlord gives notice to the Tribunal and the tenant that he will carry out the improvement himself, and does so.

The Eight and Ninth Schedules

Part I of the Eighth Schedule comprises short-term improvements, such as mole drainage and works to secure its efficient functioning, the protection of fruit trees against animals, the chalking and liming of land and clay-burning. Part II of the Schedule refers to other matters known as tenant-right matters, such as growing crops and severed or harvested crops and produce, grown on the agricultural holding in the last year of the tenancy. Crops or produce which the tenant has a right to sell or remove are not included.

Part II also includes seeds sown and cultivations, fallows and acts of husbandry performed on the holding at the expense of the tenant, and pasture laid down with clover, grass or other seeds voluntarily by the tenant at his own expense or paid for by him when he entered, and acclimatisation, hefting or settlement of hill sheep on high ground.

The consent of the landlord or of the Tribunal is not required for the improvements in Part I and the matters in Part II of the Eighth Schedule. In respect of mole drainage and works carried out to make them work effectively, however, no compensation is payable unless the tenant gave written notice to the landlord within the month before the improvement was begun, to the effect that he intended carrying out the improvement.

No compensation is payable for improvements mentioned in Part I or Part II if it is an improvement made or effected for the purposes of the proviso to section 15 (1) of the Act. This proviso requires the tenant to return to the holding the full equivalent manurial value of all crops sold off or removed from the holding in contravention of custom or agreement and, in the case of the practice of any system of cropping permitted by section 15 (1), to protect the holding from injury or deterioration.

Incoming tenants. An incoming tenant may have paid, with written consent of the landlord, compensation under the Act to the outgoing tenant, in respect of improvements. Where he has done this he is entitled, on quitting the holding, to claim compensation for that improvement in the same manner as the outgoing tenant could have claimed if he had remained in possession of the holding until that time.

Similarly, the tenant is entitled to claim compenstion on quitting the holding if he paid an amount, in respect of an improvement, to the landlord when he entered into occupation, unless he and the landlord have made some written agreement to the contrary. He will claim and be entitled in the same manner as if he had been the tenant when the improvement was carried out and as though the improvement had been carried out by him.

Successive tenancies. Where the tenant has remained in the holding during two or more tenancies he is not deprived of his right to compensation under the Act in respect of improvements by reason only that the improvements were made during a tenancy other than one at the termination of which he quits the holding.

Custom. No claim based merely on custom can be made in respect of improvements begun on or after March 1, 1948, whether or not the improvement is one for which the Act provides compensation.

Schedule Nine gives the tenant the right to compensation for improvements carried out before March 1st 1948, called "old improvements".

Compensation for special system of farming

If the value of the holding to an incoming tenant has been increased during the tenancy by the continuous adoption of a system of farming which has been more beneficial to the holding than the system required by the contract of tenancy, or, if no system is specified, the system of farming normally practised on comparable agricultural holdings, compensation may be payable under section 70.

The section states that the tenant is entitled on quitting the holding to compensation representing the increase in the value of the holding as a holding attributable to the adoption of the special system. Regard is paid to the character and situation of the holding and the average requirements of tenants reasonably skilled in husbandry.

It should be noted that a written notice of intention to claim compensation under this section must be given not later than one month before the termination of the tenancy.

Compensation for deterioration

It is not only a tenant who can claim compensation. Section 72 of the Act gives a landlord a right of compensation on termination of a tenancy.

His right arises where the value of the holding has been reduced by reason of dilapidation, or deterioration of, or damage to, any part of the holding by the tenant's non-fulfilment of his responsibilities to farm the holding according to the rules of good husbandry.

Once again, notice in writing of the intention to claim compensation must be given not later than one month before termination of the tenancy.

By section 71 the landlord can also claim compensation in respect of dilapidation, deterioration or damage to particular parts of the holding when the tenant quits on termination of the tenancy. The measure of compensation will be the cost of reinstatement. No notice of intention to claim under section 71 is necessary.

If the landlord obtains compensation under section 71 and also claims under section 72 he must bring that compensation into account; he cannot recover compensation twice over.

Section 71 preserves the landlord's right to claim under a term of the contract instead of section 71 if he wishes — he cannot claim under both.

Compensation for damage by game

If a tenant of a holding has sustained damage to his crops from game, section 20 gives him the right to compensation from the landlord. This will be so where the right to kill and take the game is vested neither in him nor in anyone claiming under him other than the landlord, and the game is not game which the tenant has permission in writing to kill.

The tenant must give to the landlord.

(i) notice in writing of the damage before the expiration of one month after the tenant first became, or ought reasonably to have become, aware of its occurrence;

(ii) a reasonable opportunity to inspect the damage before the crop is reaped, raised, consumed or begun to be removed;

(iii) notice in writing of the claim within one month of the end of the year to which the claim relates.

Compensation for disturbance

By section 60, if the tenancy of an agricultural holding terminates by reason either

(i) of a notice to quit given by the landlord; or

(ii) of a counter-notice given by the tenant under section 32, after the giving to him of notice to quit part of the holding, and the tenant consequently quits the holding, then compensation in respect of the disturbance will be payable by the landlord to the tenant, subject to the provisions of section 34.

Basic and additional compensation will not be payable if the notice to quit is excluded by S. 26 cases c, d, e, f or g.

Additional compensation will not be payable if the operation of the notice to quit in S26 is excluded by case a or case h or if the notice to quit is for any reason detailed in sub-sections (3) and (4) of section 61.

The compensation payable under this section is divided into basic and additional compensation. Basic compensation for disturbance is the amount of one years rent or if the tenant has complied with sub-section 6 (Notice of claim or reasonable opportunity for landlord to value stock) the tenant's actual loss or two years rent whichever of the latter is the smaller. Additional compensation of four years rent is a sum to assist in the reorganisation of the tenant's affairs. The definition of the tenant's actual loss is the amount of the loss or expense, directly attributable to the quitting of the holding and unavoidably incurred by the tenant upon, or in connection with, the sale or removal of his household goods, implements of husbandry, fixtures, farm produce or farm stock on, or used in connection with, the holding. It also includes any expenses reasonably incurred by the tenant in the preparation of his claim for compensation (not being costs of arbitration to determine any question arising under section 60 or 61).

Where the tenant has sub-let his holding and in consequence of a notice to quit he becomes liable to pay compensation under this section to the sub-tenant, the tenant will not be debarred from recovering compensation merely because he is not in occupation of the holding and so does not quit the holding on termination of the tenancy.

If the tenancy is determined by a counter-notice from the tenant after the landlord has given notice to quit part of the holding, and the part of the holding affected by the landlord's notice is less than one quarter of the holding and the remainder is reasonably capable of being farmed as a separate holding compensation is only payable in relation to the part of the holding to which the notice to quit relates.

Compensation payable under section 60 is in addition to any compensation to which the tenant may be entitled apart from the section.

Compensation in special cases

By sections 79 and 80 the rules as to compensation in respect of tenancies or market gardens are modified. By section 76 no compensation of any kind is payable for anything done in pursuance of an order under section 14 (4) of the Act. Such order will be one by an arbitrator varying the terms of the tenancy in consequence of a direction made by him reducing the area of land which is to be maintained under the contract of tenancy as permanent pasture.

Agreements for compensation

If the Act provides for compensation, the tenant or landlord will be entitled to compensation only under the Act in spite of any contrary agreement unless the Act allows such agreement, as in sections 20, 66 and 71.

Where the Act makes no provision for compensation, neither party is disentitled by the Act to compensation under an agreement in writing (except in those matters specified in Part II of the Eighth Schedule).

Arbitration under the Act

Section 83 provides that if a claim by landlord or tenant against the other arises.

(i) under the Act or any custom or agreement; and

(ii) on or out of the termination of the tenancy of the agricultural holding or part of it,

it shall, subject to the provisions of the section, be determined by arbitration.

The claimant must have served notice in writing upon the other party of his intention to make the claim. The notice must specify the nature of the claim and must have been served before the expiration of two months from termination of the tenancy. Subject to the terms of the section, the parties may settle the claim within a period of four months from termination of the tenancy.

The arbitration will be by a single arbitrator in accordance with the provisions of the Eleventh Schedule to the Act; the appointment of the arbitrator and the procedure at arbitration are governed by this Schedule and by section 84. The arbitrator may at any stage of the proceedings state in the form of a special case for the opinion of the county court any question of law arising in the course of the arbitration. He *must* do so if directed by the judge of the county court upon the application of either party.

It should be noted that the provisions of the Arbitration Acts have no application to arbitrations under the Agricultural Holdings Act.

By its terms, section 83 only affects the determination of claims arising on or out of the termination of the tenancy. It follows, therefore, that arbitration is not obligatory in respect of claims arising during the course of the tenancy, unless express provision is made for arbitration — such as in section 20 where arbitration is called for to decide the amount of compensation in default of agreement where there is damage by game.

Claims for compensation for disturbance, improvements and tenant-right matters, and for the increased or diminished value of the holding, arising on termination of the tenancy can be resolved only by arbitration, however. It is then irrelevant whether the claim arises under the Act or by custom or agreement.

The right of the landlord or tenant remains to pursue any contractural right of remedy *except where the Act provides otherwise.* It should be noted that section 83 covers *any* claim arising on or out of the *termination* of the tenancy. An action of ejectment against a tenant under an expired notice to quit, or proceedings claiming a declaration that the tenancy had been determined by a valid notice to quit are however outside section 83 as that section assumes that the tenancy has been properly terminated.

Recovery of compensation

Where a sum has been agreed or awarded under the Act to be paid for compensation costs or otherwise, it will be recoverable in the county court by the landlord or tenant of the holding if it is not paid within fourteen days after it becomes due.

CHAPTER EIGHTEEN

SMALLHOLDINGS AND ALLOTMENTS

A smallholding is defined by the Agriculture Act 1947 (s. 67) as a holding used or intended to be used for agriculture and the area of which does not exceed fifty acres but which is at least one acre in extent.

An allotment is variously defined: the most usual form provided is the allotment garden, which is defined in the Allotments Act 1922 as an allotment not exceeding a quarter of an acre (forty poles) in area, wholly or mainly cultivated by the occupier for the production of fruit and vegetables for consumption by himself or his family. By definition, therefore, it is not an agricultural holding under the Agricultural Holdings Act 1986 but in *Stevens v. Sedgman* (1951) it was held that an allotment other than an allotment garden is an agricultural holding if it is used for the purposes of a trade or business. Similarly a smallholding may be an agricultural holding.

The powers and duties of local authorities as far as the provision of allotments and smallholdings are contained in the Allotments Acts 1908-50 and the Agriculture Act 1970 and the Agricultural Holdings Act 1986.

COMPENSATION

The tenant of an allotment has a right to compensation on determination of the tenancy in respect of crops and other matters under the Allotments Act 1922. By section 3 of the Act he can claim in respect of:

(a) crops, including fruit, growing upon the land in the ordinary course of cultivation and labour expended upon, and manure applied to, the land; and

(b) fruit trees and bushes provided and planted by the tenant with the previous consent in writing of the landlord, and drains, outbuildings, pigsties, fowlhouses or other structural improvements made or erected by and at the expense of the tenant on the land with such consent.

The compensation recoverable in these respects is based on their value to an incoming tenant and if the parties do not agree, the difference is settled by a valuation by a person appointed, in default of agreement, by the county court judge for the area.

If the allotment is an agricultural holding compensation may be payable under the 1986 Act.

Local authority allotments

If a council lets a smallholding or allotment to a tenant he has the same right to compensation for improvements for

(1) planting standard or other fruit trees or fruit bushes permanently set out;

(2) planting strawberry plants;

(3) planting asparagus, rhubarb and other vegetable crops which continue to be productive for two or more years, as he would have, had the holding been one to which section 42 of the Agricultural Holdings Act 1908 applies. The relevant provisions now are in section 79 of the 1986 Act which relates to market gardens.

A tenant cannot claim, however, if he acted in spite of an express prohibition of the countil; a tenant aggrieved by such prohibition has the right of appeal to the Minister of Agriculture Fisheries and Food.

Allotment gardens

If land is used as an allotment garden the tenant can claim compensation under section 2 of the 1922 Act when he quits the land on termination if the tenancy is ended by the landlord by re-entry for building, industrial or public purposes (but not re-entry for non-payment of rent, breach of contractual terms, or bankruptcy or compounding with creditors). This applies notwithstanding agreement to the contrary.

What compensation can he recover? A sum in respect of crops growing on the land in the ordinary course of cultivation as an allotment garden and for manure applied to the land.

In addition to compensation under section 2, compensation can be claimed under the contract of tenancy itself and for disturbance.

Compensation for disturbance

The tenant who quits an allotment garden can, by section 3 of the Allotments Act 1950, claim compensation for disturbance in certain cases and the contract of tenancy cannot exclude the right. These are where the tenancy is terminated as to the whole or any part:

(a) by re-entry under the Allotments Act 1922; or

(b) if the landlord is himself a tenant, by the termination of his tenancy; or

(c) if the landlord is a local authority which has let the land under section 10 of the 1922 Act, by the termination of the authority's right of occupation.

The amount of compensation if tenancy of the whole is terminated is one year's rent of the land at the rate payable immediately before termination; if termination is as to part, a proportionate amount can be recovered.

Compensaion for deterioration

If a tenant of an allotment garden quits the land when the tenancy determines, the landlord, in spite of agreement to the contrary, may obtain compensation for deterioration. This will be so if the tenant has failed to maintain the land in a clean and good state of cultivation and fertility. The amount will be the cost, at quitting, of making good the deterioration (Allotments Act 1950, s. 4). S 15 of the Agricultural Holdings Act 1986 regarding disposal of product and cropping is not applicable to smallholdings (Section s. 2 1986 Act).

SECURITY OF TENURE

Determination of tenancies of allotment gardens

Reference was made above to re-entry under the Allotments Act 1922. The provisions as to determination of tenancies of allotment gardens are dealt with in section 1 of that Act (as amended) by which such tenancies can be determined only by:

(a) a twelve months' or longer notice to quit expiring on or before the sixth day of April, or on or after, the twenty-ninth day of September in any year; or

(b) re-entry after three months' notice in writing to the tenant under a power of re-entry contained in, or affecting, the contract of tenancy, the land being required for building, mining, or any other industrial purposes or for roads or sewers necessary in connection with any of those purposes; or

(c) re-entry under a power contained in, or affecting, the contract of tenancy in the case of land let by a corporation or company, being the owners or lessees of a railway, dock, canal, water or other public undertaking, the land being required for any purpose (other than agriculture) for which it has been held by the statutory body or appropriated by it. Except in a case of emergency, three months' notice in writing of the intended re-entry must be given to the tenant; or

(d) re-entry under a power contained in, or affecting, the contract of tenancy in the case of land let by a local authority, being required for the purposes of the Housing Acts 1890 to 1921 and, in the case of other land let by a local authority, after three months' previous notice in writing to the tenant if the land is required by the local authority for a purpose (other than agriculture) for which it was acquired or appropriated; or

(e) re-entry for non-payment of rent or breach of any contractual term or condition or for bankruptcy, or compounding with creditors, or, where the tenant is an association, on account of its liquidation;

There are no statutory restrictions on the termination of a tenancy of an allotment other than allotment gardens or an allotment which is an agricultural holding under the Agricultural Holdings Act 1986.

CHAPTER NINETEEN

THE LEASEHOLD REFORM ACT 1967

ENFRANCHISEMENT OR EXTENSION

Introduction

One of the results of Victorian enterprise in this country was the creation of vast numbers of leasehold dwelling-houses. This arose because land in the growing industrial cities was, at that time, mainly in the ownership of a few men who used their monopoly power to prevent development taking place on other than leasehold terms. These terms were that the owner provided the land at a nominal ground rent for, say, a period of ninety-nine years while the tenant built a house on it at his own cost and over the years maintained and improved it. At the end of the lease the successor in title to the original owner of the land acquired both land and the dwelling-house, while the tenant's successor in title lost the right to both. Since many of these long leases of ninety-nine years or more were granted in the 1860's the problems today are obvious.

A White Paper[1] published prior to the Leasehold Reform Act stated:

'It is ... quite indefensible, if justice is to be done as between freeholder and occupying leaseholder, that at the end of the term, the law should allow the ownership of the house to revert to the freeholder without his paying anything for it so that he gets not only the land but also the house, the improvements and everything the leaseholder and his predecessors have added to it. ... The Government will, therefore, introduce a Bill to give leaseholders with an original long lease greater security and to enable them to acquire the freehold on fair terms. The Bill will be based on the principle that the land belongs in equity to the land owner and the house belongs in equity to the occupying leaseholder. It follows that the leaseholder will have the right to retain his house after the lease expires and the right to enfranchise his lease".

Adopting these principles, the Leasehold Reform Act 1967 was enacted setting out the terms under which a holder of a long lease can extend that lease or acquire the freehold version.

[1] White Paper, Cmnd. 2916.

Qualifications

The Leasehold Reform Act 1967 gives to a tenant occupying a long leasehold house as his residence a right to purchase the freehold reversion, or to obtain an extension of his lease for a period of fifty years at a revised ground rent. These rights apply only to a tenant of premises used for residential purposes. Thus, business premises are excluded, though where premises are used partly for both but the residential part is the tenant's main residence, the Act may well apply. It was held in *Tandan v. Trustees of Spurgeons Homes* (1982) that so long as a building of mixed use can reasonably be called a house it falls within the requirements of the Act. The presmises must have a rateable value on the appropriate day, 23rd March, 1965, of not more than £400 in Greater London or £200 in the provinces.

If the premises were not shown in the valuation lists on that date the appropriate day is the date a value is first listed. Where that date is on or after 1st April, 1973, the rateable value must not exceed £1,500 in Greater London or £750 elsewhere. If the tenant through his own improvements has increased the rateable value that value can be reduced accordingly for the purposes of the Act.

The tenant must have occupied the premises as his only or main residence for the five years, or for five years out of the ten years, which precede his giving notice in the prescribed form to the landlord claiming enfranchisement or an extended lease. The occupation must be under a long tenancy at a low rent. Therefore where a tenant had had a 99 year lease for one year of a low rent after occupying as a regulared tenant at a rack rent for many years the occupancy was not sufficient (*Harris v. Plentex,* 1980). In addition, by section 7 of the Act a member of the tenant's family who inherits the lease and is resident in the house at the tenant's death, can include his residence before the death in computing the five years. The members of the family included are a spouse, parents, children and parents and children-in-law.

The act strictly defines the nature of a residence that can benefit from enfanchisement or a claim to an extended lease. It must be a house that is the only or main residence of the claimant. Horizontally divided flats are excluded but not vertically divided premises. However, the tenant need not occupy the whole of the premises, and indeed his dividing them into horizontal flats will not prevent his rights accruing provided he occupies one of them, and provided also that he fulfills the other conditions laid down.

Section 1 of the Act lays down a double-barrelled condition that goes to the core of the matter. The lease must be *a long one at a low rent. First,* a long lease means a term of years exceeding twenty-one years (irrespective of any right on the part of either party to pre-determine it before the end of that period — for example, by notice or forfeiture) and includes a perpertually renewable lease unless it is one by sub-demise out of a lease that is not a long one. It also includes a lease granted for less than twenty-one years but subsequently renewed under a covenant or obligations, thus having an actual running period of more than twenty-one years. A lease terminable by death or marriage is excluded.

Secondly, the ground rent must fulfil the definition of a "low rent": that is, where at any time such rent is less than two-thirds of the rateable value of the premises on whichwever is the latest event of the following:

(a) 23rd March, 1965;
(b) the first day it features in the valuation list; or
(c) the first day of the term.

The Act stipulates that any part of the rent that is in respect of services, repairs, maintenance or insurance must be ignored in computing the qualifying figure. Likewise, any penal additions to the rent in the event of a contravention of, or a non-compliance with, the terms of the tenancy are ignored.

One point must be noted. A tenancy granted between the end of August 1939 and the beginning of April 1963, other than by way of a building lease, is not a tenancy at a low rent if at the commencement the rent payable exceeded two-thirds of the letting value of the property on the same terms. The "letting value" is the rent obtainable on the open market. the purpose of this exemption is to protect from an unjustified enfranchisement property let between the last pre-war rating revaluation and the first post-war one.

The parties involved

The principle of enfranchisement can be exercised against charities and public bodies, for example, local authorities, nationalised interests and development corporations although these bodies can claim exemption where the land is needed for development. National Trust land cannot be enfranchised but an extended lease can be claimed.

A tenant entitled under the Act, yet unable to serve the prescribed notice because the landlord's identity or whereabouts cannot be established, may apply to the Chancery Division of the High Court for an order vesting the freehold reversion in the premises in him. The compensation, which is assessed by a valuer appointed by the President of the Lands Tribunal, is paid into court.

It should be noted, that the rights and obligations under the Act both as to enfranchisement and an extended lease, once having crystallised on the giving of a prescribed notice will devolve on the executors or administrators of both the parties in a similar manner as contracts for the sale of an interest in land.

A tenant may also assign his rights as though they were a chose in action, but only as part and parcel of his interest in the premises as a whole. Similarly an assignee of the reversion will be bound by the tenant's rights if protected by resignation — the crystallised rights are an estate contract.

Thus the rights and obligations under the Act are assignable with, but not capable of subsisting apart from, the property. The rights under the Act also add to the value of the premises if they are compulsorily acquired and their value must be taken into account in assessing the compensation payable. Once the right to enfranchise has accrued to a tenant nothing will prevent him temporarily releasing the right and reviving it later subject to the twelve year limitation period (*Collin v. Duke of Westminster*, 1985).

Procedure

As has already been pointed out a tenant has the right during the subsistence of the original lease to claim the right to enfranchise the lease or to extend it for a further fifty years. It is probably more convenient to deal with the latter first. The new tenancy arising in this situation is for a term commencing immediately, and expiring fifty years after after the term date of the existing lease. The new tenancy will, under section 15, be on the same terms as before but may be modified to take account of:

(a) the omission of property formerly included in the premises;

(b) any alterations to the premises subsequent to the original grant;

(c) if the tenant derives his rights from separate tenancies of two or more parts of the premises, the combined effect of the tenancies and the differences in their terms.

The rent under the existing tenancy will remain payable until that tenancy would have expired and thereafter a new rent will commence. That rent will represent the letting value of the site ignoring the value of any buildings on it. The letting value is the rent plus the decapitalised value of a lawfully obtainable premium (*Manson v. Duke of Westminster*, 1981). The new ground rent may be revised again after twenty-five years if the landlord claims. Where a tenancy has been extended in this way the tenant loses his right to enfranchisement forever unless he claims before the end of the original term.

There is no right to a further extension at the end of the fifty years. Two other points should be noted:

(i) the Landlord and Tenant Act 1954 does not apply on the expiration of an extended lease not of a sub-lease derived from it, or;

(ii) any sub-tenant cannot, on the expiration of the extended lease, claim the protection of the Rent Acts nor can he acquire a right to enfranchise or extend his sub-lease.

Because of the advantages of enfranchisement the right to extend a lease is not often invoked.

The remarks concerning procedural matters made in the discussion of enfranchisement below apply *mutatis mutandis* to the procedure concerning an extended lease. Enfranchisement will now be dealt with.

Enfranchisement

The tenant's notice claiming enfranchisement can be served upon the landlord during the subsistence of a long lease. The notice must specify and particularise the property and give details of the tenancy and its qualifications that bring it within the Act, as well as the date of its acquisition by the tenant and of the periods of his residence which bring him within the Act. The landlord must within two months, by notice, admit or deny the tenant's claims under the Act and give his grounds in the latter case. The Act lays down the procedural details in Schedule 3. Any disputes as to whether the tenant is entitled to enfranchisement must be resolved by the county court.

The landlord may be written notice demand a deposit from the tenant amounting to the three times the annual rent or £25 whichever is greater. The landlord may, after receiving the tenant's notice, give written notice requiring the tenant to prove his title to the tenancy. The tenant has twenty-one days to comply: (Leasehold Reform (Enfranchisement and Extension) Regulations 1967).

A landlord has two grounds for resisting a tenant's claim (called "overriding rights"). First, if he can establish that the property is required by him or his family for residential puposes and that there would be greater hardship to him or them than to the tenant if enfranchisement or extension were allowed, he may claim possession of the premises. He must compensate the tenant for the "bricks and mortar" that the tenant loses. The ground is not available to a landlord whose interest in the property was purchased or created after February 18, 1966 (White Paper day).

Secondly, the landlord can claim possession of the premises for the purposes of redevelopment if a claim is initiated for an extended lease or an extension has already been obtained. The matter is dealt with by the county court which must be satisfied by the landlord that he proposes to demolish or reconstruct the whole or a substantial part of the premises. He must pay compensation as before and he cannot apply until twelve months before the end of the original term date. The ground cannot be used to defeat the tenant's right to acquire the freehold but only an extension of the lease.

In the event of either party failing to comply with the procedural formalities leading to enfranchisement, then the aggrieved party can give notice, allowing at lease two months for the party defaulting to fulfil the obligations specified in such notice. If the tenant fails to comply with the notice then the negotiations are at an end and the landlord's costs must be paid by the tenant and any deposit paid is forfeit to the landlord. If the landlord is at fault the tenant recovers his deposit, is absolved from paying any costs and retains his other rights under the Act.

Effects of enfranchisement

After service of the prescribed notice, the parties are in a contractural relationship from a practical point of view. Thereafter, any proceedings for re-entry or forfeiture can be brought only with leave of the court. In due course the landlord must convey his freehold reversion to the tenant for an estate in fee simple. It is conveyed subject only to the tenancy and to the tenant's incumbrances. The conveyance has the "over-reaching" effect brought about by the operation of section 2 (1) of the Law of Property Act 1925. So far as concerns easements and benefits attached to the premises, these will be conveyed with the property, and the general words implied in conveyances under section 62 of the Law of Property Act 1925 will not be excluded or restrictive covenants for the protection of other property in which he has an interest, provided they do not derogate from the use under the lease. To sum up, the landlord need not convey any better title than that which he has, or could require to be vested in him, and the tenant is granted such rights as will establish in a freehold estate his enjoyment of the property in a similar manner as before.

All mortgages of the reversion must be discharged so that the tenant takes the premises free from such encumbrances. If the compensation is insufficient to effect this, what compensation there is will be paid to the mortgagee or, if he is unascertained, into court. As long as this is done the premises are free from the mortgage and the tenant is no longer concerned with the eventual outcome as between the landlord and the mortgagee.

COMPENSATION

Compensation will normally be determined by agreement between the parties by applying the formula stipulated in the Act, though if they cannot reach agreement the Lands Tribunal will do it for them.

Section 9 sets out the formula for ascertaining the compensation; it is to be assessed on the market value of the land only (that is, ignoring the value of the dwelling) But on the basis that the lease is notionally extended by fifty years at the same ground rent as before ignoring the tenant's willingness to pay over the market value but taking into account any develpment value to the landlord. If, however, the rateable value of the premises exceeds £1,000 in Greater London or £500 elsewhere a different basis of calculation (introduced by the Housing Act 1974) applies. Instead of the tenancy being extended by fifty years it must be assumed that the tenant has a right to remain in possession under Part 1 of the Landlord and Tenant Act 1954, that the tenant is not liable for repairs and that the price is to be decreased by the increase in value of the premises because of the tenant's repairs. The tenant must pay in addition to the purchase price:

(a) the landlord's costs for verifying the tenant's right to acquire the freehold;

(b) the landlord's legal costs and disbursements;

(c) the valuation fees incurred in the transaction.

Section 9 also forsees the possibility of the tenant changing his mind after serving the prescribed notice. He is given the right to withdraw provided he serves a further notice on the landlord that he is unable or unwilling to buy the premises at the price fixed. The original notice he served then ceases to have effect and if the landlord has suffered loss by the service of the original notice, he can claim compensation from the tenant who is prevented from serving another notice to enfranchise for five years from his withdrawal. Any costs incurred are borne by the tenant.

MANAGEMENT

By virtue of section 19, in the case of a comprehensively managed leasehold estate, which fulfils certain conditions laid down, the landlord may retain his powers of management of the estate by a scheme approved by the High Court. The landlord must apply to the appropriate Minster within two years from the Act applying for grant of a certification that in order to maintain adequate standards of appearance and amenity, and in order to regulate redevelopment in the area, in the event of tenants acquiring the landlord's interest in the houses and premises, the Minister is of the opinion that the landlord should be allowed to retain, in the general interest, powers of management.

Before granting the certificate the Minister must satisfy himself that the landlord has given adequate notice to persons interested, informing them of the application and inviting them to make representations to the Minister. He will also consider any representations made before he grants the certificate. Both the Minister and the court will in any case have regard to the benefit likely to result from the scheme to the area as a whole, and the extent to which it is reasonable to impose obligations on tenants acquiring freeholds. Consideration will also be given to past development, present character of the area, neighbouring areas, architectural and historical matters, and circumstances generally.

A certificate given, or scheme approved, is registerable as a local land charge.

Finally section 23 prohibits agreements attempting to exclude or modify the rights given to the tenant by the Act, no matter how effected between him and the landlord.

General

Two points should be noted in conclusion. *First,* Part I of the Landlord and Tenant Act 1954 will be looked upon with less eagerness by a tenant who can take up the alternative of an extended lease under the Act, even if he does not wish to enfranchise.

Secondly, it can be briefly mentioned that the county court will deal with the majority of the matters arising under the Act, except those concerning

(a) the compensation payable to the landlord;
(b) the rent payable under an extended lease;
(c) the compensation payable to the tenant where the landlord wishes

to redevelop or obtain possession for himself or his family;

(d) certain miscellaneous matters if an application is already before the Tribunal, such as the contents of the conveyance of the reversion and any apportionments arising under the negotiations.

These items will be dealt with by the Lands Tribunal. Naturally, the High Court is concerned with any applications under section 19.

It should be noted that Sections 172 et sec of the Housing Act 1985 modifies the 1967 Act in relation to those leases in the public housing sector which are subject to the "right to buy" legislation.

CHAPTER TWENTY

PUBLIC SECTOR HOUSING

Of recent years, considerable attention has been devoted legislatively to the position of council tenancies. The background has been one of assertion by local authorities to local control over housing provision, and central government anxiety to reduce levels of local autonomy, particularly in housing finance.

By the Housing Act 1985 the local housing authority must consider housing conditions in its district, it must carry out inspections; and it is given wide powers to act to establish the needs of the area regarding housing provision.

By and large, the needs are assessable through the local housing authority waiting lists and its housing investment programme but both are somewhat crude instruments for such assessment.

LOCAL AUTHORITY HOUSING FINANCE

Most housing authority expenditure is classified as capital expenditure. The income from rates, rents and subsidies is used mainly to pay charges arising from borrowed capital which is used to finance building projects and improvement schemes.

The Housing Act 1985 details the system of housing subsidy based on deficit financing—the subsidy is paid on the basis of costs incurred. The subsidy is decided by taking the *previous* year's subsidy (the base amount) and adding on increased costs (the housing costs differential) and subtracting the amount by which central government considers rents and rates will have increased (the local contribution differential). Protection is given to poorer tenants, who might be affected by the impact of rent increase, by the rent rebate scheme established by the Housing Finance Act 1972. In addition a Housing Investment Programme allocation is given to each authority which dictates the amount of borrowing an authority is allowed to meet their capital expenditure.

LOCAL HOUSING AUTHORITIES

The London boroughs and the London Residuary Body share housing responsibilities, but elsewhere housing is the responsibility of the district councils, with the county councils having certain reserve powers.

The functions of the housing departments include design and building, repair, maintenance, improvement schemes, housing management and welfare, the control of houses in multiple occupation, and the provision of housing advice agencies and tenancy relations officers.

The powers of such authorities regarding the provision of accommodation are found in Part II of the Housing Act 1985 which states they "shall secure that in the selection of their tenants a reasonable preference is given to persons who are occupying insanitary or overcrowded houses, have large families or are living under unsatisfactory conditions".

Additionally, the authority must provide alternative accommodation for anyone displaced as a result of authority compulsory purchase, housing orders or improvement notices. This does not apply to squatters who move into empty property.

The responsibilities of the authorities towards homeless persons are covered by the Act. Once an application is made the local authority must make "appropriate enquiries" and are under a duty to house those who appear to be homeless within the definition of the Act: A "priority need" arises where the homeless person has dependent children residing with him; he is homeless; or threatened with homelessness by flood, fire or other disaster; or he or someone residing with him is vulnerable as a result of old age, mental illness or handicap or physical disability. Pregnancy also gives rise to a priority need category.

If the authority is satisfied that there is no priority need, or that the homelessness was brought about intentionally, the duty is to provide advice and appropriate assistance. Where they are satisfied he *is* homeless accommodation must be provided until he has had a reasonable chance of getting accommodation for himself.

By the same section, if it is clear he is threatened with homelessness and has a priority need but he was not threatened intentionally, the authority must take reasonable steps to make sure the accommodation remains available to him.

The Act gives the local authority an escape clause in respect of its duty where the applicant has no local connection, or has a local connection with a different authority — unless, that is, there appears to be some threat of domestic violence.

But what is meant by "intentionally homelessness"? By section 60 of the Act;

> a person becomes homeless intentionally if he deliberately does or fails to do anything in consequence of which he ceases to occupy accommodation which is available for his occupation and which it would have been reasonable for him to continue to occupy.

It should be noted that there is no judicial review available to persons wrongfully refused help under the Act by a housing authority. There would therefore seem to be no relief available because the Act is silent on the question of relief (*R v. London Borough of Hillingdon ex parte Puhlhofer*, 1986).

HOUSING ASSOCIATIONS

There are various kinds of housing associations. Since, the Housing Act 1974, as amended by the Housing Act 1985, took effect such associations who wish to receive grants and loans from public funds must register with the Housing Corporation.

Although associations complying with section 15 of the Rent Act 1977 are not protected tenancies they are nevertheless subject to fair rent procedures. Unlike local authorities they have no general obligation to assess housing need but loans can be obtained for expenditure on housing association projects from local authorities or the Housing Corporation, provided registration has been obtained. Available to the associations are the Housing Association Grant, towards the costs of the project, Management Grants, Revenue Deficit Grants and Hostel Deficit Grants.

PUBLIC SECTOR HOUSING RIGHTS

Both with regard to the local authorities and the housing associations a new concept of public sector housing rights was introduced by the Housing Act 1980, based upon the idea of the "secure tenancy".

Such tenancies arise, under section 79 of the Housing Act 1985, where certain landlord and tenant conditions are satisfied.

The Landlord Conditions

These are that:

(a) the landlord is a local authority, a New Town Corporation, an urban development corporation, the Housing Corporation, a charitable housing trust, or the Development Board for Rural Wales; or

(b) the landlord is a housing association under section 15 of the Rent Act 1977; or

(c) the landlord is a housing co-operative and the dwelling house is within the housing co-operative agreement.

The Tenant Conditions

(a) The tenant must be an individual who occupies the dwelling house as his only or principal home, or

(b) in the case of a joint tenancy each joint tenant is an individual and at least one of them occupies the dwelling house as his only or principal home.

But what happens when a "secure tenant" dies? The tenancy will then remain a secure tenancy, where it is for a term certain, until it is vested or disposed of under administration of the estate, or until it is known that when it is so vested or disposed of it will *not* be a secure tenancy.

The Act states certain tenancies are not secure. These include; long leases (21 years or more); premises occupied under a contract of employment; tenancies of land acquired for development purposes; temporary tenancies for someone seeking employment tenancies of premises let on short term leases to the landlord; temporary tenancies while building works are completed; agricultural holding lettings; pub lettings; student lettings; business tenancies and lettings by almshouses charities.

Security of Tenure Provisions

By section 82 of the Act a secure tenancy which is a weekly or other periodic tenancy, or one for a term certain but subject to termination by the landlord, can be ended only by the landlord obtaining a court order. Where the tenancy has a provision for forfeiture or re-entry, the court will disregard it, but can order termination if circumstances giving rise to such rights occur.

The proceedings must be begun by a special notice of intending proceedings (replacing the common law requirement regarding the notice to quit).

But what are the grounds for eviction from a secure tenancy? They are:

(1) Rent due has not been paid or an obligation of the tenancy has been broken or not performed.
(2) The tenant or resident has been guilty of conduct which is a nuisance or annoyance to neighbours, or has been convicted of using the house or allowing it to be used for immoral or illegal purposes.
(3) The condition of the house or common parts has deteriorated through waste by, or neglect or default of, the tenant or resident, (or by a lodger or sub-tenant if the tenant has not taken reasonable steps to get rid of them).
(4) The condition of relevant furniture has deteriorated owing to ill-treatment by the tenant, resident, or, as in the circumstances of (3) above, the lodger or sub-tenant.
(5) The tenant induced the landlord to grant the tenancy by a false statement made knowingly or recklessly by the tenant.
(6) The tenancy was assigned under section 92 (by way of exchange on the payment of a premium) to the tenant or his predecessor in title.
(7) The dwelling forms part of a building used mainly for non housing purposes or non housing accommodation and (a) it was let as a result of the tenant's employment and (b) because of the tenant's conduct it would not be right for him to remain in occupation.
(8) The dwelling house was made available while improvements were being carried out on the tenant's previous home; the tenant was a secure tenant, he had agreed to give up possession on completion of the improvements; these have been completed; and the other dwelling house is available.

In each of the grounds noted in 1 to 6 above, the court will terminate the tenancy only where it considers it reasonable to do so.

(9) The dwelling house is overcrowded and rendering the occupant

guilty of an offence under the Act.

(10) The landlord intends to demolish, reconstruct, or carry out work on the building or land let with and treated as part of the premises, and cannot reasonably do this without obtaining possession.

(11) The landlord is a charitable housing trust and the tenant's continued occupation would conflict with the objects of the charity.

In grounds 9 to 11 the court will order termination only if satisfied that suitable accommodation will be available elsewhere when the order takes effect.

(12) The tenancy is within a building not used mainly for accommodation or accommodation which is housing accommodation and it was let as a result of the tenant's employment and the landlord reasonably requires it for the accommodation of another employee.

(13) The dwelling house has peculiar features designed for occupation by the physically disabled; no such person resides there; and the landlord wants it for such a person.

(14) The landlord is a housing association or housing trust letting to persons whose circumstances (other than financial) make it difficult for them to get accommodation; no such person resides there; and the landlord wants it for such a person.

(15) The dwelling house is one of a group usually let for persons with specil needs; a social service or special facility is provided nearby; no one with such special needs resides at the dwelling house; and the landlord wants it for such a person, whether alone or with members of his family.

(16) The premises are more extensive than required by the tenant; the tenant acquired the tenancy on the death of the previous tenant, was qualified to so succeed under section 29(2)(b) of the Act, and notice was served within more than six months but not less than twelve months of the death of the previous tenant.

Grounds 7 to 13 are largely concerned with matters of housing management, and the court will make no order of termination unless it is *reasonable* to make the order, and suitable accommodation will be available for the tenant when the order takes effect.

Suitable Accommodation

What is meant by "suitable accommodation"?

The Act states accommodation to be suitable if it is let as a separate dwelling under a secure tenancy or will be let as a separate dwelling under a protected tenancy. The accommodation must also be reasonably suitable to the needs of the tenant and his family.

It will *not* be suitable accommodation if it is under a protected tenancy whereby the landlord can recover possession under one of the Cases in Part II of Schedule 15 to the 1977 Act (see page 170, above).

What does "reasonably suitable" mean?

In deciding this, the court will have regard to: the nature of the accommodation the landlord normally allocates to such persons; its distance from the place of work or education or, if such nearness is necessary for the family member's wellbeing, the distance from the home of a member of the tenant's family. The court will also consider the needs and means of the tenant and his family; the terms of the secure tenancy and of the availability of the accommodation, and, if any furniture was provided under the secure tenancy, whether furniture is to be provided in the other accommodation. The nature of that furniture will also be considered.

If possession is sought because the tenancy is overcrowded (Ground 9) accommodation otherwise reasonably suitable shall not be regarded as *not* so, merely because the permitted number of persons already living in the other accommodation is fewer than the permitted number under the 1985 Act.

Terms of Secure Tenancies

By section 93 of the Housing Act 1985 secure tenants are given the right to take in lodgers or sublet part of the dwelling house. If these are not members of the family the landlord's consent must be obtained, otherwise it is an absolute right. The consent must not be unreasonably witheld. It should be noted also that the right applies only to a subletting of *part* of the house; by section 93, if the whole of the house is sublet, the secure tenancy comes to an end.

The secure tenant may have made improvements to the property. In such circumstances the landlord has a discretion to make appropriate payments to the tenant. There can be no increase of rent because of the improvements, though rates may be increased. The right to improve for both private sector and secure tenants is found in the 1985 Act.

Where a variation in the terms of a tenancy is contemplated certain formalities allowing the tenant the chance to comment on the proposed changes must be undertaken. These procedures do not apply, however, to changes in rent, or rates, or payments for services.

The Act demands that information about the terms of secure tenancies must be published but allows the landlord two years from the date when this part of the Act comes into effect to comply.

Assured Tenancies

The protection afforded with regard to security of tenure by Part II of the Landlord and Tenant Act 1954 is extended by section 56 of the Housing Act 1980 to *assured tenancies.* This is one which would otherwise be a protected tenancy and

(a) the landlord is an approved body;
(b) the dwelling house was built after 1980; and
(c) was not occupied by anyone as a resident.

The list of approved bodies is to be published and is likely to include bodies such as building societies.

The Right to Buy

The Housing Act 1985 gives secure tenants who have resided in a dwelling house for three years the right to buy the freehold or long lease of the dwellinghouse and the right to be offered a mortgage from the landlord. The three year qualifying period can be a continuous three years or several periods amounting to three years. Neither the landlord nor the dwelling house needs to have been the same for the whole period of three years. The period needs only to have been satisfied by one joint tenant if the tenancy is held by more than one.

The right to buy cannot be exercised if the secure tenant is obliged to give up possession of the dwelling house in pursuance of a court order or the secure tenant is an undischarged bankrupt, a bankruptcy petition is pending, a receiving order is in force or the secure tenant has made a composition or arrangement with his creditors the terms of which remain to be fulfilled.

The price to be paid by the secure tenant is the market value less the discount entitlement. The market value is defined as the price on the open market by sale by a willing vendor disregarding improvements made by the secure tenant, a previous secure tenant of the same tenancy being a member of the same family, and their failure to keep the property in repair internally. The value is determined by the District Valuer who considers representations from the landlord and the secure tenant.

The discount is 33% for residence of less than four years. In the case of residence for more than four years the discount is 33% plus 1% for each complete year by which the period exceeds three years, to a maximum discount of 50% or the prescribed sum. In the case of joint tenants the discount applicable is that which the longest residing joint tenant would be due.

The discount is repayable if the dwellinghouse is disposed of within five years.

INDEX

INDEX

INDEX

INDEX

Lewis and Holland's

LANDLORD and TENANT

SUPPLEMENT

LANDLORD AND TENANT ACT 1987

May 1988

The rights of tenants living in flats have been further extended by the Landlord and Tenant Act 1987. When this Act comes into force, on a date to be specified by the Secretary of State, tenants will have various rights: of first refusal when the landlord sells his reversion; of variation of their leases; and of management.

PART I

In Part I of the Act, section 1 gives the tenants of flats within a building the right of first refusal when the landlord proposes to sell the building. The landlord must serve a notice on his tenants in accordance with section 5, detailing his proposals for disposal of the building and offer to dispose of the property to his qualifying tenants on the same terms. If tenants holding over 50% of the flats within the building so choose they can acquire the landlord's title on those terms.

Generally by s.3 qualifying tenants are residential tenants not holding under a protected shorthold tenancy or a service tenancy. A tenant will not qualify if he is a body corporate or his demise includes more than one flat in the building or his demise includes common parts of the building.

The occasions of disposals by a landlord to which the rights attach are described in s.4 and exclude disposals

(a) by will or under the rules of intestacy,
(b) by way of gift to a member of the landlord's family,
(c) on divorce,
(d) under a compulsory purchase order,
(e) to a charity,
(f) under the terms of a trust of which landlord is a trustee,
(g) by a company to its associated company,
(h) to the crown,
(i) a disposal under an obligation created before the commencement of the Act or
(j) by a surrender of a tenancy in pursuance of any agreement within that tenancy.

The landlord's offer contained in his notice must be accepted within the specified period by a notice served on him by the requisite majority of qualifying tenants. The tenants may serve instead a notice of counter-offer. The landlord shall accept or reject the counter-offer by a notice, which notice,if a rejection, will stand as a fresh offer by the landlord. If the offer is not accepted by the tenants within 12 months of the date of service of the original landlord's notice, the landlord may dispose of the building to another purchaser.

Section 9 of the Act lays down rules for each party to have the right to withdraw from the transaction.

If the landlord in contravention of the Act sells to a new landlord the qualifying tenants may serve a notice on the new landlord forcing him to sell to them and obtain the particulars of the disposal to them (sections 11 and 12). Similarly if the disposal to a new landlord constituted a surrender of a head lease to a superior landlord under whom the qualifying tenants hold tenancies they can compel the superior landlord to grant a new head lease to a person nominated by the majority of the qualifying tenants.

Section 16 allows qualifying tenants to enforce these rights against subsequent purchasers further down a chain of transactions.

In order to protect prospective purchasers the Act lays down rules in section 18 allowing them to serve notices on qualifying tenants of the prospective proposal. If the qualifying tenants do not exercise their rights within 28 days of service of such a notice they lose their rights to enforce them in that instance.

The powers of enforcement of the above provisions lie with the court. However, any questions about the matters specified in a purchase notice must be decided by a rent assessment committee.

PART II

Part II of the Act deals with the widespread problems of landlords who breach the obligations owed to their tenants under the leases.

By section 21 a tenant may apply to the court for the appointment of a manager. The tenant must first serve a notice on the landlord requiring him to remedy his breaches if they are capable of being remedied. Service of this notice can be dispensed with by the court if the tenant shows service is not reasonably practicable, to cover the case of absentee landlords. The court may give the manager any functions it thinks fit in respect of management or of receivership, and a manager can subsequently apply to the court for directions. The court's power is wide and discretionary, and orders can be in an interim or final form.

PART III

Part III of the Act enables qualifying tenants to acquire their landlord's interest in the property without his consent if he has failed to discharge his obligations under the leases. The court will only make such an order if the appointment of a manager would be an inadequate remedy, or a manager has already been appointed and has so acted for the three years before the application for acquisition. However the Act allows this application only in respect of buildings where all or most of the flats are let on long leases. Any acquisition order will operate to discharge the premises from existing mortgages or charges unless the parties have agreed otherwise or the court thinks such discharge would not be fair and reasonable. The court also has power to make an acquisition order on such terms as it thinks fit when the landlord cannot be found or identified.

PART IV

Parties to long leases are given the right to apply to vary leases by Part IV of the Act. Section 35 lays down the grounds which are that the lease in question fails to make proper provision for such questions as repair, maintenance, insurance, services and service charges.

If the court makes such an order the respondent can apply for similar variations in other leases in respect of which he is the landlord if all those leases are defective in the same way.

Such variations of leases are by section 39 binding not only upon the parties, but also upon their predecessors in title and other third parties such as sureties. This is so whether or not they were parties to the proceedings or were served with notice of the proceedings.

Section 40 allows an application relating to a long lease of a dwelling other than a flat for variance of insurance provisions if the lease fails to make satisfactory provision.

PARV V

Part V of the Act relates to the management of leasehold property. It amends section 18 to 30 of the Landlord and Tenant Act 1985 to extend those provisions to dwellings other than flats and therefore repeals sections 45 to 51 of the Housing Act 1985 which extended these provisions only to dwellings let on long leases.

This part of the Act also limits the uses of service charges by landlords of dwellings. By section 42 the service charge is held in trust by the landlord to defray proper costs, and the money must be invested as the Secretary of State shall determine by order, rather than in any manner authorised by law.

On the termination of a lease the tenant shall no longer receive a part of his service charge back, but it shall continue to be held, in trust, to be used to defray expenses of the building, unless there are no other contributing tenants left, in which case the trust shall determine.

The Act also provides for limitations on service charges in schedule 2. There are provisions for inter alia, for reasonableness, estimates, consultation and production of accounts. These terms shall prevail over express terms in a lease.

Section 43 inserts into the Landlord and Tenant Act 1985 a new schedule conferring rights on tenants in respect of the insurance of their dwellings. Where a service charge is payable tenants may require a written summary of the insurance cover (if the service charge covers insurance) and may inspect the policy. The tenant can notify the insurers of possible claims and challenge the landlord's choice of insurer. These provisions do not apply to tenants of local authorities, new town corporations, or the Development Board for Rural Wales unless the tenancy is a long tenancy.

Section 44 inserts further provisions into the Landlord and Tenant Act 1985. Recognised tenants' associations may serve notice on landlords requiring consultation on matters relating to the appointment or employment of existing or proposed management agents. They may do so whereever their associations are required by their leases to contribute to the cost of buildings by paying a service charge.

Finally within this part of the Act is a provision extending the permissible objects of registered housing associations to allow them to manage a wider range of leasehold dwellings.

PART VI

Part VI of the Act contains provisions for information to be furnished to tenants. This information includes a landlord's name and address, and an address for service of notices. The Act extends circumstances in which notices are sufficiently served to the last address the landlord gave to the tenant, and provides that the landlord's liability to the tenants shall continue when the landlord has assigned his interest to another without notice to the tenant. The tenant shall also be able to search the propietorship register for the property at the Land Registry to get details of a landlord's name and address. These provisions do a great deal to make enforceable the rules previously contained in the Landlord and Tenant Act 1985 relating to provision of name and address of landlords.

APPLICATION

The Act does not generally apply to crown land, District County or London Borough Councils, the Commission for New Towns, Urban Development Corporations, the Development Board for Rural Wales, housing corporations, housing trusts, registered housing associations, or local authorities as landlords.

Parts I, II and III of the Act do not apply to resident landlords as defined in section 58(2).

The Act comes into force on a date to be specified by the Secretary of State. At the date of publishing (May 16) sections 1 to 20 (relating to the tenant's first refusal), 45 to 51 (relating to information to be furnished to tenants, and tenants' furnished to landlords, and tenants' associations rights of consultation about managing agents), and, lastly, the administrative provision of sections 52 to 62 have already come into force, on the 1st February 1988.